AN
E.B. WHITE
READER

*Edited with commentary
and questions by*

WILLIAM W. WATT *and*
ROBERT W. BRADFORD
Lafayette College

HARPER & ROW, PUBLISHERS   NEW YORK

AN E. B. WHITE READER

C-3

LIBRARY OF CONGRESS CATALOG CARD NUMBER: 66–10608

Printer & Binder: The Murray Printing Company

ACKNOWLEDGMENTS

All selections from *The Second Tree from the Corner* reprinted by permission of Harper & Row, Publishers, Incorporated. Copyright 1936, 1937, 1939, 1940, 1943, 1944, 1945, 1946, 1947, 1948, 1950, 1951, 1954, by E. B. White. Most of the pieces originally appeared in *The New Yorker*. "Farewell, My Lovely!": Copyright 1936 by The New Yorker Magazine, Inc., was a collaboration with Richard L. Strout and was published also as a book entitled *Farewell to Model T* published by G. P. Putnam's Sons in 1936. "Death of a Pig" appeared in the *Atlantic Monthly*. "Some Remarks on Humor" is an adaption of the Preface to *A Subtreasury of American Humor* edited by Katharine S. White and E. B. White (Coward-McCann). Copyright 1941 by Katharine S. White and E. B. White. "Don Marquis" originally appeared, in a slightly different form, as the Introduction by E. B. White to *The Lives and Times of Archy and Mehitabel* by Don Marquis. Introduction Copyright, 1950 by Doubleday & Company, Inc. Reprinted by permission of the publisher.

All selections from *The Points of My Compass* are reprinted by permission of Harper & Row, Publishers, Incorporated. Copyright © 1954, 1956, 1957, 1960, by E. B. White. All pieces originally appeared in *The New Yorker*, with the exception of "A Slight Sound at Evening" which was first published in *The Yale Review* under the title "Walden—1954." "Will Strunk" appeared originally in *The New Yorker* in 1957 in a slightly different form as part of a larger essay, and also as the Introduction by E. B. White to *The Elements of Style* by William Strunk, Jr. and E. B. White published by The Macmillan Company in 1959.

All selections from *One Man's Meat* reprinted by permission of Harper & Row, Publishers, Incorporated. Copyright 1938, 1939, 1940, 1941, 1942, 1943 by E. B. White. All pieces were originally published in *Harper's Magazine* with the exception of "The Flocks We Watch By Night," which originally appeared in *The New Yorker*.

"The Sea and the Wind that Blows" Copyright 1963 by E. B. White. The selections from *Quo Vadimus?* originally appeared in *The New Yorker* and are reprinted by permission of Harper & Row, Publishers, Incorporated. Copyright 1933 by E. B. White.

The selection from *Here Is New York* is reprinted by permission of

CONTENTS

Preface   vii

A Biographical Note   ix

Part One: SAYING THE WORDS

FROM WRITER TO READER   3

The Writer's Duty   4

"The Duty of Writers"   4

Appropriate Usage   6

"English Usage"   7

The Secret Struggle   8

"The Word-handler's Aim"   9

A Personal Problem   10

"A Study of the Clinical 'We'"   10

Style and Styles   12

"An Approach to Style"   13

"Prefer the Standard to the Offbeat"   17

Reading and Writing   19

"Calculating Machine"   20

"The Future of Reading"   23

ANGLE AND ATTITUDE   24

Point of View   24

"Western Unity"   26

"The Wild Flag"   28

Tone   30

"Two Letters, Both Open"   32

"The Day of Days"   37

"The Burning Question"   38

"Farewell, My Lovely!"   40

Part Two: THE CAREFUL FORM

FORMS OF DISCOURSE   53

Description   53

"Salt Water Farm"   56

"Business Show"   58

Narrative   59

"Coon Hunt"   61

"The Second Tree from the Corner"   66

Persuasion   72

"Withholding"   74

"Sound"   75

"The Age of Dust"   76

Exposition   78

"Motor Cars"   79

"Freedom"   82

WAYS OF DEVELOPMENT   88

Reporting the Facts   89

"Town Meeting"   91

"Twins"   93

"About Myself"   95

Definition   98

"Dudes and Flapsails"   100

"Law and Justice"   101

"Democracy"   102

"Fascism"   103

Classification and Division   104

"Poetry"   105

"Security"   108

Illustration   109

"Mrs. Wienckus"   110

"Lime"   111

Comparison and Contrast   114
"Education"   116
"Beside the Shalimar"   119
"Camp Meeting"   120
"Beloved Barriers"   127

Analysis   128
"The Shape of the U.N."   130
"A Shepherd's Life"   139

A SUITABLE DESIGN   144

"Bedfellows"   147
"Death of a Pig"   157

Part Three: ONE MAN'S WORLD

Self-Portraits   171
"First World War"   172
"Removal"   180
"Incoming Basket"   182
"Figures"   183
"Questionnaire"   184
"The Sea and the Wind
   that Blows"   184

Portraits   191
"Old Dameron"   191
"The Flocks We Watch by
   Night"   193
"Will Strunk"   198
"Don Marquis"   205

Book Country   212
"A Classic Waits for Me"   212
"Across the Street and Into
   the Grill"   215
"Some Remarks on Humor"   218
"Walden"   226

"A Slight Sound at Eve-
   ning"   234
Habitats   244
"On a Florida Key"   245
"The Cities"   251
"Trance"   252
"Here Is New York"   253
"Cold Weather"   255
Shadow of the Future   258
"The Supremacy of Uru-
   guay"   259
"The Door"   263
"Sootfall and Fallout"   268
Song Trio   278
"The Red Cow Is Dead"   280
"The Tennis"   281
"A Listener's Guide to the
   Birds"   282
Epilogue   285
"Once More to the Lake"   286
"The Ring of Time"   293

Questions for Discussion   303

Suggestions for Writing   335

Index   339

PREFACE

This book has two primary aims: to provide college undergraduates with a representative selection from the work of a distinguished contemporary writer and to supply an arrangement and commentary that will be particularly useful in composition courses in which intelligent reading is encouraged as a means to intelligible writing.

In the first part of the book the student is introduced informally to a number of general problems of writing and reading—usage, style, point of view, tone—with a large share of the pedagogical guidance given by White himself. The selections in the second part are arranged somewhat more systematically, to present an orderly discussion of rhetoric. The traditional forms of discourse and techniques of development are considered in turn, always with an emphasis on the total design of the finished product. In the third part the emphasis shifts from rhetoric to reading and the pieces are arranged in categories that suggest not only the variety of White's writing but also the dimensions of his world.

We do not presume to teach the undergraduate how to write like E. B. White or even to encourage him to cover the paper with off-White. Nor do we wish to perpetuate the familiar classroom illusion that White—like Shakespeare—wrote in order to fit the grooves of Academe. We believe that a close examination of these selections, with some informal guidance from the editors, will do more good for the student's own writing than ploughing through a miscellaneous anthology or an isolated handbook. There are special advantages to concentrating on a contemporary whose writing reveals a rare concern for style and whose characteristic performance, however subtle, is neither too long nor too specialized to serve as a model, or at least a stimulus, for the undergraduate writer. We hope also that many more readers—at both ends of the classroom—will come to enjoy E. B. White as much as we do.

With his permission we have omitted the "postscripts" to the following selections from *The Points of My Compass:* "The Shape of the U.N.", "Bedfellows," "Will Strunk," "Sootfall and Fallout," and "The Ring of Time." The piece we have called "Western

Unity" is a passage from the essay in *The Points of My Compass* entitled "Unity." We have culled a brief excerpt from the long essay "Here Is New York." All other selections are complete.

White has also permitted us the liberty of coining titles for selections that would otherwise be identified only by dates (as in *The Wild Flag*) or by the titles covering groups of short pieces (as in *One Man's Meat*). We are responsible for the following labels: "The Duty of Writers," "The Word-handler's Aim," "The Day of Days," "The Burning Question," "Dudes and Flapsails," "Law and Justice," "Democracy," "Fascism," "Beside the Shalimar," "Beloved Barriers," "Figures," "Old Dameron," and "The Cities."

The order of the pieces is not necessarily chronological, even within sections. But we have supplied dates throughout so that the reader will know precisely at which point White is fishing in the stream of time, and thus will have a better chance of separating topical allusions from those that are not of an age. The selections from the journal, *One Man's Meat,* carry the date of composition, not the month when they appeared in *Harper's Magazine*. Except for the few dates in the upper right hand corner of "letters," all other dates refer to first publication, usually in *The New Yorker*.

In addition to our general debt to our colleagues at Lafayette and elsewhere, we are especially indebted to Brooks and Warren's *Modern Rhetoric* for suggestions about definition and terminology in Part Two. We are deeply grateful to E. B. White, not only for his generosity in allowing us to put his works in a didactic frame, but for his cooperation throughout. Although he did not make the selection, he was kind enough to approve it. For anything that is said or asked about him or his writing, the editors assume complete responsibility.

W. W. W.
R. W. B.

Lafayette College
Easton, Pennsylvania

A BIOGRAPHICAL NOTE

Any student who reads all the selections, with or without benefit of the editorial remarks, will learn more about White than he can possibly get from an extended biographical essay. This note is intended merely to supply a few points of reference.

E. B. White was born on July 11, 1899, in Mount Vernon, a suburb of Manhattan. He attended the public schools of Mount Vernon and entered Cornell University in the fall of 1917. In his senior year he was editor-in-chief of the Cornell *Daily Sun*. After graduation in 1921 he wandered westward in a Model T and stopped off for a year in the state of Washington, where he served one of his writing apprenticeships as a reporter for the Seattle *Times*. In the summer of 1923 he made his way to Alaska by working in the night saloon and the firemen's mess on a trading ship. After returning to Manhattan in the fall, he worked for a short time as an advertising copy writer, but soon freed his lance to tilt in the wider lists of literature. Some of his early verses appeared in the famous "Conning Tower" of F. P. A. Shortly after the birth of *The New Yorker* in February 1925, he discovered an environment that was peculiarly congenial to his tastes and talents. He was hired as a part-time contributing editor in the fall of 1926 at a starting wage of thirty dollars a week.

As the "number one wheel horse" in *The New Yorker* stable, White edited manuscripts, invented tag lines for "newsbreaks," coined ideas and captions for cartoons, went on contributing both prose and verse in his own name or initials, and built a matchless reputation as the personal voice behind the editorial "we" of "Notes and Comment" in "The Talk of the Town" at the front of the magazine. As the magazine prospered in the depression decade, the name of E. B. White became inseparable from its fortunes and its flavor.

Four years before Pearl Harbor he moved his base of operations from Manhattan to Maine, where he had been at home since boyhood. With his wife—the distinguished *New Yorker* editor Katharine Sergeant White—and his small son, he settled in a salt water farmhouse in North Brooklin and began a brave new life as part-time shepherd, part-time writer. Between July, 1938, and January, 1943, having temporarily severed his informal official connection with *The New Yorker,* he wrote the monthly journal called "One Man's Meat" for *Harper's Magazine*. He returned to *The*

New Yorker in 1943, but continued to live the greater part of the year at his farmhouse. Although he has made extended visits to Manhattan, Florida, and South Carolina, his home-comings are still to the land of his boyhood summers.

As the range of his book titles implies, E. B. White's fame as a writer of essays, editorials, children's classics, and verse—a master of the style he recommends and represents—has spread far beyond the privileged circle of the veteran readers of two magazines. His honorary degrees—from Dartmouth, Maine, Yale, Bowdoin, Hamilton, Harvard, and Colby—and his numberless contributions to anthologies attest his reputation in the academic world. *One Man's Meat* won the gold medal of the Limited Editions Club as the book most likely to attain the stature of a classic. In 1960 he was awarded the gold medal for Essays and Criticism from the National Institute of Arts and Letters. On July 4, 1963, John Kennedy named him in the first group to receive the new Presidential Medal of Freedom, the highest civilian honor that a President can bestow in peacetime: an award reserved for those "who contribute significantly to the quality of American life." When President Johnson made the award in the following December, the citation read as follows: "An essayist whose concise comment on men and places has revealed to yet another age the vigor of the English sentence."

A CHRONOLOGICAL LIST OF HIS BOOKS

Is Sex Necessary?, 1929   (with James Thurber)
The Lady Is Cold, 1929   (verse)
Ho Hum, 1931
Another Ho Hum, 1932   (both collections of "newsbreaks")
Every Day Is Saturday, 1934   ("Notes and Comments")
The Fox of Peapack, 1938   (verse)
Quo Vadimus? or The Case for the Bicycle, 1939
A Subtreasury of American Humor, 1941 (with Katharine S. White)
One Man's Meat, 1942,   enlarged 1944
The Wild Flag, 1946
Stuart Little, 1945   (a children's book)
Here Is New York, 1949
Charlotte's Web, 1952   (a children's book)
The Second Tree from the Corner, 1953
The Elements of Style, 1959   (with William Strunk, Jr.)
The Points of My Compass, 1962

SAYING THE WORDS

"Some people, perhaps most people, think
words are not really important, but I
am a word man and I attach the very
highest importance to words."

Shortly after his graduation from Cornell, E. B. White spent eleven months learning to be a reporter for the Seattle *Times*. A piece of this experience is recorded in *The Second Tree from the Corner*. Though he had scaled the heights of undergraduate journalism, serving in his senior year as editor-in-chief of the Cornell *Daily Sun*, he was still learning how hard it is to write even a simple story well. One day he got stuck on a story and took his problem to the city editor:

> How was I to express a certain thing? (I've forgotten what it was, but I had undoubtedly got bogged down in attempting to put the intricacies of a second-string felony into deathless prose.) I asked him how I could get around my difficulty.
>
> He thought for a minute. Then he said, "Just say the words."
>
> I always remembered that. It was excellent advice and I am still [sixteen years later] trying to say the words. . . .

The anecdote conveys a fundamental lesson for any writer —apprentice or veteran: Simplicity is the key to clarity. The strenuous struggle for deathless prose does not guarantee lively writing. It is better to say what comes naturally than to strain to be impressive.

But simplicity must not be confused with simple-mindedness. Good natural writing is not random thought transferred indiscriminately to paper. Prosaic talk is not readable prose. A responsible writer, even if he is not formally schooled in rhetoric, cannot evade the problems of structure, usage, diction, style, and tone that are discussed in textbook and classroom. He does not put away these problems as childish things when, for example, he is through with or exempted from freshman English. Consciously or unconsciously he confronts them all his life.

FROM WRITER TO READER

White expressed his own faith when he wrote that "English prose composition is not only a necessary skill but a sensible pursuit as well—a way to spend one's days." His sensitive awareness of the problems of composition is implicit in all his writing. It is made explicit in numerous contexts, ranging from incidental references through one-paragraph comments to complete essays. Though White is the co-author of a celebrated guide to style, he is too humble before the elusive miracle of the written word to pose as a solemn expert on it. He is a professional writer, not a rhetorician; his voice is authoritative, not authoritarian. The following selections from his statements on writing, speaking, and reading touch a wide range of the subjects discussed more formally in the standard rhetoric textbooks.

THE WRITER'S DUTY

The first selection, "The Duty of Writers," is a short essay in which White notes a current attitude and then comments on it. Though the piece first appeared in *Harper's,* it follows the style of the "Notes and Comments" that he wrote for many years for *The New Yorker*. It emphasizes the personal responsibility of anyone who uses words, whether he is a professional writer in a time of crisis (and since when has the world known any other time) or an undergraduate creeping unwillingly to a routine deadline. White's essay is a lesson, sobering if not sober, for the student who assumes that his periodic five hundred words don't really matter because they are ephemeral effusions, read only by his instructor and perhaps his roommate.

JANUARY   1939

THE DUTY OF WRITERS

I was sorry to hear the other day that a certain writer, appalled by the cruel events of the world, had pledged himself never to write anything that wasn't constructive and significant and liberty-loving. I have an idea that this, in its own way, is bad news.

All word-mongers, at one time or another, have felt the

From "Salt Water Farm" in *One Man's Meat.*

divine necessity of using their talents, if any, on the side of right—but I didn't realize that they were making any resolutions to that effect, and I don't think they should. When liberty's position is challenged, artists and writers are the ones who first take up the sword. They do so without persuasion, for the battle is peculiarly their own. In the nature of things, a person engaged in the flimsy business of expressing himself on paper is dependent on the large general privilege of being heard. Any intimation that this privilege may be revoked throws a writer into a panic. His is a double allegiance to freedom—an intellectual one springing from the conviction that pure thought has a right to function unimpeded, and a selfish one springing from his need, as a bread-winner, to be allowed to speak his piece. America is now liberty-conscious. In a single generation it has progressed from being toothbrush-conscious, to being air-minded, to being liberty-conscious. The transition has been disturbing, but it has been effected, and the last part has been accomplished largely by the good work of writers and artists, to whom liberty is a blessed condition that must be preserved on earth at all costs.

But to return to my man who has foresworn everything but what is good and significant. He worries me. I hope he isn't serious, but I'm afraid he is. Having resolved to be nothing but significant, he is in a fair way to lose his effectiveness. A writer must believe in something, obviously, but he shouldn't join a club. Letters flourish not when writers amalgamate, but when they are contemptuous of one another. (Poets are the most contemptuous of all the writing breeds, and in the long run the most exalted and influential.) Even in evil times, a writer should cultivate only what naturally absorbs his fancy, whether it be freedom or cinch bugs, and should write in the way that comes easy.

The movement is spreading. I know of one gifted crackpot who used to be employed gainfully in the fields of humor and satire, who has taken a solemn pledge not to write anything funny or light-hearted or "insignificant" again till things get straightened around in the world. This seems to me distinctly deleterious and a little silly. A literature composed of nothing but liberty-loving thoughts is little better than the propaganda which it seeks to defeat.

In a free country it is the duty of writers to pay no attention to duty. Only under a dictatorship is literature expected to exhibit an harmonious design or an inspirational tone. A despot doesn't fear eloquent writers preaching freedom—he fears a drunken poet who may crack a joke that will take hold. His gravest concern is lest gaiety, or truth in sheep's clothing, somewhere gain a foothold, lest joy in some unguarded moment be unconfined. I honestly don't believe that a humorist should take the veil today; he should wear his bells night and day, and squeeze the uttermost jape, even though he may feel more like writing a strong letter to the *Herald Tribune*.

APPROPRIATE USAGE

Whether a writer should limit himself to the safe and significant or follow the gleam of his own fancy—that is only one of many difficult decisions. In writing anything he must choose, either consciously or not, a general level (or a variety) of language; and this major choice will influence the choice and use of individual words. The level of most of White's essays—and of much of the best contemporary writing—is *informal:* a broad and comfortable middle ground somewhere between the strict propriety of an earnest commencement address and the free-wheeling chatter of the dormitory. In "The Duty of Writers," for example, he uses colloquial contractions ("I hope he isn't serious, but I'm afraid he is") and other conversational idioms freely ("bad news," "He worries me," "in a fair way," "comes easy"). But he doesn't stoop to conquer by adopting the fashionable illiteracies (like a notorious cigarette ad does), or by avoiding polysyllabic words (*intimation, amalgamate, deleterious*) merely because they have more than one syllable and the man in the street, whoever he is, may not know their meaning.

The choice of a level of language or the test of any usage is appropriateness in context. To speak of "good English" or "bad," to call any expression "correct" or "incorrect" without regard to context is to misrepresent the nature of language. Eng-

lish, or its American cousin, is not a rigid structure governed by un-
alterable laws; it is a restless growth exposed to the winds of
cultural change and continuously affected by individual taste,
judgment, fancy, and sheer luck. In the following selection White
combines the lesson of appropriateness with related comments on
the perils of ambiguity and the intricacies of idiom and sentence
structure.

JANUARY 30, 1937

ENGLISH USAGE

We were interested in what Dr. Henry Seidel Canby
had to say about English usage, in the *Saturday Review*. Usage
seems to us peculiarly a matter of ear. Everyone has his own
prejudices, his own set of rules, his own list of horribles. Dr.
Canby speaks of "contact" used as a verb, and points out that
careful writers and speakers, persons of taste, studiously avoid it.
They do—some of them because the word, so used, makes their
gorge rise, others because they have heard that we sensitive lit'ry
folk consider it displeasing. The odd thing is that what is true of
one noun-verb is not necessarily true of another. To "contact a
man" makes us wince; but to "ground a plane because of bad
weather" sounds all right. Further, although we are satisfied to
"ground a plane," we object to "garaging an automobile." An
automobile should not be "garaged"; it should either be "put in a
garage" or left out all night.

The contraction "ain't," as Dr. Canby points out, is a
great loss to the language. Nice Nellies, schoolteachers, and
underdone grammarians have made it the symbol of ignorance
and ill-breeding, when in fact it is a handy word, often serving
where nothing else will. "Say it ain't so" is a phrase that is right
the way it stands, and couldn't be any different. People are afraid
of words, afraid of mistakes. One time a newspaper sent us to a
morgue to get a story on a woman whose body was being held for
identification. A man believed to be her husband was brought in.

From *The Second Tree from the Corner*.

Somebody pulled the sheet back; the man took one agonizing look, and cried, "My God, it's her!" When we reported this grim incident, the editor diligently changed it to "My God, it's she!"

The English language is always sticking a foot out to trip a man. Every week we get thrown, writing merrily along. Even Dr. Canby, a careful and experienced craftsman, got thrown in his own editorial. He spoke of "the makers of textbooks who are nearly always reactionary, and often unscholarly in denying the right to change to a language that has always been changing . . ." In this case the word "change," quietly sandwiched in between a couple of "to's," unexpectedly exploded the whole sentence. Even inverting the phrases wouldn't have helped. If he had started out "In denying to a language . . . the right to change," it would have come out this way: "In denying to a language that has always been changing the right to change . . ." English usage is sometimes more than mere taste, judgment, and education—sometimes it's sheer luck, like getting across a street.

THE SECRET STRUGGLE

"English Usage" presents the dilemma of any conscientious writer: If he is "afraid of words, afraid of mistakes," afraid of rules or the reader who threatens to enforce them with a red pencil, the genuine warmth of his feeling may turn cold, and his natural human speech may grow stiff with bookish correctness. On the other hand, if he relaxes too far, if he assumes an attitude of casual indifference to the complexities of language, he may hit every trap in the course. In the words of a Connecticut highway warning—cutely tailored for rapid reading and easy remembering—*relax but don't be lax*. No matter how hard a piece of writing comes, the final product should never advertise the struggle. As Maugham once wrote, "you would not believe a man was very intent on ploughing a furrow if he carried a hoop with him and jumped through it at every step. A good style should show no sign of effort. What is written should seem a happy accident." White, in this next piece, makes the same point in his contrast of photography with writing.

JULY 24, 1937

THE WORD-HANDLER'S AIM

Photography is the most self-conscious of the arts. The act of photography has been glorified in the newspicture magazines, and even in the newspapers. Publisher and reader enjoy shoptalk together. The editor continually points to "best shots," or "news-picture of the week," confident that his clientele is following every move of the shutter. Even the staid *Times* published a couple of views of John L. Lewis the other day, and remarked that they were "unretouched." (Imagine retouching a picture of John L. Lewis!) *Life* describes how Margaret Bourke-White leans far out of her plane to snap "such stunning pictures as the one on p. 26." In the writing profession, there is nothing that quite corresponds to this sort of cameraderie. We feel rather left out. Perhaps we make a mistake not to make more fuss about the mechanics of our writing. When we toss off a particularly neat ablative absolute, or kill a hanging participle in the last three seconds of play, maybe our editor should call the matter to the attention of the reader. A writer does a lot of work the reader isn't conscious of, and never gets any credit. This paragraph was exposed for eighteen minutes, in a semi-darkened room. The writer was leaning far out over his typewriter, thinking to beat the band.

Of course, it may be that the art of photography and the art of writing are antithetical. The hope and aim of a word-handler is that he may communicate a thought or an impression to his reader without the reader's realizing that he has been dragged through a series of hazardous or grotesque syntactical situations. In photography, the goal seems to be to prove beyond a doubt that the cameraman, in his great moment of creation, was either

From "Peaks in Journalism" in *The Second Tree from the Corner*.

hanging by his heels from the rafters or was wedged under the floor with his lens at a knothole.

A PERSONAL PROBLEM

One of the elementary dilemmas confronting any writer when he begins to write is: "What shall I call myself?" The answer is not always easy. The question is related to the subtle literary problem of *point of view* (to be considered later) and—eventually—to one of the central questions of liberal education and human existence: "Who am I?" A natural personal essayist, White is a literary and spiritual descendant of Montaigne, who wrote on the first page of his sixteenth-century *Essays:* "I am myself the matter of my book." The use of the first person singular pronoun comes naturally to White. But the student will have noted already that White sometimes calls himself "I" and sometimes—conforming to the journalistic convention followed in the first section of *The New Yorker*—uses the editorial "we."

As he reveals in the following piece, he is never completely at home posing as a plural person. By gently mocking one universal species of "we-uns," he illustrates the relation between language and its social context and shows how an entrenched idiom —whether grammatical or not—can degenerate into an automatic and ambiguous cliché. Though this piece is primarily concerned with the spoken language, a broader lesson can be inferred. The writer should always make it clear who "we" are and—unless conforming to an accepted convention or consciously assuming another point of view, personal or impersonal—should not be afraid to look himself squarely in the "I."

JUNE 10, 1933

A STUDY OF THE CLINICAL "WE"

A recent article on grammar, which I read in a magazine, has led me to the preparation of a paper on the clinical "we." The clinical "we" is a bedside form in use among practical

From *Quo Vadimus?*

nurses, who find, in the sound of the plural, a little of the faded romance that still attaches to life. It is also used universally by baby nurses, who think of themselves in groups of four.

Unlike the editorial "we," which is a literary device used to protect writers from the fumes of their own work, the clinical "we" is simply a spoken form, and is rarely written. A baby nurse employs the "we" in the belief that no single person could have as much special knowledge as she has, and that therefore when she speaks it must be three other people too. Thus, when I once asked a baby nurse if she wouldn't please put a hat on my son before she took him out in a sandstorm that happened to be raging at the moment, her reply was: "We never put hats on him after June first." "You and who else don't?" I remember answering. It was my first clash with the clinical "we."

Since then I have studied it, not only in baby nurses but in dentists' assistants, ward witches, and the developers of X-ray plates. It is common to all of them, but hospital nurses use it to denote the patient, not the nurse. I know of one hospital case in which the sudden use of the clinical "we," in the presence of an elderly gentleman convalescing from an operation, threw him into a paroxysm that proved a serious setback to his recovery. It was early in the morning, and a pretty little Southern nurse, coming into his room, sang out: "We didn't change our pajamas this morning, did we?"

"No, let's do it right now!" replied the aged patient somewhat bitterly. The wry joke so excited him that he had to be given a sedative, and later a talking to.

It is probably apparent from the above examples that the clinical "we" can seldom be taken lying down, but almost always provokes a rejoinder. In hospitals the "we" is merely an unattractive figure of speech in a world of strange and unattractive details, but in the home it is intolerable. To live under the same roof with a user of the "we" is a fairly good test of a man's character. During the winter of 1931 I employed twenty-two baby nurses, one after another, before I found one who could make a sentence beginning with the word "I." I used to call them "we-uns." Every morning I would go upstairs to the nursery. "Morning, Nurse," I would say, "how you feeling?"

"We are just fine, sir," would be the courteous but silly reply.

"Canst make a sentence beginning with the word 'I'?" I would ask.

"We never make sentences that-a-way, sir," she would say. So I would fire her and get another. Finally a little Irish girl named McGheogheoghan (pronounced McVeigh) came along, and one morning I went up and asked her how she was feeling.

"I feel terrible," she answered.

That nurse is still with us, and grows, I am happy to say, more singular every day.

STYLE AND STYLES

The elusive word *style* has no ultimate definition. In the clothing business—euphemistically called "the fashion world"—the latest styles are designed and decreed by a coterie of experts. Fashionable clothes are an adornment, assumed from without and often more closely related to the wearer's purse than to his personality. It is commercially agreed that style makes the man—or the woman.

The most familiar epigram concerning word-fashions is Buffon's assertion that "the style is the man himself." A more recent word man, John Mason Brown, has put it this way: "An author's style is his written voice; his spirit and mind caught in ink." It is not an adornment to cover up or to beautify naked, natural prose. A fashionable writer may set a style for a season, and thousands of earnest followers may try tailoring it to their own personal dimensions. But in the long run it is useless for any writer to play the sedulous ape to another. The imitator will soon learn that every versatile writer has both a style and many styles, each of them peculiarly his. The product of imitation will be parody, not self-expression. This truth does not, however, invalidate the central thesis of this book: An undergraduate can improve his own writing by closely examining White's method of expressing himself.

When the personal element is distilled out of any effective style, the basic residue is common to all good writing. The conventions of grammar and punctuation, the structure of sentences and paragraphs, the use or misuse of familiar words and expressions—all these are considered in *The Elements of Style* by White's teacher at Cornell, the late William Strunk, Jr. For the new edition of "the little book," published in 1959, White added a chapter of his own. Here he approaches style in the broader sense of "what is distinguished and distinguishing" in the use of English. The next two selections are from that chapter. Taken together, they illustrate the mysterious attractions of a personal style and the menaces in the jungle of impersonal jargon.

1959

AN APPROACH TO STYLE

Up to this point, the book has been concerned with what is correct, or acceptable, in the use of English. In this final chapter, we approach style in its broader meaning: style in the sense of what is distinguished and distinguishing. Here we leave solid ground. Who can confidently say what ignites a certain combination of words, causing them to explode in the mind? Who knows why certain notes in music are capable of stirring the listener deeply, though the same notes, slightly rearranged, are impotent? These are high mysteries, and this chapter is a mystery story, thinly disguised. There is no satisfactory explanation of style, no infallible guide to good writing, no assurance that a person who thinks clearly will be able to write clearly, no key that unlocks the door, no inflexible rule by which the young writer may shape his course. He will often find himself steering by stars that are disturbingly in motion.

The preceding chapters contain instructions drawn from established English usage; this one contains advice drawn from a writer's experience of writing. Since the book is a rulebook,

From *The Elements of Style*.

these cautionary remarks, these subtly dangerous hints, are presented in the form of rules, but they are, in essence, mere gentle reminders: they state what most of us know and, at times, forget.

Style is an increment in writing. When we speak of Fitzgerald's style, we don't mean his command of the relative pronoun, we mean the sound his words make on paper. Every writer, by the way he uses the language, reveals something of his spirit, his habits, his capacities, his bias. This is inevitable, as well as enjoyable. All writing is communication; creative writing is communication through revelation—it is the Self escaping into the open. No writer long remains incognito.

If the student doubts that style is something of a mystery, let him try rewriting a familiar sentence and see what happens. Any much-quoted sentence will do. Suppose we take "These are the times that try men's souls." Here we have eight short, easy words, forming a simple declarative sentence. The sentence contains no flashy ingredient, such as "Damn the torpedoes!" and the words, as you see, are ordinary. Yet in that arrangement they have shown great durability; the sentence is well along in its second century. Now compose a few variations:

> Times like these try men's souls.
> How trying it is to live in these times!
> These are trying times for men's souls.
> Soulwise, these are trying times.

It seems unlikely that Thomas Paine could have made his sentiment stick if he had couched it in any of these forms. But why not? No fault of grammar can be detected in them, and in every case the meaning is clear. Each version is correct, and each, for some reason that we can't readily put our finger on, is marked for oblivion. We could, of course, talk about "rhythm" and "cadence," but the talk would be vague and unconvincing. We could declare "soulwise" to be a silly word, inappropriate to the occasion; but even that won't do—it does not answer the main question. Are we even sure "soulwise" is silly? If "otherwise" is a serviceable word, what's the matter with "soulwise"?

Here is another sentence, this one by a later Tom. It is not a famous sentence, although its author (Thomas Wolfe) is well known. "Quick are the mouths of earth, and quick the teeth that fed upon this loveliness." The sentence would not take a prize for clarity, and rhetorically it is at the opposite pole from "These are the times." Try it in a different form, without the inversions:

> The mouths of earth are quick, and the teeth
> that fed upon this loveliness are quick, too.

The author's meaning is still intact, but not his overpowering emotion. What was poetical and sensuous has become prosy and wooden; instead of the secret sounds of beauty, we are left with the simple crunch of mastication. (Whether Mr. Wolfe was guilty of overwriting is, of course, another question—one that is not pertinent here.)

With some writers, style not only reveals the spirit of the man, it reveals his identity, as surely as would his fingerprints. Here, following, are two brief passages from the works of two American novelists. The subject in each case is languor. In both, the words used are ordinary, and there is nothing eccentric about the construction.

> He did not still feel weak, he was merely luxuriating in that supremely gutful lassitude of convalescence in which time, hurry, doing, did not exist, the accumulating seconds and minutes and hours to which in its well state the body is slave both waking and sleeping, now reversed and time now the lip-server and mendicant to the body's pleasure instead of the body thrall to time's headlong course.

> Manuel drank his brandy. He felt sleepy himself. It was too hot to go out into the town. Besides there was nothing to do. He wanted to see Zurito. He would go to sleep while he waited.

Anyone acquainted with Faulkner and Hemingway will have recognized them in these passages and perceived which was which. How different are their languors!

Or take two American poets, stopping at evening. One stops by woods, the other by laughing flesh.

> My little horse must think it queer
> To stop without a farmhouse near
> Between the woods and frozen lake
> The darkest evening of the year.[1]

> I have perceived that to be with those I like is enough,
> To stop in company with the rest at evening is enough,
> To be surrounded by beautiful, curious, breathing,
>   laughing flesh is enough . . .

Because of the characteristic styles, there is little question of identity here, and if the situations were reversed, with Whitman stopping by woods and Frost by laughing flesh (not one of his regularly scheduled stops), the reader would still know who was who.

Young writers often suppose that style is a garnish for the meat of prose, a sauce by which a dull dish is made palatable. Style has no such separate entity; it is non-detachable, unfilterable. The beginner should approach style warily, realizing that it is himself he is approaching, no other; and he should begin by turning resolutely away from all devices that are popularly believed to indicate style—all mannerisms, tricks, adornments. The approach to style is by way of plainness, simplicity, orderliness, sincerity.

Writing is, for most, laborious and slow. The mind travels faster than the pen; consequently, writing becomes a question of learning to make occasional wing shots, bringing down the bird

---

[1] Excerpt from "Stopping by Woods on a Snowy Evening" from *Complete Poems of Robert Frost*. Copyright 1923 by Holt, Rinehart and Winston, Inc. Copyright 1936, 1951 by Robert Frost. Copyright © 1964 by Lesley Frost Ballantine. Reprinted by permission of Holt, Rinehart and Winston, Inc.

of thought as it flashes by. A writer is a gunner, sometimes waiting in his blind for something to come in, sometimes roaming the countryside hoping to scare something up. Like other gunners, he must cultivate patience: he may have to work many covers to bring down one partridge.

1959

PREFER THE STANDARD TO THE OFFBEAT

The young writer will be drawn at every turn toward eccentricities in language. He will hear the beat of new vocabularies, the exciting rhythms of special segments of his society, each speaking a language of its own. All of us come under the spell of these unsettling drums; the problem, for the beginner, is to listen to them, learn the words, feel the excitement, and not be carried away.

Today, the language of advertising enjoys an enormous circulation. With its deliberate infractions of grammatical rules and its crossbreeding of the parts of speech, it profoundly influences the tongues and pens of children and adults. Your new kitchen range is so revolutionary it *obsoletes* all other ranges. Your counter top is beautiful because it is *accessorized* with gold-plated faucets. Your cigarette tastes good *like* a cigarette should. And *like the man says,* you will want to try one. You will also, in all probability, want to try writing that way, using that language. You do so at your peril, for it is the language of mutilation.

Advertisers are quite understandably interested in what they call "attention getting." The man photographed must have lost an eye or grown a pink beard, or he must have three arms or be sitting wrong end to on a horse. This technique is proper in its place, which is the world of selling, but the young writer had best not adopt the device of mutilation in ordinary composition, whose purpose is to engage, not paralyze, the reader's senses. Our

From *The Elements of Style.*

advice is to buy the gold-plated faucets if you will, but do not accessorize your prose. To use the language well, do not begin by hacking it to bits; accept the whole body of it, cherish its classic form, its variety, and its richness.

Another segment of society that has constructed a language of its own is business. The businessman says that ink erasers are *in short supply,* that he has *updated* the next shipment of these erasers, and that he will *finalize* his recommendations at the next meeting of the board. He is speaking a language that is familiar to him and dear to him. Its portentous nouns and verbs invest ordinary events with high adventure; the executive walks among ink erasers caparisoned like a knight. This we should be tolerant of—every man of spirit wants to ride a white horse. The only question is whether his vocabulary is helpful to ordinary prose. Usually, the same ideas can be expressed less formidably, if one wishes to do so. A good many of the special words of business seem designed more to express the user's dreams than his precise meaning. Not all such words, of course, can be dismissed summarily—indeed, no word in the language can be dismissed offhand by anyone who has a healthy curiosity. *Update* isn't a bad word; in the right setting it is useful. In the wrong setting, though, it is destructive, and the trouble with adopting coinages too quickly is that they will bedevil one by insinuating themselves where they do not belong. This may sound like rhetorical snobbery, or plain stuffiness; but the writer will discover, in the course of his work, that the setting of a word is just as restrictive as the setting of a jewel. The general rule, here, is to prefer the standard. *Finalize,* for instance, is not standard: it is special, and it is a peculiarly fuzzy and silly word. Does it mean *terminate,* or does it mean *put into final form?* One can't be sure, really, what it means, and one gets the impression that the person using it doesn't know either, and doesn't want to know.

The special vocabularies of the law, of the military, of government, are familiar to most of us. Even the world of criticism has a modest pouch of private words (*luminous, taut*), whose only virtue is that they are exceptionally nimble and can escape from the garden of meaning over the wall. Of these Critical words, Wolcott Gibbs once wrote: ". . . they are detached from the language and inflated like little balloons." The young writer should learn to spot them—words that at first glance seem freighted with delicious meaning but that soon burst in air, leaving nothing but a memory of bright sound.

The language is perpetually in flux: it is a living stream, shifting, changing, receiving new strength from a thousand tributaries, losing old forms in the backwaters of time. To suggest that a young writer not swim in the main stream of this turbulence would be foolish indeed, and such is not the intent of these cautionary remarks. The intent is to suggest that in choosing between the formal and the informal, the regular and the offbeat, the general and the special, the orthodox and the heretical, the beginner err on the side of conservatism, on the side of established usage. No idiom is taboo, no accent forbidden; there simply is a better chance of doing well if the writer holds a steady course, enters the stream of English quietly, and does not thrash about.

"But," the student may ask, "what if it comes natural to me to experiment rather than conform? What if I am a pioneer, or even a genius?" Answer: then be one. But do not forget that what may seem like pioneering may be merely evasion, or laziness— the disinclination to submit to discipline. Writing good standard English is no cinch, and before you have managed it you will have encountered enough rough country to satisfy even the most adventurous spirit.

READING AND WRITING

Before the hickory stick gave way to the audio-visual aid in the schools, the 3 R's were memorably associated by rhythmic alliteration. Now that 'rithmetic is yielding to set theory and the computer, the time-honored trio has dwindled to a tired fundamentalist chant. The marriage of reading and 'riting is also threat-

ened by divorce. Some prophets assume that the first two R's—
swept along on the tide of better living and swifter dying—will
soon give way to mechanical processes efficiently programmed
by technicians in white coats.

Meanwhile, pending the day of mechanized doom, our era
has been peopled by new tribes of experts on how to read and
write. Many are serious teachers giving useful training; others
promise misleading shortcuts to general literacy. Too often compre-
hension is sacrificed to speed, and subtlety to simplicity. Though
the calculated techniques for hurried reading may increase the
efficiency of the harassed executive or undergraduate, the ultimate goals of serious reflection cannot be reached by rapid
transit. Nor is it the serious writer's duty to reduce his prose to
the lowest common denominator so that he who skims may read.
To be clear to a reader is not to condescend to a consumer. The
problems of literacy have not been solved yet by substituting in a
formula, or a whole series of formulas. Neither reading nor writing
is a process or an isolated subject confined to a school curriculum;
both are arts to be imperfectly learned in a lifetime of patient,
lonely application. Because the two arts are subtly related, one
rarely finds a good writer who is not a thorough and omniverous
reader.

In the two pieces that follow, White expresses his faith in
this old-fashioned doctrine. He takes his text, not from the latest
expert, but from his favorite nineteenth-century guide, a writer
who will turn up again in this book: the author of *Walden*.

MARCH 3, 1951

CALCULATING MACHINE

A publisher in Chicago has sent us a pocket calculating
machine by which we may test our writing to see whether it is
intelligible. The calculator was developed by General Motors,
who, not satisfied with giving the world a Cadillac, now dream

From *The Second Tree from the Corner*.

of bringing perfect understanding to men. The machine (it is simply a celluloid card with a dial) is called the Reading-Ease Calculator and shows four grades of "reading ease"—Very Easy, Easy, Hard, and Very Hard. You count your words and syllables, set the dial, and an indicator lets you know whether anybody is going to understand what you have written. An instruction book came with it, and after mastering the simple rules we lost no time in running a test on the instruction book itself, to see how *that* writer was doing. The poor fellow! His leading essay, the one on the front cover, tested Very Hard.

Our next step was to study the first phrase on the face of the calculator: "How to test Reading-Ease of written matter." There is, of course, no such thing as reading ease of written matter. There is the ease with which matter can be read, but that is a condition of the reader, not of the matter. Thus the inventors and distributors of this calculator get off to a poor start, with a Very Hard instruction book and a slovenly phrase. Already they have one foot caught in the brier patch of English usage.

Not only did the author of the instruction book score badly on the front cover, but inside the book he used the word "personalize" in an essay on how to improve one's writing. A man who likes the word "personalize" is entitled to his choice, but we wonder whether he should be in the business of giving advice to writers. "Whenever possible," he wrote, "personalize your writing by directing it to the reader." As for us, we would as lief Simonize our grandmother as personalize our writing.

In the same envelope with the calculator, we received another training aid for writers—a booklet called "How to Write Better," by Rudolf Flesch. This, too, we studied, and it quickly demonstrated the broncolike ability of the English language to throw whoever leaps cocksurely into the saddle. The language not only can toss a rider but knows a thousand tricks for tossing him, each more gay than the last. Dr. Flesch stayed in the saddle only a moment or two. Under the heading "Think Before You Write," he wrote, "The main thing to consider is your *purpose* in writing. Why are you sitting down to write?" An echo answered: Because, sir, it is more comfortable than standing up.

Communication by the written word is a subtler (and more beautiful) thing than Dr. Flesch and General Motors imagine. They contend that the "average reader" is capable of reading only what tests Easy, and that the writer should write at or below this level. This is a presumptuous and degrading idea. There is no average reader, and to reach down toward this mythical character is to deny that each of us is on the way up, is ascending. ("Ascending," by the way, is a word Dr. Flesch advises writers to stay away from. Too unusual.)

It is our belief that no writer can improve his work until he discards the dulcet notion that the reader is feeble-minded, for writing is an act of faith, not a trick of grammar. Ascent is at the heart of the matter. A country whose writers are following a calculating machine downstairs is not ascending—if you will pardon the expression—and a writer who questions the capacity of the person at the other end of the line is not a writer at all, merely a schemer. The movies long ago decided that a wider communication could be achieved by a deliberate descent to a lower level, and they walked proudly down until they reached the cellar. Now they are groping for the light switch, hoping to find the way out.

We have studied Dr. Flesch's instructions diligently, but we return for guidance in these matters to an earlier American, who wrote with more patience, more confidence. "I fear chiefly," he wrote, "lest my expression may not be *extra-vagant* enough, may not wander far enough beyond the narrow limits of my daily experience, so as to be adequate to the truth of which I have been convinced. . . . Why level downward to our dullest perception always, and praise that as common sense? The commonest sense is the sense of men asleep, which they express by snoring."

Run that through your calculator! It may come out Hard, it may come out Easy. But it will come out whole, and it will last forever.

MARCH 24, 1951

THE FUTURE OF READING

In schools and colleges, in these audio-visual days, doubt has been raised as to the future of reading—whether the printed word is on its last legs. One college president has remarked that in fifty years "only five per cent of the people will be reading." For this, of course, one must be prepared. But how prepare? To us it would seem that even if only one person out of a hundred and fifty million should continue as a *reader,* he would be the one worth saving, the nucleus around which to found a university. We think this not impossible person, this Last Reader, might very well stand in the same relation to the community as the queen bee to the colony of bees, and that the others would quite properly dedicate themselves wholly to his welfare, serving special food and building special accommodations. From his nuptial, or intellectual, flight would come the new race of men, linked perfectly with the long past by the unbroken chain of the intellect, to carry on the community. But it is more likely that our modern hive of bees, substituting a coaxial cable for spinal fluid, will try to perpetuate the race through audio-visual devices, that ask no discipline of the mind and that are already giving the room the languor of an opium parlor.

Reading is the work of the alert mind, is demanding, and under ideal conditions produces finally a sort of ecstasy. As in the sexual experience, there are never more than two persons present in the act of reading—the writer, who is the impregnator, and the reader, who is the respondent. This gives the experience of reading a sublimity and power unequalled by any other form of communication. It would be just as well, we think, if educators clung to this great phenomenon and did not get sidetracked, for although books and reading may at times have played too large a part in the educational process, that is not what is happening

From *The Second Tree from the Corner.*

today. Indeed, there is very little true reading, and not nearly as much writing as one would suppose from the towering piles of pulpwood in the dooryards of our paper mills. Readers and writers are scarce, as are publishers and reporters. The reports we get nowadays are those of men who have not gone to the scene of the accident, which is always farther inside one's own head than it is convenient to penetrate without galoshes.

ANGLE AND ATTITUDE

The student who has read "A Study of the Clinical 'We'" and the attached editorial comments should be aware that when the nurse uses the plural pronoun the implications of her choice are not strictly grammatical. Consciously or not, she is speaking no longer as one fallible female, endowed with both practical wisdom and human ignorance, but as a representative of a race of experts, with all rights and privileges. She is looking at the job from a professional angle. Moreover, her attitude toward herself, her profession, and her employer is reflected in both her choice of words and the intonations of her voice. Does she condescend to her employer with the cool haughtiness of the expert consigning the layman to the lowest circle of stupidity? What is her cribside manner? Does she remove her professional mask, adopt the point of view of a tender intimate, and assume a tone of infantile idiocy in a language too primitive for pronouns? (Diddums wettums didums again?) In everyday speech, point of view and tone are always related and very often ambiguous. (Is this your opinion? Are you speaking for yourself? Are you serious? Are you kidding? What's so funny about that?) In writing, where the personal pronoun is sometimes absent and the tone of voice is always still, the nuances of point of view and tone can be even more subtle.

POINT OF VIEW

In most compositions for an elementary course the writer will be himself and call himself "I," whether or not the assignment is "An Autobiographical Theme" or "A Personal Essay." He may assume a more disinterested point of view by referring to himself in the third person. ("He was a young man who had entered college with a National Merit Scholarship.") In describing habitual experience or explaining a process, he may resort to the impersonal "you" or the more formal "one." ("You find yourself in a dormitory peopled with high school valedictorians." "One can't drive legally without a license, can one?") Or he may—as in much technical or critical writing—avoid the pronoun choice entirely, perhaps in a conscious attempt to assume scientific or aesthetic detachment. ("*Titus Andronicus* is the bloodiest of Shakespeare's plays.") But the writer should not escape the choice of pronouns only to fall headlong into the trap of the passive voice. ("From the foregoing illustrations it can be observed that the following conclusions can be drawn.")

The study of point of view in fiction—short story or novel—can become a complex problem of literary criticism. In simplified form it amounts to the writer implying and the reader discovering the answers to the following questions: Are the author and narrator one person or two? What kind of person is he (are they)? Where is the author (or narrator) in relation to the events of the story?

If, instead of using a narrator, the author chooses to tell the story himself, he may tell it from the God's-eye view of one who can fathom the innermost secrets of all his creations (*author omniscient*); he may assume the angle of a limited observer who is on the scene but not involved in the action (*author observant*); he may thrust himself into the middle of the action (*author participant*). Obvious as this may be to the student in a literature course, it is too often forgotten by the same student in a writing course. The undergraduate writer may even violate the most elementary rule: *Once you assume a point of view, stick to it with complete consistency unless you prepare your reader for a switch.*

Each of the next two selections has the same theme: the search for unity in a divided world. But there are two distinctly different points of view with regard to technique.

In the first selection—a part of a longer essay—White expresses his opinion directly in the first person. If the "I's" were exchanged for "we's" and the humility of the modest citizen were replaced by the omniscience of the pundit, the point of view (not the writer's opinion) would be that of a standard newspaper editorial. But here, as in all the pieces in *The Points of My Compass,* White adopts the frank first-person attitude (but not aimless chitchat) of the writer of a friendly letter. (For his explanation of his personal compass see pages 244–245.) He is not handing down anonymous editorial pronouncements from a city room on Olympus; he is sitting at a typewriter, an undisguised mortal, sharing his private yearnings for higher ground and cleaner air. The point of view is typical of the *personal* (or *familiar,* or *informal*) essay.

The second piece (written before the division of China) illustrates an ancient form in an ancient frame: a parable in a dream. A parable—and White has written many—is a short fictitious anecdote with a clear moral implication. It is a branch of allegory, which is an abundant literary tree bearing such profoundly simple parables as "The Good Samaritan" or Dickens's *Christmas Carol* and such masterpieces as *The Divine Comedy, The Faerie Queene,* and Joyce's *Ulysses.* The technique of the parable is a far cry from that of the typical personal essay. The point is approached implicitly through narrative, not explicitly through exposition; the reader is gradually led—often teased—to an inevitable conclusion and he is not confronted with a direct assertion. The point of view is more impersonal, detached, objective. Take the Christmas parable of "The Wild Flag," for example. Though the dream may be an intense personal experience, White does not appear as a direct participant in the miracle he reports. He is not speaking in his own voice from the front of the stage; he is the dreamer in the wings, less intimately involved with the actors than the puppeteer with the puppets— the occidental innocent bemused by the wisdom of the Orient.

JUNE 18, 1960

WESTERN UNITY

Avenue of the Americas, June 4, 1960

Perhaps this is not the proper time to explore the foundations of unity of the West. Many people would say that although

From "Unity," a "Letter from the West" in *The Points of My Compass.*

the vision of a federal union of free democratic capitalist states is a pleasing prospect for dreamers, actual work on it would be too upsetting, would shake us at a ticklish time. We might become so absorbed in establishing order on a higher level that we'd lose what little order we now enjoy, and thus play into the hands of our enemies. Others would say that if the political unity of free powers were to become an accomplished fact, it would merely increase the challenge and the fury of the East. Others would argue that most people find unity repugnant; it spoils the fun.

These are all good arguments against trying to bring greater order into Western society. As an American citizen, though, I would welcome the stirrings of political union with the United Kingdom, with Scandinavia, with the Western European nations—with any nation, in fact, that could show a long, successful record of government by the consent of the governed. For I would feel that although I was being placed temporarily in a more dangerous position, I was nevertheless occupying higher ground, where the view was better. I would know my destination at last. If from the shambles of the summit there were to emerge the first positive thrust of Western unity, then the summit would, in my book, go down as a smashing success, not a bleak failure.

The Communists have a shape they pursue; they propose an Eastern union that will eventually erode the West and occupy the globe. In a day when imperialism is despised and languishing, they brazenly construct an empire. To do this they engage us in a Cold War. I believe this war would be easier to fight if we, too, could find a shape to pursue, a proposal to make. Let us pursue the shape of English liberty—what Santayana once described as "this slow cooperation of free men, this liberty in democracy." English liberty in a federal hall—there's a shape to conjure with! "Far from being neutralized by American dash and bravura," wrote Santayana, "or lost in the opposite instincts of so many alien races, it seems to be adopted at once in the most mixed circles and in the most novel predicaments." A federation of free states, with its national units undisturbed and its people elevated to a new and greater sovereignty, is a long way off, by

anybody's guess; but if we could once settle on it among ourselves, and embrace it unashamedly, then we would begin to
advance in a clear direction and enjoy the pleasures and disci-
plines of a political destination. Liberty is never out of bounds or
off limits; it spreads wherever it can capture the imagination of
men.

In the long debate on disarmament, I encountered a
statement that has proved memorable; it was in a piece in the
Times magazine last October, by Salvador de Madariaga, who
for a number of years watched disarmament from the vantage
point of the League of Nations. Señor de Madariaga ended his
article with an observation that should inform and enliven every
free nation.

"The trouble today," he wrote, "is that the Communist
world understands unity but not liberty, while the free world
understands liberty but not unity. Eventual victory may be won
by the first of the two sides to achieve the synthesis of both
liberty and unity."

I have never seen the matter stated more succinctly, nor
have I ever read a prediction I felt more confidence in.

DECEMBER 25, 1943

THE WILD FLAG

This is the dream we had, asleep in our chair, thinking of
Christmas in lands of the fir tree and pine, Christmas in lands of
the palm tree and vine, and of how the one great sky does for all
places and all people.

After the third war was over (this was our curious
dream), there was no more than a handful of people left alive,
and the earth was in ruins and the ruins were horrible to behold.
The people, the survivors, decided to meet to talk over their
problem and to make a lasting peace, which is the customary
thing to make after a long, exhausting war. There were eighty-
three countries, and each country sent a delegate to the conven-

From *The Wild Flag.*

tion. One Englishman came, one Peruvian, one Ethiopian, one Frenchman, one Japanese, and so on, until every country was represented. Each delegate brought the flag of his homeland with him—each, that is, except the delegate from China. When the others asked him why he had failed to bring a flag, he said that he had discussed the matter with another Chinese survivor, an ancient and very wise man, and that between them they had concluded that they would not have any cloth flag for China any more.

"What kind of flag *do* you intend to have?" asked the delegate from Luxembourg.

The Chinese delegate blinked his eyes and produced a shoebox, from which he drew a living flower that looked very like an iris.

"What is that?" they all inquired, pleased with the sight of so delicate a symbol.

"That," said the Chinese, "is a wild flag, *Iris tectorum*. In China we have decided to adopt this flag, since it is a convenient and universal device and very beautiful and grows everywhere in the moist places of the earth for all to observe and wonder at. I propose all countries adopt it, so that it will be impossible for us to insult each other's flag."

"Can it be waved?" asked the American delegate, who wore a troubled expression and a Taft button.

The Chinese gentleman moved the flag gently to and fro. "It can be waved, yes," he answered. "But it is more interesting in repose or as the breeze stirs it."

"I see it is monocotyledonous," said the Dutch delegate, who was an amiable man.

"I don't see how a strong foreign policy can be built around a wild flag which is the same for everybody," complained the Latvian.

"It can't be," said the Chinese. "That is one of the virtues of my little flag. I should remind you that the flag was once yours, too. It is the oldest flag in the world, the original one, you might say. We are now, gentlemen, in an original condition again. There are very few of us."

The German delegate arose stiffly. "I would be a poor man indeed," he said, "did I not feel that I belonged to the master race. And for that I need a special flag, *natürlich*."

"At the moment," replied the Chinaman, "the master race, like so many other races, is suffering from the handicap of being virtually extinct. There are fewer than two hundred people left in the entire world, and we suffer from a multiplicity of banners."

The delegate from Patagonia spoke up. "I fear that the wild flag, one for all, will prove an unpopular idea."

"It will, undoubtedly," sighed the Chinese delegate. "But now that there are only a couple of hundred people on earth, even the word 'unpopular' loses most of its meaning. At this juncture we might conceivably act in a sensible, rather than a popular, manner." And he produced eighty-two more shoeboxes and handed a wild flag to each delegate, bowing ceremoniously.

Next day the convention broke up and the delegates returned to their homes, marveling at what they had accomplished in so short a time. And that is the end of our dream.

TONE

Tone can be defined broadly as a blend of the writer's attitudes toward both his subject and his reader. The range of possible tones is as limitless as the gamut of human emotions and the adjectives used to describe them. A writer may be solemn, sober, earnest, serious, ironic, sentimental, or playful; respectful to his reader or condescending, reverent or contemptuous. He may kid his material or his reader or both. If he is solemn, he may be stately or merely stuffy. His irony may be gentle ridicule of human foibles or savage indignation at human failures. A sentimental tone may reveal natural tenderness or a calculated effort to drown the stage in tears sweetened with saccharine. A playful tone may mask a serious observer—as it often does in White's essays—or a facetious wisecracker.

Obviously the words describing tone are not mutually exclusive categories. A writer may be stuffy in order to be funny or funny to avoid sounding stuffy. No reader who understands the intimate relation between tears and laughter should make the familiar mistake of assuming that the choice between seriousness and humor is arbitrary and that never the twain should meet. As James Thurber once said of writers of short humorous pieces, "the little wheels of their invention are set in motion by the damp hand of melancholy." This does not mean that every humorist is a Pagliacci deep in his broken heart. "It would be more accurate . . . to say," White once wrote, "that there is a deep vein of melancholy running through everyone's life and that the humorist, perhaps more sensible of it than some others, compensates for it actively and positively."

A single work may employ many tones well; so long as the reader is not misled into taking irony literally or confusing soul-searching with leg-pulling. But it is better, on the whole, for an apprentice writer, especially in a short piece, to select a single tone and try to preserve it consistently throughout.

There are no formulas for doing this. The overall tone of any writing depends on numerous elements—on sound as well as sense, on rhythm as well as grammar and sentence structure, even on spelling and punctuation. But the clearest clue to a writer's tone is his choice of words.

Take, for example, the first selection in the following group. White addresses a pair of anonymous officials who have accused him of violating the law. If he had intended only to register the customary complaint of the benighted private citizen, he might have composed stiffly formal models of business correspondence, as impersonal and colorless as the dun from the tax bureau. The letters begin with the conventional rubber stamps ("Dear Sir: I have your notice about a payment . . ."). But it is soon evident that White's motives are not strictly utilitarian: He intends to open the letters to other readers who may enjoy both the confusion of his own dilemma and his ridicule of the toils and toilers of officialdom. Instead of playing the outraged taxpayer, heaping contemptuous scorn on his accusers, he assumes the point of view of a misunderstood innocent and adopts a tone of ostensibly friendly cooperation.

He conveys this tone, not in the words of an urbane professional writer from Manhattan, but in the folksy idiom of a frustrated farmer who is too busy to be a good businessman. The letters are pervaded by gentle irony. The essence of irony is contrast—implied contrast here between genuine and assumed friendship, between the impersonal voice of authority and the folksy talk of a puzzled human being, between the memo-minded bureaucrat whose time means money and the tender-hearted husbandman who intrudes on that time—with a show of complete insouciance—to beguile the bureaucrat with an interminable dog-and-goose story.

The student could go back over any of the other pieces considered so far and study them for tone. He might learn, for example, that effective irony is not, as many undergraduates apparently assume, a forced tone of "oh yeah" sarcasm: It may lurk unobtrusively beneath the surface of an ostensibly literal statement. ("The people, the survivors, decided to meet to talk over their problem and to make a lasting peace, which is the customary thing to make after a long war.")

The following four selections have been chosen to illustrate a variety of tones. "The Day of Days" and "The Burning Question" are both short seasonal pieces about animals in Maine; or, to put it more abstractly, about the subtle relations between Man and Nature. But in tone or in mood, they are so different that no sensitive reader could have the same reaction to them both. The longer piece, "Farewell, My Lovely!", runs a wide tonal gamut of nostalgia, ridicule, humor, and neutral literal statement—all blended to convey a considerable amount of accurate information.

APRIL 21, 1951

TWO LETTERS, BOTH OPEN

New York, N.Y.
12 April 1951

The American Society for the Prevention of Cruelty to Animals
York Avenue and East 92nd Street
New York 28, N.Y.
Dear Sirs:

I have your letter, undated, saying that I am harboring an unlicensed dog in violation of the law. If by "harboring" you

From *The Second Tree from the Corner.*

mean getting up two or three times every night to pull Minnie's blanket up over her, I am harboring a dog all right. The blanket keeps slipping off. I suppose you are wondering by now why I don't get her a sweater instead. That's a joke on you. She has a knitted sweater, but she doesn't like to wear it for sleeping; her legs are so short they work out of a sweater and her toenails get caught in the mesh, and this disturbs her rest. If Minnie doesn't get her rest, she feels it right away. I do myself, and of course with this night duty of mine, the way the blanket slips and all, I haven't had any real rest in years. Minnie is twelve.

In spite of what your inspector reported, she has a license. She is licensed in the State of Maine as an unspayed bitch, or what is more commonly called an "unspaded" bitch. She wears her metal license tag but I must say I don't particularly care for it, as it is in the shape of a hydrant, which seems to me a feeble gag, besides being pointless in the case of a female. It is hard to believe that any state in the Union would circulate a gag like that and make people pay money for it, but Maine is always thinking of something. Maine puts up roadside crosses along the highways to mark the spots where people have lost their lives in motor accidents, so the highways are beginning to take on the appearance of a cemetery, and motoring in Maine has become a solemn experience, when one thinks mostly about death. I was driving along a road near Kittery the other day thinking about death and all of a sudden I heard the spring peepers. That changed me right away and I suddenly thought about life. It was the nicest feeling.

You asked about Minnie's name, sex, breed, and phone number. She doesn't answer the phone. She is a dachshund and can't reach it, but she wouldn't answer it even if she could, as she has no interest in outside calls. I did have a dachshund once, a male, who was interested in the telephone, and who got a great many calls, but Fred was an exceptional dog (his name was Fred) and I can't think of anything offhand that he *wasn't* interested in. The telephone was only one of a thousand things. He loved life—that is, he loved life if by "life" you mean "trouble," and of course the phone is almost synonymous with trouble.

Minnie loves life, too, but her idea of life is a warm bed, preferably with an electric pad, and a friend in bed with her, and plenty of shut-eye, night and day. She's almost twelve. I guess I've already mentioned that. I got her from Dr. Clarence Little in 1939. He was using dachshunds in his cancer-research experiments (that was before Winchell was running the thing) and he had a couple of extra puppies, so I wheedled Minnie out of him. She later had puppies by her own father, at Dr. Little's request. What do you think about *that* for a scandal? I know what Fred thought about it. He was some put out.

Sincerely yours,
E. B. White

New York, N.Y.
12 April 1951

Collector of Internal Revenue
Divisional Office
Bangor, Maine
Dear Sir:

I have your notice about a payment of two hundred and some-odd dollars that you say is owing on my 1948 income tax. You say a warrant has been issued for the seizure and sale of my place in Maine, but I don't know as you realize how awkward that would be right at this time, because in the same mail I also received a notice from the Society for the Prevention of Cruelty to Animals here in New York taking me to task for harboring an unlicensed dog in my apartment, and I have written them saying that Minnie is licensed in Maine, but if you seize and sell my place, it is going to make me look pretty silly with the Society, isn't it? Why would I license a dog in Maine, they will say, if I don't live there? I think it is a fair question. I have written the Society, but purposely did not mention the warrant of seizure and sale. I didn't want to mix them up, and it might have sounded like just some sort of cock and bull story. I have always paid my taxes promptly, and the Society would think I was kidding, or something.

Anyway, the way the situation shapes up is this: I am being accused in New York State of dodging my dog tax, and accused in Maine of being behind in my federal tax, and I believe I'm going to have to rearrange my life somehow or other so that everything can be brought together, all in one state, maybe Delaware or some state like that, as it is too confusing for everybody this way. Minnie, who is very sensitive to my moods, knows there is something wrong and that I feel terrible. And now *she* feels terrible. The other day it was the funniest thing, I was packing a suitcase for a trip home to Maine, and the suitcase was lying open on the floor and when I wasn't looking she went and got in and lay down. Don't you think that was cute?

If you seize the place, there are a couple of things I ought to explain. At the head of the kitchen stairs you will find an awfully queer boxlike thing. I don't want you to get a false idea about it, as it looks like a coffin, only it has a partition inside, and two small doors on one side. I don't suppose there is another box like it in the entire world. I built it myself. I made it many years ago as a dormitory for two snug-haired dachshunds, both of whom suffered from night chill. Night chill is the most prevalent dachshund disorder, if you have never had one. Both these dogs, as a matter of fact, had rheumatoid tendencies, as well as a great many other tendencies, especially Fred. He's dead, damn it. I would feel a lot better this morning if I could just see Fred's face, as he would know instantly that I was in trouble with the authorities and would be all over the place, hamming it up. He was something.

About the tax money, it was an oversight, or mixup. Your notice says that the "first notice" was sent last summer. I think that is correct, but when it arrived I didn't know what it meant as I am no mind reader. It was cryptic. So I sent it to a lawyer, fool-fashion, and asked him if *he* knew what it meant. I asked him if it was a tax bill and shouldn't I pay it, and he wrote back and said, No, no, no, no, it isn't a tax bill. He advised me to wait till I got a bill, and then pay it. Well, that was all right, but I was building a small henhouse at the time, and when I get building something with my own hands I lose all sense of time and place. I don't even show up for meals. Give me some tools and some second-handed lumber and I get completely absorbed in what I am doing. The first thing I knew, the summer was gone, and the fall was gone, and it was winter. The lawyer must have been building something, too, because I never heard another word from him.

To make a long story short, I am sorry about this non-payment, but you've got to see the whole picture to understand it, got to see my side of it. Of course I will forward the money if you haven't seized and sold the place in the meantime. If you have, there are a couple of other things on my mind. In the barn, at the far end of the tieups, there is a goose sitting on eggs. She is a young goose and I hope you can manage everything so as not to disturb her until she has brought off her goslings. I'll give you one, if you want. Or would they belong to the federal government anyway, even though the eggs were laid before the notice was mailed? The cold frames are ready, and pretty soon you ought to transplant the young broccoli and tomato plants and my wife's petunias from the flats in the kitchen into the frames, to harden them. Fred's grave is down in the alder thicket beyond the dump. You have to go down there every once in a while and straighten the headstone, which is nothing but a couple of old bricks that came out of a chimney. Fred was restless, and his headstone is the same way—doesn't stay quiet. You have to keep at it.

I am sore about your note, which didn't seem friendly. I am a friendly taxpayer and do not think the government should take a threatening tone, at least until we have exchanged a couple of letters kicking the thing around. Then it might be all right to talk about selling the place, if I proved stubborn. I showed the lawyer your notice about the warrant of seizure and sale, and do you know what he said? He said, "Oh, that doesn't mean anything, it's just a form." What a crazy way to look at a piece of plain English. I honestly worry about lawyers. They never write plain English themselves, and when you give them a bit of plain English to read, they say, "Don't worry, it doesn't mean anything." They're hopeless, don't you think they are? To me a word is a word, and I wouldn't dream of writing anything like "I am going to get out a warrant to seize and sell your place" unless I meant it, and I can't believe that my government would either.

The best way to get into the house is through the wood-shed, as there is an old crocus sack nailed on the bottom step and you can wipe the mud off on it. Also, when you go in through the woodshed, you land in the back kitchen right next to the cooky jar with Mrs. Freethy's cookies. Help yourself, they're wonderful.

Sincerely yours,
E. B. White

APRIL　1941

THE DAY OF DAYS

There is a stanza in Robert Frost's poem "Two Tramps in Mud Time" that describes an April moment when air and sky have a vernal feeling, but suddenly a cloud crosses the path of the sun and a bitter little wind finds you out, and you're back in the middle of March. Everyone who has lived in the country knows that sort of moment—the promise of warmth, the raised hope, the ruthless rebuff.

There is another sort of day that needs celebrating in song—the day of days when spring at last holds up her face to be kissed, deliberate and unabashed. On that day no wind blows either in the hills or in the mind; no chill finds the bone. It is a day that can come only in a northern climate, where there has been a long background of frigidity, a long deficiency of sun.

We've just been through this magical moment—which

From "Spring" in *One Man's Meat*.

was more than a moment and was a whole morning—and it lodges in memory like some old romance, with the same subtlety of tone, the same enrichment of the blood, and the enchantment and the mirth and the indescribable warmth. Even before break-fact I felt that the moment was at hand, for when I went out to the barn to investigate twins I let the kitchen door stay open, lazily, instead of closing it behind me. This was a sign. The lambs had nursed and the ewe was lying quiet. One lamb had settled itself on the mother's back and was a perfect miniature of the old one—they reminded me of a teapot we have, whose knob is a tiny replica of the pot itself. The barn seemed warmer and sweeter than usual, but it was early in the day, and the hint of springburst was still only a hint, a suggestion, a nudge. The full impact wasn't felt until the sun had climbed higher. Then came, one after another, the many small caresses that added up to the total embrace of warmth and life—a laziness and contentment in the behavior of animals and people, a tendency of man and dog to sit down somewhere in the sun. In the driveway, a deep rut that for the past week had held three or four inches of water and had alternately frozen and thawed, showed clear indications of drying up. On the window ledge in the living room, the bare brown forsythia cuttings suddenly discovered the secret of yel-low. The goose, instead of coming off her nest and joining her loud companions, settled down on her eleven eggs, pulled some feathers from her breast, and resigned herself to the twenty-eight-day grind. When I went back through the kitchen I noticed that the air that had come in was not like an invader but like a friend who had stopped by for a visit.

OCTOBER   1938

THE BURNING QUESTION

The burning question around here now is what I am going to do about my deer. They always speak of it as "my" deer,

From "Clear Days" in *One Man's Meat*.

and it has come to seem just that. I often think of this not impossible animal, walking statelily through the forest paths and wearing a studded collar with "E. B. White, phone Waterlot 40 Ring 3," engraved on it.

"You goin' to get your deer?" I am asked by every man I meet—and they all wait for an answer. My deer-slaying program is a matter of considerable local import, much to my surprise. It is plain that I now reside in a friendly community of killers, and that until I open fire myself they cannot call me brother.

The truth is I have never given serious thought to the question of gunning. My exploits have been few. Once I shot a woodchuck that my dog had already begun to take apart; and once, in the interests of science, I erased a domestic turkey—crouching silently on a log six feet from the bird's head, as cool as though I were aiming at my own cousin. But by and large my hunting has been with a .22 rifle and a mechanical duck, with dusk falling in gold and purple splendor in the penny arcades along Sixth Avenue. I imagine I would feel mighty awkward discharging a gun that wasn't fastened to a counter by a small chain.

This business of going after some deer meat is a solemn matter hereabouts. My noncommittal attitude has marked me as a person of doubtful character, who will bear watching. There seems to be some question of masculinity involved: until I slay my dragon I am still in short pants, as far as my fellow-countrymen are concerned. As for my own feelings in the matter, it's not that I fear buck fever, it's more that I can't seem to work up a decent feeling of enmity toward a deer. Toward *my* deer, I mean. I think I'd rather catch it alive and break it to harness.

Besides, I don't really trust myself alone in the woods with a gun. The woods are changing. I see by the papers that our Eastern forests this season are full of artists engaged in making pencil sketches of suitable backgrounds for Walt Disney's proposed picture "Bambi"—which is about a deer. My eyesight isn't anything exceptional; it is quite within the bounds of probability that I would march into the woods after my deer and come home with a free-hand artist draped across my running board, a tiny crimson drop trickling from one nostril.

MAY 16, 1936

FAREWELL, MY LOVELY!
(An aging male kisses an old flame goodbye)

I see by the new Sears Roebuck catalogue that it is still possible to buy an axle for a 1909 Model T Ford, but I am not deceived. The great days have faded, the end is in sight. Only one page in the current catalogue is devoted to parts and accessories for the Model T; yet everyone remembers springtimes when the Ford gadget section was larger than men's clothing, almost as large as household furnishings. The last Model T was built in 1927, and the car is fading from what scholars call the American scene—which is an understatement, because to a few million people who grew up with it, the old Ford practically *was* the American scene.

It was the miracle God had wrought. And it was patently the sort of thing that could only happen once. Mechanically uncanny, it was like nothing that had ever come to the world before. Flourishing industries rose and fell with it. As a vehicle, it was hardworking, commonplace, heroic; and it often seemed to transmit those qualities to the persons who rode in it. My own generation identifies it with Youth, with its gaudy, irretrievable excitements; before it fades into the mist, I would like to pay it the tribute of the sigh that is not a sob, and set down random entries in a shape somewhat less cumbersome than a Sears Roebuck catalogue.

The Model T was distinguished from all other makes of cars by the fact that its transmission was of a type known as planetary—which was half metaphysics, half sheer friction. Engineers accepted the word "planetary" in its epicyclic sense, but I

From *The Second Tree from the Corner*.

was always conscious that it also meant "wandering," "erratic." Because of the peculiar nature of this planetary element, there was always, in Model T, a certain dull rapport between engine and wheels, and even when the car was in a state known as neutral, it trembled with a deep imperative and tended to inch forward. There was never a moment when the bands were not faintly egging the machine on. In this respect it was like a horse, rolling the bit on its tongue, and country people brought to it the same technique they used with draft animals.

Its most remarkable quality was its rate of acceleration. In its palmy days the Model T could take off faster than anything on the road. The reason was simple. To get under way, you simply hooked the third finger of the right hand around a lever on the steering column, pulled down hard, and shoved your left foot forcibly against the low-speed pedal. These were simple, positive motions; the car responded by lunging forward with a roar. After a few seconds of this turmoil, you took your toe off the pedal, eased up a mite on the throttle, and the car, possessed of only two forward speeds, catapulted directly into high with a series of ugly jerks and was off on its glorious errand. The abruptness of this departure was never equalled in other cars of the period. The human leg was (and still is) incapable of letting in a clutch with anything like the forthright abandon that used to send Model T on its way. Letting in a clutch is a negative, hesitant motion, depending on delicate nervous control; pushing down the Ford pedal was a simple, country motion—an expansive act, which came as natural as kicking an old door to make it budge.

The driver of the old Model T was a man enthroned. The car, with top up, stood seven feet high. The driver sat on top of the gas tank, brooding it with his own body. When he wanted gasoline, he alighted, along with everything else in the front seat; the seat was pulled off, the metal cap unscrewed, and a wooden stick thrust down to sound the liquid in the well. There were always a couple of these sounding sticks kicking around in the ratty sub-cushion regions of a flivver. Refuelling was more of a social function then, because the driver had to unbend, whether he wanted to or not. Directly in front of the driver was the windshield—high, uncompromisingly erect. Nobody talked about air resistance, and the four cylinders pushed the car through the atmosphere with a simple disregard of physical law.

There was this about a Model T: the purchaser never regarded his purchase as a complete, finished product. When you bought a Ford, you figured you had a start—a vibrant, spirited framework to which could be screwed an almost limitless assortment of decorative and functional hardware. Driving away from the agency, hugging the new wheel between your knees, you were already full of creative worry. A Ford was born naked as a baby, and a flourishing industry grew up out of correcting its rare deficiencies and combatting its fascinating diseases. Those were the great days of lily-painting. I have been looking at some old Sears Roebuck catalogues, and they bring everything back so clear.

First you bought a Ruby Safety Reflector for the rear, so that your posterior would glow in another's car's brilliance. Then you invested thirty-nine cents in some radiator Moto Wings, a popular ornament which gave the Pegasus touch to the machine and did something godlike to the owner. For nine cents you bought a fan-belt guide to keep the belt from slipping off the pulley.

You bought a radiator compound to stop leaks. This was as much a part of everybody's equipment as aspirin tablets are of a medicine cabinet. You bought special oil to prevent chattering, a clamp-on dash light, a patching outfit, a tool box that you bolted to the running board, a sun visor, a steering-column brace to keep the column rigid, and a set of emergency containers for gas, oil, and water—three thin, disc-like cans that reposed in a case on the running board during long, important journeys—red for gas, gray for water, green for oil. It was only a beginning. After the car was about a year old, steps were taken to check the alarming disintegration. (Model T was full of tumors, but they were benign.) A set of anti-rattlers (ninety-eight cents) was a popular panacea. You hooked them on to the gas and spark rods, to the brake pull rod, and to the steering-rod connections. Hood silencers, of black rubber, were applied to the fluttering hood. Shock-absorbers and snubbers gave "complete relaxation." Some people bought rubber pedal pads, to fit over the standard metal pedals. (I didn't like these, I remember.) Persons of a suspicious or pugnacious turn of mind bought a rear-view mirror; but most Model T owners weren't worried by what was coming from behind because they would soon enough see it out in front. They rode in a state of cheerful catalepsy. Quite a large mutinous clique among Ford owners went over to a foot accelerator (you could buy one and screw it to the floor board), but there was a certain madness in these people, because the Model T, just as she stood, had a choice of three foot pedals to push, and there were plenty of moments when both feet were occupied in the routine performance of duty and when the only way to speed up the engine was with the hand throttle.

Gadget bred gadget. Owners not only bought ready-made gadgets, they invented gadgets to meet special needs. I myself drove my car directly from the agency to the blacksmith's, and had the smith affix two enormous iron brackets to the port running board to support an army trunk.

People who owned closed models builded along different lines: they bought ball grip handles for opening doors, window anti-rattlers, and de-luxe flower vases of the cut-glass anti-splash type. People with delicate sensibilities garnished their car with a device called the Donna Lee Automobile Disseminator—a porous vase guaranteed, according to Sears, to fill the car with a "faint clean odor of lavender." The gap between open cars and closed cars was not as great then as it is now: for $11.95, Sears Roebuck converted our touring car into a sedan and you went forth renewed. One agreeable quality of the old Fords was that they had no bumpers, and their fenders softened and wilted with the years and permitted the driver to squeeze in and out of tight places.

Tires were 30 x 3½, cost about twelve dollars, and punctured readily. Everybody carried a Jiffy patching set, with a nutmeg grater to roughen the tube before the goo was spread on. Everybody was capable of putting on a patch, expected to have to, and did have to.

During my association with Model T's, self-starters were not a prevalent accessory. They were expensive and under suspicion. Your car came equipped with a serviceable crank, and the first thing you learned was how to Get Results. It was a special trick, and until you learned it (usually from another Ford owner, but sometimes by a period of appalling experimentation) you might as well have been winding up an awning. The trick was to leave the ignition switch off, proceed to the animal's head, pull the choke (which was a little wire protruding through the radiator) and give the crank two or three nonchalant upward lifts. Then, whistling as though thinking about something else, you would saunter back to the driver's cabin, turn the ignition on, return to the crank, and this time, catching it on the down stroke, give it a quick spin with plenty of That. If this procedure was followed, the engine almost always responded—first with a few scattered explosions, then with a tumultuous gunfire, that you checked by racing around to the driver's seat and retarding the throttle. Often, if the emergency brake hadn't been pulled all the way back, the car advanced on you the instant the first explosion occurred and you would hold it back by leaning your weight against it. I can still feel my old Ford nuzzling me at the curb, as though looking for an apple in my pocket.

In zero weather, ordinary cranking became an impossibility, except for giants. The oil thickened, and it became necessary to jack up the rear wheels, which, for some planetary reason, eased the throw.

The lore and legend that governed the Ford were boundless. Owners had their own theories about everything; they discussed mutual problems in that wise, infinitely resourceful way old women discuss rheumatism. Exact knowledge was pretty scarce, and often proved less effective than superstition. Dropping a camphor ball into the gas tank was a popular expedient; it seemed to have a tonic effect on both man and machine. There wasn't much to base exact knowledge on. The Ford driver flew blind. He didn't know the temperature of his engine, the speed of his car, the amount of his fuel, or the pressure of his oil (the old Ford lubricated itself by what was amiably described as the "splash system"). A speedometer cost money and was an extra, like a windshield-wiper. The dashboard of the early models was bare save for an ignition key; later models, grown effete, boasted an ammeter which pulsated alarmingly with the throbbing of the car. Under the dash was a box of coils, with vibrators that you adjusted, or thought you adjusted. Whatever the driver learned of his motor, he learned not through instruments but through sudden developments. I remember that the timer was one of the vital organs about which there was ample doctrine. When everything else had been checked, you "had a look" at the timer. It was an extravagantly odd little device, simple in construction, mysterious in function. It contained a roller, held by a spring, and there were four contact points on the inside of the case against which, many people believed, the roller rolled. I have had a timer apart on a sick Ford many times. But I never really knew what I was up to—I was just showing off before God. There were almost as many schools of thought as there were timers. Some people, when things went wrong, just clenched their teeth and gave the timer a smart crack with a wrench. Other people opened it up and blew on it. There was a school that held that the timer needed large amounts of oil; they fixed it by frequent baptism. And there was a school that was positive it was meant to run dry as a bone; these people were continually taking it off and wiping it. I remember once spitting into a timer; not in anger, but in a spirit of research. You see, the Model T driver moved in the realm of metaphysics. He believed his car could be hexed.

One reason the Ford anatomy was never reduced to an exact science was that, having "fixed" it, the owner couldn't honestly claim that the treatment had brought about the cure.

There were too many authenticated cases of Fords fixing themselves—restored naturally to health after a short rest. Farmers soon discovered this, and it fitted nicely with their draft-horse philosophy: "Let 'er cool off and she'll snap into it again."

A Ford owner had Number One Bearing constantly in mind. This bearing, being at the front end of the motor, was the one that always burned out, because the oil didn't reach it when the car was climbing hills. (That's what I was always told, anyway.) The oil used to recede and leave Number One dry as a clam flat; you had to watch that bearing like a hawk. It was like a weak heart—you could hear it start knocking, and that was when you stopped to let her cool off. Try as you would to keep the oil supply right, in the end Number One always went out. "Number One Bearing burned out on me and I had to have her replaced," you would say, wisely; and your companions always had a lot to tell about how to protect and pamper Number One to keep her alive.

Sprinkled not too liberally among the millions of amateur witch doctors who drove Fords and applied their own abominable cures were the heaven-sent mechanics who could really make the car talk. These professionals turned up in undreamed-of spots. One time, on the banks of the Columbia River in Washington, I heard the rear end go out of my Model T when I was trying to whip it up a steep incline onto the deck of a ferry. Something snapped; the car slid backward into the mud. It seemed to me like the end of the trail. But the captain of the ferry, observing the withered remnant, spoke up.

"What's got her?" he asked.

"I guess it's the rear end," I replied, listlessly. The captain leaned over the rail and stared. Then I saw that there was a hunger in his eyes that set him off from other men.

"Tell you what," he said, carelessly, trying to cover up his eagerness, "let's pull the son of a bitch up onto the boat, and I'll help you fix her while we're going back and forth on the river."

We did just this. All that day I plied between the towns of Pasco and Kennewick, while the skipper (who had once worked in a Ford garage) directed the amazing work of resetting the bones of my car.

Springtime in the heyday of the Model T was a delirious season. Owning a car was still a major excitement, roads were still wonderful and bad. The Fords were obviously conceived in madness: any car that was capable of going from forward into reverse without any perceptible mechanical hiatus was bound to be a mighty challenging thing to the human imagination. Boys used to veer them off the highway into a level pasture and run wild with them, as though they were cutting up with a girl. Most everybody used the reverse pedal quite as much as the regular foot brake—it distributed the wear over the bands and wore them all down evenly. That was the big trick, to wear all the bands down evenly, so that the final chattering would be total and the whole unit scream for renewal.

The days were golden, the nights were dim and strange. I still recall with trembling those loud, nocturnal crises when you drew up to a signpost and raced the engine so the lights would be bright enough to read destinations by. I have never been really planetary since. I suppose it's time to say goodbye. Farewell, my lovely!

THE CAREFUL FORM

"Here, then, is the very nub of the conflict: the careful form of art, and the careless shape of life itself."

For a writer, material and form stand in a relation of conflict that art can domesticate but never dominate. One enters college to sit at the feet of a Plato and ends up arguing a grade average with a Polonius. One goes to hear a concert and remembers only the cacophony of street traffic to and from the hall. In the midst of this confusion of sense impression a writer tries to communicate with other minds that are inside sets of experiences different from his own—tries, that is, to write letters to other worlds. A writer must be acutely aware of what White calls "the careless shape of life itself." To make it bear the burden of his messages is the purpose of "the careful form of art."

Common sense insists that the writer should begin with something to say, some vision to proclaim. The anodyne for the glassy stare at the blank sheet of paper is not a pill of rhetoric but a good look at the world. A writer, like Antaeus, draws strength from contact with the earth, from experience with living. It is sophomoric, of course, to confuse experience with leaving home for distant and therefore better places. Eagerly lived, any life—in Boston or Bombay, in Podunk or Potsdam—yields rich experience. White himself offers professional testimony to this point:

> I think the best writing is often done by persons who are snatching the time from something else—something that is either burning them up, as religion, or love, or politics, or that is boring them to tears, as prison, or a brokerage house, or an advertising firm.

A good look at the careless shape of life produces not just raw material or inert slides stored in a film tray to be projected through a typewriter, but an energy of mind resulting from emotional as well as intellectual contact with environment. A plumber who is not trapped in the clichés of his trade can write cogently about ninety-degree bends for an audience that longs to give a different direction to copper pipe. A freshman biology student who has used his microscope as a window on an amusing world, rather than as a mirror of what his laboratory manual has shown him, is prepared to say something real, however microscopic, even to an English professor.

Though writing begins in the bucking saddle of experience, it comes finally to rhetoric. Experience with things, with people, with books, and, above all, with reflection, will leave a lively person bored or burning up. Nevertheless, energy without purpose cannot be useful or even exist, except inchoately within the individual psyche. Form, often a word of protean meanings, may be understood as the application of purpose to energy. Even a meandering stream, pleasant as its random curves are to an eye jaded by discipline, follows a physics that a poet can explain. Even the crudest freshman theme moves within necessities of form that an aspiring physicist should be eager to master. Rhetoric is the art of ordering words to effect a purpose.

The remarks on rhetoric that introduce the selections by White in this second part are focused on problems of immediate concern to a writer. Behind these remarks lies the assumption that no writer who successfully reaches an audience lacks a main intention. He may meander over the whole countryside of rhetoric, but a careful consideration of his wanderings will discern that he remains responsible to a main intention. The terms *description, narrative, persuasion,* and *exposition* are used as convenient abstractions to warn that different intentions demand different strategies. These strategies, which make up a ring of rhetoric composed of interdependent ways of developing thought, can best be studied in an order that begins with observation and culminates in explanation.

The selections from White are chosen both for their merit and for their usefulness in illustrating the careful form of art. Writing begins not only with first hand experience but also with imitation; for the soul cannot "clap its hands and sing," as Yeats wrote in "Sailing to Byzantium," until the writer is aware of the example of the work of sensitive artists:

> Nor is there singing school but studying
> Monuments of its own magnificence.

The student should not confuse imitation with assiduous copying. He should not understand tradition as rule, or form as prefabricated pattern. He should critically examine White's letters to other worlds and by doing so he may learn how to build his own cabin in his own wilderness.

FORMS OF DISCOURSE

DESCRIPTION

Description, like leisure, is indispensable, but cloying in large doses. It is an art in miniature, often incidental to another purpose such as telling a story or explaining a point. Discreetly used, as it is sometimes in daily conversation, vivid description stirs the imagination. Consequently it is valued not by its quantity, but by its impact.

Description adds zest to living. As Thoreau suggested, to be alert is to be alive. A deer can pick up a scent better than a man. A wily crow has keen sight. But man reflects on his primary sense experiences and communicates verbally. Whether one describes the sound of a bassoon or the sight of a hooked black bass is immaterial. To put impressions of the world in words is to live close to primary experience in a way that is uniquely human.

The intent of description (exclusive of technical description) is sharing experience, real or imagined. Joseph Conrad once wrote: "My task which I am trying to achieve is, by the power of the written word to make you hear, to make you feel—it is, before all to make you *see*." Description—of the color of the marsh grass beside a turnpike or the sound of music carried on still night air—must be grasped vicariously by a reader through his senses. Though the problems of a student writer may not be Conrad's, the same principles obtain.

Anyone who is seriously trying to share an experience uses abstract language at the peril of being vague. Although the language most appropriate to all forms of discourse is concrete, this principle is especially pertinent to description. Particular nouns like *muzzle* and *bowsprit* are concrete. Active verbs like *sting* are more effective than linking verbs like *are*. In the following passage, White, with concrete language, describes his dachshund Fred in a way that shows the reader that he has taken the trouble to really look rather than to just stumble over the dog in a dark hallway:

> Noticed this morning how gray Fred is becoming, our elderly dachshund. His trunk and legs are still red but his muzzle, after dozens of major operatons for the removal of porcupine quills, is now a sort of strawberry roan, with many white hairs, the result of worry.

Once White made up his mind about the dog he could have used an abstract word such as *elderly*:

> Noticed this morning how elderly Fred, our dachshund, is becoming.

If White had used this abstraction he would have sacrificed control of his reader's imagination and also created a sentence with the flavor of used chewing gum. A reader might think of "elderly Fred" not as a grizzled worrier but as a gay old dog, perhaps sporting an aluminum prosthetic splint, the result of an accident to a paw in a revolving door. Silly, indeed, but who can predict what will happen to a reader's imagination coasting down an abstract word in neutral, with no control?

Another unhappy solution to the problem of sharing experience is the use of technical description. To give a dog's vital statistics—height, weight, color, daily consumption of dog food, and length of tongue when yawning—might seem like brisk and efficient description. But unless the audience is very special indeed, all the reader wants is the sense of the living Fred, not his statistics, however informative they may be. In "Salt Water Farm" White conveys experience through concrete language in a way that a technical description cannot duplicate:

> My neighbor Mr. Dameron, who goes after the lobsters from early spring till late fall, tethers his cow a few paces from his landing, so that he can pick her up handily when he comes in from hauling his traps. The two of them walk up together through the field, he with his empty gas can, she with her full bag of milk.

No matter how graphically a writer describes a world he has carefully examined, he must curb any desire to send up a

Roman candle display of details. To avoid the random burst, he must assume a clear point of view and follow an orderly structure. If White, for example, had chosen to depict his seacoast farm as it might have been seen by a sea rover making in of an evening toward a mooring, the description might begin out in the lonely bay. Instead he sees the farm from the viewpoint of a part-time farmer, amused by his kinship with more experienced "maritime agriculturalists." His actual order is not a simple, methodical progression from door to dock. His purpose is not merely to describe a farm but rather to use description to communicate the expansiveness of farming where the pasture stretches out to sea. Thus in each of the first three paragraphs he takes the reader from near to far—from farm, to shore, to the restless fields of protein. Finally, having set the stage, he devotes the last two paragraphs to the actors.

Of crucial importance to description is the writer's *dominant impression*. Such an impression may be a memory of a physical detail that identifies an experience, as a person may visit Dartmouth College and forever after associate Hanover, New Hampshire, with the spire of Baker Library. Frequently a dominant impression will be a feeling, a mood, an atmosphere associated with memory, as an old song may bring back a distant Junior Prom. The remark in "Salt Water Farm" about "gulls like gnats round your ears, and the threat of fog always in the pit of your stomach" underscores the impression of expansiveness, the feeling that "beyond one blue acre is another." To share an experience a writer may focus on those details that will best convey his dominant impression.

In "Business Show" White develops an unusual impression. The description is as impersonal on the surface as the glittering calculating machines it describes. The language is concrete ("smoke rising in straws of light"). The observer seems as impressed as "a traveller before a shrine"; yet a reader may sense that he is less than thrilled by the robot implications of chromium chairs and chattering calculators. The blonde girls in white satin tapping keys with "nails shining pink the color of chrysanthemums" turn the description from photograph to painting. Into a strange, mechanistic world intrudes some ineffable straw of power, as evanescent as clouds the color of chrysanthemums. This single paragraph, organized around a dominant impression of a current more powerful than a utility company's, achieves an impact that will remain in focus.

JANUARY 1939

SALT WATER FARM

A seacoast farm, such as this, extends far beyond the boundaries mentioned in the deed. My domain is arable many miles offshore, in the restless fields of protein. Cultivation begins close to the house with a rhubarb patch, but it ends down the bay beyond the outer islands, hand-lining for cod and haddock, with gulls like gnats round your ears, and the threat of fog always in the pit of your stomach.

I think it is the expansiveness of coastal farming that makes it so engrossing: the knowledge that your fence, on one side at least, shuts out no neighbor—you may climb it and keep going if you have a boat and the strength to raise a sail. The presence in the offing of the sea's fickle yield, those self-sown crops given up grudgingly to the patient and the brave, is an attraction few men are proof against. Beyond one blue acre is another, each one a little farther from the house than the last. On a summer's day I may start out down the lane with a pail to pick a few berries for my wife's piemaking, but there is always the likelihood that I will turn up hours later with two small flounders and a look of profound accomplishment. A man who has spent much time and money in dreary restaurants moodily chewing filet of sole on the special luncheon is bound to become unmanageable when he discovers that he can produce the main fish course directly, at the edge of his own pasture, by a bit of trickery on a fine morning.

Below the barn are the asparagus and the potatoes and the potato bugs in season. Beyond is the pasture, where, amid

From *One Man's Meat.*

juniper and granite and lambkill, grow the wild strawberries and the tame heifers. Keep walking and you come to the blueberries and cranberries. Take off your shoes, advance, and you are on the clam beds—the only crop on the place that squirts water at you in time of drought. Beyond the clams are the cunners and the flounders, hanging round the dock piles on the incoming tide. Near the ledges, off the point, are the lobsters. Two miles farther, off the red rocks, are the mackerel, flashing in schools, ready for the Sunday afternoon sociable when the whole village turns out for the harvest of fishes. Mackereling is the accepted Sabbath engagement in summertime; there are two or three spots known to be good and the boats bunch up at these points, a clubby arrangement for man and fish. It is where you meet your friends, and, if the tide serves you, reap the benefit from your friends' toll bait, which drifts down over your hook. Farthest from home are the cod and haddock. You must rise early the day you go to bring them in.

The salt water farms hereabouts give ample evidence that their owners have a great deal on their minds. Rocks and alders are the most conspicuous crops, and if a man can get a job firming the public highway he gives small thought to loosening the soil in his own garden. With the whole sea bottom to rake, he isn't going to spend all his time weeding a bean row. He puts in a vegetable garden in spring, gives it a few vicious pokes with a hoe in June, and devotes the remainder of the year to lustier pursuits—grinding the valves of an old boat-engine, or mending a weir. My neighbor Mr. Dameron, who goes after the lobsters from early spring till late fall, tethers his cow a few paces from his landing, so that he can pick her up handily when he comes in from hauling his traps. The two of them walk up together through the field, he with his empty gas can, she with her full bag of milk.

There is a lively spirit here among us maritime agriculturalists. My neighbors are mostly descendants of sea rovers and are stifled by the confinements of a farm acre. The young men fit easier on an Indian motorcycle than on a disc harrow. And I have noticed that it is the easy-going ones among us who have the best time; in this climate, at the rate a stove eats wood, if a man were to grow too thrifty or forehanded he'd never be able to crawl out from under his own woodpile.

OCTOBER 31, 1936

BUSINESS SHOW

It was a soft afternoon with smoke rising in straws of light from the chimneys, and pink clouds the color of chrysanthemums folded gently against a pale sky. Even Eighth Avenue seemed to dwell in heavenly pallor when we left it to plunge into the Business Show and walk in the chattering aisles of calculators, addressographs, electric tabulation machines, where girls in purest white satin, enthroned on chromium chairs, their blonde hair gleaming like clouds, their nails shining pink the color of chrysanthemums, pushed the little shining keys—tick, tap, PULL, tick, tap, PULL—adding, subtracting, filing, assembling, addressing, dictaphoning, typing, silhouetted firmly against the pure walls of steel that was grained to look like wood, and the murmurous mysteries of business enlarged a hundred times, staggering the mind. Adoringly we paused before each machine, as a traveller before a shrine; and it all seemed more mechanistic than any play we had ever seen, even than the plays produced by the little groups who take the theatre seriously. But what we noticed was that the seeming dominance of the machines was an illusion of the senses, that the electric current was in fact impotent, for everywhere we saw men standing gravely talking to the girls in purest white satin, and always something passed between them, something a little extra in their look, the eyes of the girls returning the clear, desirous gaze of the builders of the incredible machines, giving back desire for desire, and that

From *The Second Tree from the Corner.*

the current of this exchange (the exciting unfulfillment) was the thing in all the room, and not the chattering mysteries of the addition, tabulation, punctuation, subtraction, which were as nothing, which were as an accompaniment (tick, tap, PULL) to the loud, insistent, throbbing song of beauty unattainable, hair (like clouds) infinitely desirable (in a hall on Eighth Avenue), with smoke rising in straws of light from the chimneys.

NARRATIVE

Telling a story is as natural and familiar an act as describing a person or place. On buses, in corridors, and before check-out counters in stores, the amount of he-said-and-then-she-said-and-then-we-went conversation is formidable. It is only when people begin to put narrative on paper that drought can suddenly threaten the scene. Knowledge of a few simple principles of narrative will not make a Faulkner out of everyone, but it may irrigate unsuspected garden plots.

Narrative presents an action, real or imaginary. "Coon Hunt," among the selections which follow, reports events one can imagine White recording in a journal after the experience; "The Second Tree from the Corner" leads behind a door that no ordinary recital of fact would unlock. Yet these contrasting selections have in common with each other the author's intention to arrange events in an ordered time sequence; to tell what happened. The subject of each narrative is a series of events closely tied together and ultimately called an action.

Whether the action is great and the sum of many smaller ones, as in full-scale biography, or minor and concerned with a single event, as in one of Hemingway's early short stories, it must be complete in order to make sense. Description may be complete and have unity if it develops one dominant impression vividly, but narrative has a form governed by different circumstances. This difference is clarified when an action is considered as a process: a sequence that leads to a definite conclusion and that involves a change. Narrative intended to explain a technical operation— how clothes flow through a modern laundry and emerge clean and tidily wrapped—differs greatly from the narrative in "Coon Hunt," which lets the reader participate imaginatively in the experience. In both types, however, the writer's fundamental concern is with unity defined by the time during which the process unfolds, and by the stated or implied interpretation that gives point to the action.

The way in which the point of an action is elucidated influences the shape of a narrative. The following two selections from White relate complete processes, but these actions are meaningful units for quite different reasons. "Coon Hunt" sets forth a series of events that happen to White and the bewildered dog. The dog, in particular, is victim rather than participant, and is in no way responsible for actually influencing the sequence of accidental events. On the other hand, "The Second Tree from the Corner" describes an action that Trexler causes rather than one that just happens to him. A whole bizarre sequence of events develops not from the impact of a single event on Trexler, but from his own motivation when he struggles to conceal his vision from the doctor. The meaning of the first narrative is defined in terms of response to events; the meaning of the second stems from the motivation of the participant.

Different meanings require different narrative methods. "Coon Hunt" is chiefly an account of what happened, of the steps that led White to experience his first coon hunt more vividly through the experience of the dog. "The Second Tree from the Corner" is dramatic in method, presenting Trexler's haunting tilt with conflicting norms and values as if it were happening before the reader's eyes.

Once the meaning of an action is understood, the time duration of the process ceases to be arbitrary. The puppy on the coon hunt passes through his violent and drastic change from innocence to experience in the hours of one mysterious and exciting night. But Trexler sits in the patient's chair on five occasions over a period of several weeks before his startling identification with the doctor leads to his vision of the small tree "saturated with evening." The puppy's change begins when he is placed in the truck, Trexler's when he hears the doctor's first question. Each story ends when the process of change has run its course.

NOVEMBER   1941

COON HUNT

There were two dogs with us the night we went coon hunting. One was an old hound, veteran of a thousand campaigns, who knew what we were up to and who wasted no time in idle diversions. The other was a puppy, brought along to observe and learn; to him the star-sprinkled sky and the deep dark woods and the myriad scents and the lateness of the hour and the frosty ground were intoxicating. The excitement of our departure was too much for his bowels. Tied in the truck, he was purged all the way over to Winkumpaw Brook and was hollow as a rotten log before the night was well under way. This may have had something to do with what happened.

It was great hunting that night, perfect for man and beast, a fateful night for coon. The stars leaned close, and some lost their hold and fell. I was amazed at how quickly and easily the men moved through the woods in strange country, guided by hunches and a bit of lantern gleam. The woods hit back at you if you let your guard down.

We were an odd lot. A couple of the men were in coveralls—those bunny suits garage mechanics wear. One old fellow had been all stove to pieces in a car accident; another was down with a hard cold and a racking cough; another had broken two ribs the day before and had been strapped up that afternoon by a doctor. He had killed the pain with a few shots of whisky and the spirits had evidently reminded him of coon hunting. This fellow had a terrible thirst for water all during the night and he had a way of straying off from the main party and hugging the water courses where he could kneel and drink when the need was great. We could sometimes follow the progress of his thirst

From *One Man's Meat*.

in the winking of his buglight, in some faraway valley. After a bit he would rejoin us. "I'm drier'n a covered bridge," he would say disconsolately.

I felt a strong affinity for the puppy because he and I were the new ones to this strange game, and somehow it seemed to me we were sharing the same excitement and mystery of a night in the woods. I had begun to feel the excitement back in the kitchen of the farmhouse, where the hunters had gathered, dropping in and standing about against the walls of the room. The talk began right away, all the cooning lore, the tales of being lost from three in the morning until six, and the tricks a coon would play on a dog. There was a woman in the room, wife of the owner of the old dog, and she was the only one for whom the night held no special allure. She sat knitting a huge mitten. Mostly, the hunters paid no attention to her. Only one remark went her way. One of the men, observing the mitten, asked:

"Gettin' that man o' yours ready for winter?"

She nodded.

"I should kill him before winter if he was mine—he's no good for anything else," the fellow continued, pleasantly.

The woman raised a grudging smile to this sure-fire witticism. She plied the needles without interruption. This obviously was not the first time she had been left at home while men and dogs went about their business, and it wasn't going to be the last time either. For her it was just one night in a long succession of nights. This was the fall and in the fall the men hunted coon. They left after sundown and returned before sunup. That was all there was to that.

The best coon country is always far away. Men are roamers, and getting a long way from home is part of the sport. Our motorcade consisted of two vehicles, a truck for the dogs and owners, and a sedan for the hangers-on, lantern-bearers, and advisory committee. The old dog jumped into place the minute he was let out of the barn; the puppy was hoisted in and tied. The two of them sat on a pile of straw just behind the cab. The man with the broken ribs got into the sedan. Nobody seemed to think it was in the least odd that he was going coon hunting, to walk twelve or fifteen miles in rough country. He said the adhesive tape held everything O.K. and anyway, he said, the only time his chest hurt was when he breathed.

We advanced without stealth, the truck leading. The headlights of our car shone directly in the faces of the dogs. The old dog leaned back craftily against the sideboards, to steady himself against the motion. He half closed his eyes and was as quiet on the journey as a middle-aged drummer on a way train. The pup crouched uneasily and was frequently thrown. He would rare up and sniff, then crouch again, then a curve would throw him and he would lose his balance and go down. He found a hole in the sideboards and occasionally would press his nose through to sniff the air. Then the excitement would attack his bowels and he would let go all over everything—with some difficulty because of the violent motion of the truck. The old dog observed this untidiness with profound contempt.

We got away from the highway after a while and followed a rough back road up into some country I had never been into. At last we got out and let the old hound go. He went to work instantly, dropping downhill out of sight. We could hear his little bell tinkling as he ranged about in the dim valley between us and a night-struck lake. When he picked up a scent, suddenly his full round tones went through you, and the night was a gong that had been struck. The old dog knew his business. The men, waiting around, would discuss in great detail his hunting and would describe what he was doing off there, and what the coon was doing; but I doubted that they knew, and they just kept making things up the way children do. As soon as the hound barked tree, which is a slightly different sound than the sound of the running, we followed his voice and shot the coon.

Once the dog led us to an old apple tree in an almost impenetrable thicket, and when the flashlights were shined up into the topmost branches no coon was there. The owner was puzzled and embarrassed. Nothing like this had ever happened before, he said. There was a long period of consultation and speculation, all sorts of theories were advanced. The most popular was that the coon had climbed the apple tree, then crossed, squirrel-like, into the branches of a nearby hackmatack, then descended, fooling the hound. Either this was the case or the dog had made an error. Upward of an hour was spent trying every angle of this delicious contretemps.

The puppy was held in leash most of the time, but when the first coon was treed he was allowed to watch the kill. Lights from half a dozen flashlights swept the tree top and converged to make a halo, with the coon's bright little sharp face in the center of the luminous ring. Our host lethargically drew his pistol, prolonging the climax with a legitimate sense of the theater. No one spoke while he drew a bead. The shot seemed to puncture first the night, then the coon. The coon lost his grip and landed with a thud, still alive and fighting. The old hound rushed in savagely, to grab him by the throat and finish him off. It was a big bull coon; he died bravely and swiftly, and the hound worked with silent fury. Then the puppy, in leash, was allowed to advance and sniff. He was trembling in every muscle, and was all eyes and ears and nose—like a child being allowed to see something meant only for grownups. (I felt a little that way myself.) As he stretched his nose forward timidly to inhale the heady smell of warm coon the old hound, jealous, snarled and leaped. The owner jerked back. The puppy yelped in terror. Everyone laughed. It was a youngster, getting burned by life— that sort of sight. Made you laugh.

After midnight we moved into easier country about ten miles away. Here the going was better—old fields and orchards, where the little wild apples lay in thick clusters under the trees. Old stone walls ran into the woods, and now and then there would be an empty barn as a ghostly landmark. The night grew frosty and the ground underfoot was slippery with rime. The bare birches wore the stars on their fingers, and the world rolled seductively, a dark symphony of brooding groves and plains. Things had gone well, and everyone was content just to be out in the small hours, following the musical directions of a wise and busy dog.

The puppy's owner had slipped the leash and allowed his charge to range about a bit. Nobody was paying much attention to him. The pup stayed with the party mostly, and although he was aware of the long-range operations of the older dog, he seemed to know that this was out of his class; he seemed timid of the woods and tended to stay close, contenting himself with sniffing about and occasionally jumping up to kiss someone's face. We were stepping along through the woods, the old hound near at hand, when the thing happened. Suddenly the puppy (who had not made a sound up to this point) let out a loud whoop and went charging off on a tangent. Everybody stopped dead in surprise.

"What goes on here anyway?" said somebody quietly.

The old hound was as mystified as the rest of us. This was a show-off stunt apparently, this puppy trying to bark coon. Nobody could make it out. Obviously there was no coon scent or the old dog would have picked it up instantly and been at his work.

"What in *the* devil?" asked somebody.

The puppy was howling unmercifully as though possessed. He charged here and there and came back along his own track passing us at a crazy mad pace, and diving into the woods on the other side of the trail. The yelps sounded hysterical now. Again the puppy charged back. This time as he passed we could see that he had a queer look in his eye and that his movements were erratic. He would dive one way at a terrible clip, then stop and back off as though ducking an enemy, half cringing; but he kept putting up this terrible holler and commotion. Once he came straight at me. I stepped aside and he went by screaming.

"Runnin' fit," said his owner. "That's the trouble. I can tell now by the way he acts. He's took with cramps in his bowwils and he don't know anythin' to do 'cept run and holler. C'mon, Dusty, c'mon, boy!"

He kept calling him softly. But Dusty was in another world and the shapes were after him. It was an eerie business, this crazy dog tearing around in the dark woods, half coming at you, half running from you. Even the old dog seemed disturbed and worried, as though to say: "You see—you *will* bring a child along, after his bedtime."

The men were patient, sympathetic now.

"That's all it is, he's took with a fit."

Dusty charged into the midst of us, scattering us. He stopped, bristling, his eyes too bright, a trace of froth at his mouth. He seemed half angry, half scared and wanting comfort. "Nothing much you can do, he'll run it off," they said.

And Dusty ran it off, in the deep dark woods, big with imaginary coons and enormous jealous old hounds, alive with the beautiful smells of the wild. His evening had been too much for him; for the time being he was as crazy as a loon. Someone suggested we go home.

We started moving up toward the cars, which were two or three fields away over where you could see the elms black against the sky. The thought of home wasn't popular. A counter suggestion was made to prolong the hunting, and we separated off into two parties, one to return to the cars, the other to cut across country with the old dog and intercept the main body where a certain woods road met the highway. I walked several more miles, and for the first time began to feel cold. It was another hour before I saw Dusty again. He was all right. All he needed was to be held in somebody's arms. He was very, very sleepy. He and I were both sleepy. I think we will both remember the first night we ever went coon hunting.

MAY 31, 1947

THE SECOND TREE FROM THE CORNER

"Ever have any bizarre thoughts?" asked the doctor.

Mr. Trexler failed to catch the word. "What kind?" he said.

"Bizarre," repeated the doctor, his voice steady. He watched his patient for any slight change of expression, any

From *The Second Tree from the Corner.*

wince. It seemed to Trexler that the doctor was not only watching him closely but was creeping slowly toward him, like a lizard toward a bug. Trexler shoved his chair back an inch and gathered himself for a reply. He was about to say "Yes" when he realized that if he said yes the next question would be unanswerable. Bizarre thoughts, bizarre thoughts? Ever have any bizarre thoughts? What kind of thoughts *except* bizarre had he had since the age of two?

Trexler felt the time passing, the necessity for an answer. These psychiatrists were busy men, overloaded, not to be kept waiting. The next patient was probably already perched out there in the waiting room, lonely, worried, shifting around on the sofa, his mind stuffed with bizarre thoughts and amorphous fears. Poor bastard, thought Trexler. Out there all alone in that misshapen antechamber, staring at the filing cabinet and wondering whether to tell the doctor about that day on the Madison Avenue bus.

Let's see, bizarre thoughts. Trexler dodged back along the dreadful corridor of the years to see what he could find. He felt the doctor's eyes upon him and knew that time was running out. Don't be so conscientious, he said to himself. If a bizarre thought is indicated here, just reach into the bag and pick anything at all. A man as well supplied with bizarre thoughts as you are should have no difficulty producing one for the record. Trexler darted into the bag, hung for a moment before one of his thoughts, as a hummingbird pauses in the delphinium. No, he said, not that one. He darted to another (the one about the rhesus monkey), paused, considered. No, he said, not that.

Trexler knew he must hurry. He had already used up pretty nearly four seconds since the question had been put. But it was an impossible situation—just one more lousy, impossible situation such as he was always getting himself into. When, he asked himself, are you going to quit maneuvering yourself into a pocket? He made one more effort. This time he stopped at the asylum, only the bars were lucite—fluted, retractable. Not here, he said. Not this one.

He looked straight at the doctor. "No," he said quietly. "I never have any bizarre thoughts."

The doctor sucked in on his pipe, blew a plume of smoke toward the rows of medical books. Trexler's gaze followed the smoke. He managed to make out one of the titles, "The Genito-Urinary System." A bright wave of fear swept cleanly over him, and he winced under the first pain of kidney stones. He remembered when he was a child, the first time he ever entered a doctor's office, sneaking a look at the titles of the books—and the flush of fear, the shirt wet under the arms, the book on t.b., the sudden knowledge that he was in the advanced stages of consumption, the quick vision of the hemorrhage. Trexler sighed wearily. Forty years, he thought, and I still get thrown by the title of a medical book. Forty years and I still can't stay on life's little bucky horse. No wonder I'm sitting here in this dreary joint at the end of this woebegone afternoon, lying about my bizarre thoughts to a doctor who looks, come to think of it, rather tired.

The session dragged on. After about twenty minutes, the doctor rose and knocked his pipe out. Trexler got up, knocked the ashes out of his brain, and waited. The doctor smiled warmly and stuck out his hand. "There's nothing the matter with you—you're just scared. Want to know how I know you're scared?"

"How?" asked Trexler.

"Look at the chair you've been sitting in! See how it has moved back away from my desk? You kept inching away from me while I asked you questions. That means you're scared."

"Does it?" said Trexler, faking a grin. "Yeah, I suppose it does."

They finished shaking hands. Trexler turned and walked out uncertainly along the passage, then into the waiting room and out past the next patient, a ruddy pin-striped man who was seated on the sofa twirling his hat nervously and staring straight ahead at the files. Poor, frightened guy, thought Trexler, he's probably read in the *Times* that one American male out of every two is going to die of heart disease by twelve o'clock next Thursday. It says that in the paper almost every morning. And he's also probably thinking about that day on the Madison Avenue bus.

A week later, Trexler was back in the patient's chair. And for several weeks thereafter he continued to visit the doctor, always toward the end of the afternoon, when the vapors hung thick above the pool of the mind and darkened the whole region of the East Seventies. He felt no better as time went on, and he found it impossible to work. He discovered that the visits were becoming routine and that although the routine was one to which he certainly did not look forward, at least he could accept it with cool resignation, as once, years ago, he had accepted a long spell with a dentist who had settled down to a steady fooling with a couple of dead teeth. The visits, moreover, were now assuming a pattern recognizable to the patient.

Each session would begin with a résumé of symptoms—the dizziness in the streets, the constricting pain in the back of the neck, the apprehensions, the tightness of the scalp, the inability to concentrate, the despondency and the melancholy times, the feeling of pressure and tension, the anger at not being able to work, the anxiety over work not done, the gas on the stomach. Dullest set of neurotic symptoms in the world, Trexler would think, as he obediently trudged back over them for the doctor's benefit. And then, having listened attentively to the recital, the doctor would spring his question: "Have you ever found anything that gives you relief?" And Trexler would answer, "Yes. A drink." And the doctor would nod his head knowingly.

As he became familiar with the pattern Trexler found that he increasingly tended to identify himself with the doctor, transferring himself into the doctor's seat—probably (he thought) some rather slick form of escapism. At any rate, it was nothing new for Trexler to identify himself with other people. Whenever he got into a cab, he instantly became the driver, saw everything from the hackman's angle (and the reaching over with the right hand, the nudging of the flag, the pushing it down, all the way down along the side of the meter), saw every-thing—traffic, fare, everything—through the eyes of Anthony Rocco, or Isidore Freedman, or Matthew Scott. In a barbershop, Trexler was the barber, his fingers curled around the comb, his hand on the tonic. Perfectly natural, then, that Trexler should soon be occupying the doctor's chair, asking the questions, wait-ing for the answers. He got quite interested in the doctor, in this way. He liked him, and he found him a not too difficult patient.

It was on the fifth visit, about halfway through, that the doctor turned to Trexler and said, suddenly, "What do you want?" He gave the word "want" special emphasis.

"I d'know," replied Trexler uneasily. "I guess nobody knows the answer to that one."

"Sure they do," replied the doctor.

"Do you know what you want?" asked Trexler narrowly.

"Certainly," said the doctor. Trexler noticed that at this point the doctor's chair slid slightly backward, away from him. Trexler stifled a small, internal smile. Scared as a rabbit, he said to himself. Look at him scoot!

"What *do* you want?" continued Trexler, pressing his advantage, pressing it hard.

The doctor glided back another inch away from his in-quisitor. "I want a wing on the small house I own in Westport. I want more money, and more leisure to do the things I want to do."

Trexler was just about to say, "And what are those things you want to do, Doctor?" when he caught himself. Better not go too far, he mused. Better not lose possession of the ball. And besides, he thought, what the hell goes on here, anyway—me paying fifteen bucks a throw for these séances and then doing the work myself, asking the questions, weighing the answers. So he wants a new wing! There's a fine piece of theatrical gauze for you! A new wing.

Trexler settled down again and resumed the role of patient for the rest of the visit. It ended on a kindly, friendly note. The doctor reassured him that his fears were the cause of his sickness, and that his fears were unsubstantial. They shook hands, smiling.

Trexler walked dizzily through the empty waiting room and the doctor followed along to let him out. It was late; the secretary had shut up shop and gone home. Another day over the dam. "Goodbye," said Trexler. He stepped into the street, turned west toward Madison, and thought of the doctor all alone there, after hours, in that desolate hole—a man who worked longer hours than his secretary. Poor, scared, overworked bastard, thought Trexler. And that new wing!

It was an evening of clearing weather, the Park showing green and desirable in the distance, the last daylight applying a high lacquer to the brick and brownstone walls and giving the street scene a luminous and intoxicating splendor. Trexler meditated, as he walked, on what he wanted. "What do you want?" he heard again. Trexler knew what he wanted, and what, in general, all men wanted; and he was glad, in a way, that it was both inexpressible and unattainable, and that it wasn't a wing. He was satisfied to remember that it was deep, formless, enduring, and impossible of fulfillment, and that it made men sick, and that when you sauntered along Third Avenue and looked through the doorways into the dim saloons, you could sometimes pick out from the unregenerate ranks the ones who had not forgotten, gazing steadily into the bottoms of the glasses on the long chance that they could get another little peek at it. Trexler found himself renewed by the remembrance that what he wanted was at once great and microscopic, and that although it borrowed from the nature of large deeds and of youthful love and of old songs and early intimations, it was not any one of these things, and that it had not been isolated or pinned down, and that a man who attempted to define it in the privacy of a doctor's office would fall flat on his face.

Trexler felt invigorated. Suddenly his sickness seemed health, his dizziness stability. A small tree, rising between him and the light, stood there saturated with the evening, each gilt-edged leaf perfectly drunk with excellence and delicacy. Trexler's spine registered an ever so slight tremor as it picked up this natural disturbance in the lovely scene. "I want the second tree from the corner, just as it stands," he said, answering an imaginary question from an imaginary physician. And he felt a slow pride in realizing that what he wanted none could bestow, and that what he had none could take away. He felt content to be sick, unembarrassed at being afraid; and in the jungle of his fear he glimpsed (as he had so often glimpsed them before) the flashy tail feathers of the bird courage.

Then he thought once again of the doctor, and of his being left there all alone, tired, frightened. (The poor, scared guy, thought Trexler.) Trexler began humming "Moonshine Lullaby," his spirit reacting instantly to the hypodermic of Merman's healthy voice. He crossed Madison, boarded a downtown bus, and rode all the way to Fifty-second Street before he had a thought that could rightly have been called bizarre.

PERSUASION

Conflict is as inevitable in human affairs as wash day. To live is to affirm values and to affirm values is to clash with someone, somewhere. The conflict that results must be resolved and the art of persuasion attempts to fulfill this need.

As a literary form, persuasion should be distinguished from argument. "Argument" designates writing that has as its purpose the resolution of human conflicts by an appeal to reason. Persuasion is an effort to assuage conflicts through appeals to emotion. This distinction is useful because it allows for discrimination between a reasonable examination of conflicts over policy and a direct appeal for action; but it is not common in contemporary prose, which tends to be more relaxed than yesterday's formal debates and therefore more concerned with man as a fallible creature. Some writers, influenced by the impact of the discoveries in the behavioral sciences, are primarily concerned with what will motivate an audience. This is a method of manipulation that sees the reader as a puppet or a prey. But White scorns the implied contempt of such an attitude and persuades in a manner that is informal, flexible, and human.

However informal, convincing persuasion—in a good editorial, for example—is implicitly based on the premise that human conflicts can be settled by an appeal to reason that will lead the contestants to change their minds. Without this assumption the whole effort would be silly and the writer would be better advised to reach for a blackjack. In an inept hand an appeal to reason often degenerates to the as-all-right-minded-people-know approach, though even this cliché preserves the fiction that reason is at the heart of the matter. In responsible persuasion the basic concern is to find a common ground between the conflicting views of men of good will.

Such a search will lead a writer to analyze with exactitude the problem that has provoked the conflict. This analysis will help him to state his solution to the problem clearly. It will also provide disproof of the opposing arguments and support for his proposed solution. Although the writer is bound to no rigid formula, there are four steps in traditional formal argument which will help when approaching the problem of persuasion: analysis, statement, disproof, and proof.

In each of the following pieces White takes a stand on one side of a controversial issue. The withholding principle of taxation is inconsistent with democracy because it implies that a citizen, though he is expected to vote, is "incapable of handling his own affairs." The sound truck, or Free Speech on Wheels, is out of place because "loud speaking is not the same thing as plain speaking." The world needs a delegate in the Security Council who is not "a good chess player studying the future" but "a memoirist remembering the past." It needs not a technician with "purity of detachment" but a man sensitive to the peril that threatens humanity. Working in the brief confines of editorial pieces as short as one paragraph, White suggests broad policy rather than specific solutions. He speaks plainly and forcefully in defense of values devoid of selfishness: a faith in the competence of citizens; the belief that confusing free speech with "free extension-of-speech" will aggravate resentment against the whole principle of freedom of speech; an awe before "the

world of the child in the swing." His common ground is the sur-
vival of humanity. His persuasive words are directed against a
too hasty acceptance of the word of the expert or a too rapid
adjustment to the miracles of the inventor.

FEBRUARY 5, 1944

WITHHOLDING

We have given about a year's thought to the withholding
principle of taxation (not to be confused with the pay-as-you-go
plan) and are now ready with our conclusion. Our belief is that
withholding is a bad way to go about collecting tax money, even
though the figures may show that it gets results. It is bad because
it implies that the individual is incapable of handling his own
affairs. The government as much as says: We know that, if left
to your own devices, you will fritter away your worldly goods
and tax day will catch you without cash. Or it says: We're not
sure you'll come clean in your return, so we will just take the
money before it reaches you and you will be saved the trouble
and fuss of being honest. This implication is an unhealthy thing
to spread around, being contrary to the old American theory that
the individual is a very competent little guy indeed. The whole
setup of our democratic government assumes that the citizen is
bright, honest, and at least as fundamentally sound as a common
stock. If you start treating him as something less than that, you
are going to get into deep water, in our opinion. The device of
withholding tax money, which is clearly confiscatory, since the
individual is not allowed to see, taste, or touch a certain percent-
age of his wages, tacitly brands him as negligent or unthrifty or
immature or incompetent or dishonest, or all of those things at
once. There is, furthermore, a bad psychological effect in earning
money that you never get your paws on. We believe this effect to
be much stronger than the government realizes. At any rate, if
the American individual is in truth incapable of paying his tax

From *The Second Tree from the Corner.*

all by himself, then he should certainly be regarded as incapable of voting all by himself, and the Secretary of the Treasury should accompany him into the booth to show him where to put the X.

JUNE 19, 1948

SOUND

The sound truck, or Free Speech on Wheels, won its first brush with the law by a close decision in the Supreme Court. We have an idea, however, that the theme of amplification is not dead and will recur in many variations. The Court found itself in a snarl; free speech became confused with free extension-of-speech, noise with ideas wrapped in noise. A sound truck, it seems to us, is not a man on a soapbox—it is Superman on a tower of suds. The distinction will eventually have to be drawn. Loud speaking is not the same thing as plain speaking; the loud-speaker piles decibel on decibel and not only is capable of disturbing the peace but through excess of volume can cause madness and death, whereas the human voice is a public nuisance only to the extent that it aggravates the normal human resentment against the whole principle of free speech. Amplified sound is already known among military men as a weapon of untried potency, and we will probably suffer from it if there is another war.

Up till now, modern man has meekly accepted the miracle of his enlarged vocal cords. He has acquiesced in jumbo-ism. A modern baby is born amplified, for even the nursery is wired for sound and the infant's earliest cries are carried over a private distress system to the ears of its mother in the living room—along with street noises that drift in through the open nursery window. (Note to political candidates: Always park your sound truck under nursery windows and your remarks will be

From *The Second Tree from the Corner.*

picked up by an interior network and carried to uneasy elders.)
One wonders, though, how much longer the human race will
string along with its own electrical gifts, and how long the right
to speak can remain innocent of wattage. We have a feeling that
only if this issue is met will the principle of free speech survive.
There are always plenty of people who are eager to stifle opinion
they don't admire, and if the opinion happens to be expressed in
a volume of sound that is in itself insufferable, the number of
people who will want to stifle both the sound *and* the fury will
greatly increase. Amplification, therefore, is something like alco-
hol: it can heighten our meanings, but it can also destroy our
reason.

AUGUST 26, 1950

THE AGE OF DUST

On a sunny morning last week, we went out and put up a
swing for a little girl, age three, under an apple tree—the tree
being much older than the girl, the sky being blue, the clouds
white. We pushed the little girl for a few minutes, then returned
to the house and settled down to an article on death dust, or
radiological warfare, in the July *Bulletin of the Atomic Scientists*, Volume VI, No. 7.

The article ended on a note of disappointment. "The area
that can be poisoned with the fission products available to us
today is disappointingly small; it amounts to not more than two
or three major cities per month." At first glance, the sentence
sounded satirical, but a rereading convinced us that the scientist's
disappointment was real enough—that it had the purity of
detachment. The world of the child in the swing (the trip to the
blue sky and back again) seemed, as we studied the ABC of
death dust, more and more a dream world with no true relation

From *The Second Tree from the Corner.*

to things as they are or to the real world of discouragement over the slow rate of the disappearance of cities.

Probably the scientist-author of the death-dust article, if he were revising his literary labors with a critical eye, would change the wording of that queer sentence. But the fact is, the sentence got written and published. The terror of the atom age is not the violence of the new power but the speed of man's adjustment to it—the speed of his acceptance. Already bomb-proofing is on approximately the same level as mothproofing. Two or three major cities per month isn't much of an area, but it is a start. To the purity of science (which hopes to enlarge the area) there seems to be no corresponding purity of political thought, never the same detachment. We sorely need, from a delegate in the Security Council, a statement as detached in its way as the statement of the scientist on death dust. This delegate (and it makes no difference what nation he draws his pay from) must be a man who has not adjusted to the age of dust. He must be a person who still dwells in the mysterious dream world of swings, and little girls in swings. He must be more than a good chess player studying the future; he must be a memoirist remembering the past.

We couldn't seem to separate the little girl from radiological warfare—she seemed to belong with it, although inhabiting another sphere. The article kept getting back to her. "This is a novel type of warfare, in that it produces no destruction, except to life." The weapon, said the author, can be regarded as a horrid one, or, on the other hand, it "can be regarded as a remarkably humane one. In a sense, it gives each member of the target population [including each little girl] a choice of whether he will live or die." It turns out that the way to live—if that be your choice—is to leave the city as soon as the dust arrives, holding "a folded, dampened handkerchief" over your nose and mouth. We went outdoors again to push the swing some more for the little girl, who is always forgetting her handkerchief. At lunch we watched her try to fold her napkin. It seemed to take forever.

As we lay in bed that night, thinking of cities and target

populations, we saw the child again. This time she was with the other little girls in the subway. When the train got to 242nd Street, which is as far as it goes into unreality, the children got off. They started to walk slowly north. Each child had a handkerchief, and every handkerchief was properly moistened and folded neatly—the way it said in the story.

EXPOSITION

Of the four forms of discourse, exposition is the least likely to have roots in everyday conversation; but it is the one most commonly required in educated life, where the need to explain is greatest. Paradoxically, skill in exposition undergirds the effective use of the three other forms. For example, description, when it is more complicated than the quick turns of phrase in daily speech or the figurative insights of native intelligence, can draw upon expository skills, for example comparison. Or, to pick a different kind of problem, the writer of persuasion may need to spend most of his time explaining before he can persuade.

The main intention of exposition is to clarify a subject for better understanding. Since exposition engages the intellect more than the passions, at first glance it may not seem as exciting to the inexperienced writer as narrative or persuasion. Although the primary aim of exposition does not lie in sharing a vivid experience with the reader or resolving a specific conflict, the writer is under no special obligation to be dull just because he is trying to inform. The curse of much writing palmed off as exposition in manuals, textbooks, reports, and often in speeches is a jargon that usurps standard English in an effort, conscious or not, to express or imitate the impersonal tone of an expert. ("In conclusion, it may be reported that the personnel practices surveyed in this study validate the hypothesis originally postulated.") Fortunately, some expository writing in the better scientific journals demonstrates that large amounts of information may be quickly conveyed in a manner that is simple, lucid, and lively.

The special virtue of White's exposition is that it is lively as well as informative. In pieces such as "Motor Cars" and "Freedom" he is speaking out of a passion that affects his own adrenal glands as well as the reader's. And he is not writing for an audience of experts in Detroit or Manhattan. In clarifying his ideas of the danger implicit in treacherous design both to a nation's character and to its motor cars, he illustrates how exposition can be flexible in appeal and style while conveying essential information. He has no compunction about using humorous hyperbole for a serious purpose, as when he speaks about the designers huffing and puffing (like the big bad wolf) to produce wonderful fenders "that would reach out and claw at anything that came anywhere near them." In his piece on freedom, as it existed in what W. H. Auden called a "low dishonest decade," he explains frankly and with sadness exactly where he stands. On a theme often characterized by solemn jargon, he composes a spirited personal credo.

"Motor Cars" and "Freedom" may appear informal, but they follow designs that are far from haphazard. The former is built around an explanation of the process evolving a self-defacing car. White's own *reductio ad absurdum* is no more absurd than the concept of planned obsolescence that became fashionable twenty years after his essay. "Freedom," on the other hand, begins with some samples of the "defeatism and disillusion" that disturbed White in 1940 and continues with an analysis of the instinct for freedom and its expression in practical liberties. With this double-surfaced touchstone, he tests Hitler's stand, contrasting the dictator's beliefs with his own. Though White makes it seem so, neither essay explains points that are inherently simple. In both, the writing is translucent without being transparent.

OCTOBER 1940

MOTOR CARS

The motor car is, more than any other object, the expression of the nation's character and the nation's dream. In the free billowing fender, in the blinding chromium grilles, in the fluid control, in the ever-widening front seat, we see the flowering of

From *One Man's Meat.*

the America that we know. It is of some interest to scholars and historians that the same autumn that saw the abandonment of the window crank and the adoption of the push button (removing the motorist's last necessity for physical exertion) saw also the registration of sixteen million young men of fighting age and symphonic styling. It is of deep interest to me that in the same week Japan joined the Axis, DeSoto moved its clutch pedal two inches to the left—and that the announcements caused equal flurries among the people.

I have long been interested in motor-car design, or the lack of it, and this for two reasons. First, I used to like motoring. Second, I am fascinated by the anatomy of decline, by the spectacle of people passively accepting a degenerating process that is against their own interests. A designer sitting at his drafting board blowing up a mudguard into some new fantastic shape is no more responsible to his public than is a political ruler who is quietly negotiating a treaty for the extension of his power. In neither case is the public in on the deal.

Some years ago car manufacturers maliciously began reducing the size of windows and increasing the size of mudguards, or "fenders" as the younger generation calls them. By following no particular principle of design and by ignoring the functional aspects of an automobile, these manufacturers eventually achieved a vehicle that not only was stranger looking than anything that had heretofore been evolved, but because it cut off the driver's view, was capable of getting into more scrapes. At first the advantages of this design were not apparent, but it didn't take long before the motor-car industry realized that it had hold of something that, from a commercial angle, was pure gold. Every automobile was intrinsically self-defacing—and sometimes self-destructive—and this soon made the market ever so much brisker.

I shall go into the evolution of this modern car in a little more detail. The way it happened was that a rumor got started (I don't know why) that a motor car should be "longer" and "lower." Now, obviously it was impractical to reduce, to any great extent, the height of a motor car. And it was just as impractical to increase, to any great extent, the length of a motor car. So the designers had to produce an *illusion* of great length and extreme lowness. The first thing they did was to raise the hood, so that the rest of the car would appear lower by contrast. Having raised the hood, they also raised the line of the doors, to carry out the illusion clear to the bitter end. This of course reduced the size of the windows, and the motorist began the long sinking process which was to end, in 1941, in his total immersion. Fenders also had to be raised (you notice that in order to build a "low" car everything was raised). But it was impossible to raise fenders without also enlarging them—otherwise they would rise right up off the wheels. So the designers began playing with new shapes in fenders, and they huffed and they puffed, and they produced some wonderful fenders—fenders that not only were a very odd shape indeed, but that would reach out and claw at everything that came anywhere near them.

Meanwhile wheels had shrunk so small, and tires had grown so big, that the fenders were still further enlarged in a downward direction, so that they would not only be readily bumped, but would scrape along the tops of curbings and culverts and miscellaneous mounds. They also made it impossible for anyone but a contortionist to change tires.

The decrease in the size of windows, simultaneously with the increase in the size of fenders, produced astounding results in the automobile industry. Millions of motorists who had become reasonably proficient in driving their cars without denting them suddenly lost that proficiency because they no longer could see where they were going (or where they had been), and because the dentable surfaces had been so drastically enlarged. Car owners who were accustomed to keeping a car for six or eight years, found that their modern car was all dented up after a single season of blind flying. So they would trade it in for a new one. Here was a most favorable turn of events for the manufacturer. He wasn't slow in catching on.

The ultimate goal of automobile designers is to produce a car into whose driving seat the operator will sink without a trace. They have very nearly achieved this goal. I know several women whose heads are permanently slanted backward because of the neck cramps they have developed trying to peek out over the cowl of a modern super-matic automobile. Incidentally, the steering wheel has been a big help to the designers in producing this type of cramp. If, after the hood had been raised, there still lingered any doubt that the operator's vision had been blocked off, the designer settled it once and for all by moving the wheel up an inch or two till the top of it was exactly on eye level. Even a skinny little steering wheel can cut off about an acre of visibility if properly placed by a skillful designer.

Mr. Arthur W. Stevens of Boston has computed that since 1900 the motorist's angle of visibility has been reduced thirty-six degrees. That is nice figuring. All I know is that for almost two decades I owned cars and never dented them up, and a couple of years ago I bought a new sedan in the low-price group, and after two years of my conservative driving it looks as though it had been dropped from a rather high building. This doesn't mean that I have become less skillful in driving a car; it means that the designers have become more determined that I shall not be given an even show.

The public's passive acceptance of this strange vehicle is disheartening, as is the acceptance by other peoples of the strange modern governments which are destroying them in a dulcet fashion. I think there will some day be an awakening of a rude sort, just as there will some day inevitably be a union of democracies, after many millions have died for the treacherous design of nationalism.

JULY   1940

FREEDOM

I have often noticed on my trips up to the city that people have recut their clothes to follow the fashion. On my last trip, however, it seemed to me that people had remodeled their ideas

From *One Man's Meat*.

too—taken in their convictions a little at the waist, shortened the sleeves of their resolve, and fitted themselves out in a new intellectual ensemble copied from a smart design out of the very latest page of history. It seemed to me they had strung along with Paris a little too long.

I confess to a disturbed stomach. I feel sick when I find anyone adjusting his mind to the new tyranny which is succeeding abroad. Because of its fundamental strictures, fascism does not seem to me to admit of any compromise or any rationalization, and I resent the patronizing air of persons who find in my plain belief in freedom a sign of immaturity. If it is boyish to believe that a human being should live free, then I'll gladly arrest my development and let the rest of the world grow up.

I shall report some of the strange remarks I heard in New York. One man told me that he thought perhaps the Nazi ideal was a sounder ideal than our constitutional system "because have you ever noticed what fine alert young faces the young German soldiers have in the newsreel?" He added: "Our American youngsters spend all their time at the movies—they're a mess." That was his summation of the case, his interpretation of the new Europe. Such a remark leaves me pale and shaken. If it represents the peak of our intelligence, then the steady march of despotism will not receive any considerable setback at our shores.

Another man informed me that our democratic notion of popular government was decadent and not worth bothering about—"because England is really rotten and the industrial towns there are a disgrace." That was the only reason he gave for the hopelessness of democracy; and he seemed mightily pleased with himself, as though he were more familiar than most with the anatomy of decadence, and had detected subtler aspects of the situation than were discernible to the rest of us.

Another man assured me that anyone who took *any* kind of government seriously was a gullible fool. You could be sure, he said, that there is nothing but corruption "because of the way Clemenceau acted at Versailles." He said it didn't make any difference really about this war. It was just another war. Having relieved himself of this majestic bit of reasoning, he subsided.

Another individual, discovering signs of zeal creeping into my blood, berated me for having lost my detachment, my pure skeptical point of view. He announced that he wasn't going to be swept away by all this nonsense, but would prefer to remain in the role of innocent bystander, which he said was the duty of any intelligent person. (I noticed, however, that he phoned later to qualify his remark, as though he had lost some of his innocence in the cab on the way home.)

Those are just a few samples of the sort of talk that seemed to be going round—talk which was full of defeatism and disillusion and sometimes of a too studied innocence. Men are not merely annihilating themselves at a great rate these days, but they are telling one another enormous lies, grandiose fibs. Such remarks as I heard are fearfully disturbing in their cumulative effect. They are more destructive than dive bombers and mine fields, for they challenge not merely one's immediate position but one's main defenses. They seemed to me to issue either from persons who could never have really come to grips with freedom, so as to understand her, or from renegades. Where I expected to find indignation, I found paralysis, or a sort of dim acquiescence, as in a child who is dully swallowing a distasteful pill. I was advised of the growing anti-Jewish sentiment by a man who seemed to be watching the phenomenon of intolerance not through tears of shame but with a clear intellectual gaze, as through a well-ground lens.

The least a man can do at such a time is to declare himself and tell where he stands. I believe in freedom with the same burning delight, the same faith, the same intense abandon which attended its birth on this continent more than a century and a half ago. I am writing my declaration rapidly, much as though I were shaving to catch a train. Events abroad give a man a feeling of being pressed for time. Actually I do not believe I am pressed for time, and I apologize to the reader for a false impression that may be created. I just want to tell, before I get slowed down, that I am in love with freedom and that it is an affair of long standing and that it is a fine state to be in, and that I am deeply suspicious of people who are beginning to adjust to fascism and dictators merely because they are succeeding in war. From such adaptable natures a smell rises. I pinch my nose.

For as long as I can remember I have had a sense of living somewhat freely in a natural world. I don't mean I enjoyed freedom of action, but my existence seemed to have the quality of free-ness. I traveled with secret papers pertaining to a divine conspiracy. Intuitively I've always been aware of the vitally important pact which a man has with himself, to be all things to himself, and to be identified with all things, to stand self-reliant, taking advantage of his haphazard connection with a planet, riding his luck, and following his bent with the tenacity of a hound. My first and greatest love affair was with this thing we call freedom, this lady of infinite allure, this dangerous and beautiful and sublime being who restores and supplies us all.

It began with the haunting intimation (which I presume every child receives) of his mystical inner life; of God in man; of nature publishing herself through the "I." This elusive sensation is moving and memorable. It comes early in life: a boy, we'll say, sitting on the front steps on a summer night, thinking of nothing in particular, suddenly hearing as with a new perception and as though for the first time the pulsing sound of crickets, overwhelmed with the novel sense of identification with the natural company of insects and grass and night, conscious of a faint answering cry to the universal perplexing question: "What is 'I'?" Or a little girl, returning from the grave of a pet bird leaning with her elbows on the windowsill, inhaling the unfamiliar draught of death, suddenly seeing herself as part of the complete story. Or to an older youth, encountering for the first time a great teacher who by some chance word or mood awakens something and the youth beginning to breathe as an individual and conscious of strength in his vitals. I think the sensation must develop in many men as a feeling of identity with God—an eruption of the spirit caused by allergies and the sense of divine existence as distinct from mere animal existence. This is the beginning of the affair with freedom.

But a man's free condition is of two parts: the instinctive free-ness he experiences as an animal dweller on a planet, and the practical liberties he enjoys as a privileged member of human society. The latter is, of the two, more generally understood, more widely admired, more violently challenged and discussed. It is the practical and apparent side of freedom. The United States, almost alone today, offers the liberties and the privileges and the tools of freedom. In this land the citizens are still invited to write their plays and books, to paint their pictures, to meet for discussion, to dissent as well as to agree, to mount soapboxes in the public square, to enjoy education in all subjects without censorship, to hold court and judge one another, to compose music, to talk politics with their neighbors without wondering whether the secret police are listening, to exchange ideas as well as goods, to kid the government when it needs kidding, and to read real news of real events instead of phony news manufactured by a paid agent of the state. This is a fact and should give every person pause.

To be free, in a planetary sense, is to feel that you belong to earth. To be free, in a social sense, is to feel at home in a democratic framework. In Adolf Hitler, although he is a freely flowering individual, we do not detect either type of sensibility. From reading his book I gather that his feeling for earth is not a sense of communion but a driving urge to prevail. His feeling for men is not that they co-exist, but that they are capable of being arranged and standardized by a superior intellect—that their existence suggests not a fulfillment of their personalities but a submersion of their personalities in the common racial destiny. His very great absorption in the destiny of the German people somehow loses some of its effect when you discover, from his writings, in what vast contempt he holds *all* people. "I learned," he wrote, ". . . to gain an insight into the unbelievably primitive opinions and arguments of the people." To him the ordinary man is a primitive, capable only of being used and led. He speaks continually of people as sheep, halfwits, and impudent fools—the same people from whom he asks the utmost in loyalty, and to whom he promises the ultimate in prizes.

Here in America where our society is based on belief in the individual, not contempt for him, the free principle of life has a chance of surviving. I believe that it must and will survive. To understand freedom is an accomplishment that all men may acquire who set their minds in that direction; and to love freedom is a tendency that many Americans are born with. To live in the same room with freedom, or in the same hemisphere, is still a profoundly shaking experience for me.

One of the earliest truths (and to him most valuable) that the author of *Mein Kampf* discovered was that it is not the written word, but the spoken word, that in heated moments moves great masses of people to noble or ignoble action. The written word, unlike the spoken word, is something that every person examines privately and judges calmly by his own intellectual standards, not by what the man standing next to him thinks. "I know," wrote Hitler, "that one is able to win people far more by the spoken than by the written word. . . ." Later he adds contemptuously: "For let it be said to all knights of the pen and to all the political dandies, especially of today: the greatest changes in this world have never yet been brought about by a goose quill! No, the pen has always been reserved to motivate these changes theoretically."

Luckily I am not out to change the world—that's being done for me, and at a great clip. But I know that the free spirit of man is persistent in nature; it recurs, and has never successfully been wiped out, by fire or flood. I set down the above remarks merely (in the words of Mr. Hitler) to motivate that spirit, theoretically. Being myself a knight of the goose quill, I am under no misapprehension about "winning people"; but I am inordinately proud these days of the quill, for it has shown itself, historically, to be the hypodermic that inoculates men and keeps the germ of freedom always in circulation, so that there are individuals in every time in every land who are the carriers, the Typhoid Mary's, capable of infecting others by mere contact and example. These persons are feared by every tyrant—who shows his fear by burning the books and destroying the individuals. A writer goes about his task today with the extra satisfaction that comes from knowing that he will be the first to have his head lopped off—even before the political dandies. In my own case this is a double satisfaction, for if freedom were denied me by force of earthly circumstance, I am the same as dead and would infinitely prefer to go into fascism without my head than with it, having no use for it any more and not wishing to be saddled with so heavy an encumbrance.

WAYS OF DEVELOPMENT

Developing an idea is often more of a problem than finding one. An understanding of the four forms of discourse, the four main intentions behind writing, helps a student judge approximately where to begin a subject and where to end it, and roughly what ground to cover in between. But how to expand a good intention into an idea that will be clear and convincing to a reader—this is a troublesome matter. Six general ways of confronting the problem are discussed in the following pages.

Two illusions cause many writers to waste much time and paper. One is that the writer must be inspired. There is a flaw inherent in this assumption because much of the world's work is done on blue Monday or fatigued Friday, when inspiration is a bird just flown. The second illusion is that a truly disciplined and informed master of rhetoric will understand so well what he is doing that he will have plotted the course of every paragraph before he engages the gears of his typewriter. Judged by this majestic standard any humble attempt at planning looks confused and futile.

Faced with inevitable frustration, a student may take comfort in the attitude of the helmet-and-goggles flier who said that any landing from which you walk away is a successful landing. If a student reaches his objective, shakily but in one piece, he need not fret that his skill is less than a master artist's.

To a master or an apprentice, the six methods of development are useful in exposition and in the other forms of discourse. They are part of the basic resources of rhetoric, the art of effective expression. They are neither miraculous shortcuts to instant success nor iron maidens fiendishly devised to confine and torture inspiration, but simply six guides to turning a main intention into an effective piece of writing.

REPORTING THE FACTS

When White was learning to "say the words" as a reporter for the Seattle *Times,* he discovered that, although he was a "literary man in the highest sense of the term, a poet who met every train," as a newspaper reporter he was "almost useless." Years later, as he looked back on his years of wonder and wander after graduation, he noticed that the diary he had kept during the period offered "few crumbs of solid information":

> As a diarist, I was a master of suspense, leaving to the reader's imagination everything pertinent to the action of my play. I operated, generally, on too high a level for routine reporting, and had not at that time discovered the eloquence of facts. I can see why the *Times* fired me. A youth who persisted in rising above the facts must have been a headache to a city editor.

White's phrase "the eloquence of facts" succinctly and accurately states a simple principle of good writing. Facts are eloquent. Few lessons are harder to learn; few are more useful. The writer who persists in rising above facts will rise above his reader. Even a reader aching for understanding cannot fight his way through generalizations frozen in abstract language, while a lazy reader may be touched by accurately reported facts. The editors who called the New England town meeting the "quintessence of democracy" spoke less eloquently, though more loftily, than White when he reported, in "Town Meeting," the remark of a neighbor:

> "Well," he said, as he climbed into our car balancing a pot of baked beans wrapped in a paper bag, "here we go to the Chase and Sanborn hour."

Whether a writer aspires to hold a job on a newspaper or merely to submit an effective paper in a history course or a poem to a campus magazine, he is up against a stubborn fact of language: Specific and concrete words are more useful to a reader than general and abstract words. For example, "mansard roof," in "Town Meeting," is more specific than "roof." "Ugly" is an abstract word, but the idea of ugly is made concrete in the description of four voting booths "looking perilously like pay toilets." The writer who is both specific and concrete is less likely to be vague and more likely to strike a reader sharply and convincingly. White's tender and factual observations of the twins at the Bronx Zoo are far more effective than the familiar generalizations about the wonder of birth.

The standard assumption that accurate facts are for reporters or scientists, not for novelists or poets, is rooted in an ignorance of the relation of literature and reality. Hemingway wrote of his unending struggle to pin down "the real thing, the sequence of motion and fact which made the emotion." The most intricate poem of the imagination may be as closely fastened to fact as the simplest song. Consider this, for example, from Coleridge:

> And ice, mast-high, came floating by,
> As green as emerald.

Or this from Housman:

> Now, of my threescore years and ten,
> Twenty will not come again,
> And take from seventy springs a score,
> It only leaves me fifty more.

Those who resist using facts in their writing from the mistaken notion that they will be bound to a pedestrian plod should look carefully at "About Myself." Such a tour de force is not the ham and eggs we need daily, but it illustrates that a deft use of the dullest and most prosaic detail—the numbers on pill bottles or the cryptic symbols on department store receipts at which we stare dumbly in daily life—can yield a subtle comment on existence in a classified and impersonal world. Isolated facts may be trivial flotsam; selected and arranged by a responsible writer they can become useful, even eloquent.

MARCH   1940

TOWN MEETING

We had our annual town meeting last week, in the old town hall next to the church and across from the cemetery. I see that *Life* Magazine calls the New England town meeting the quintessence of democracy; but one of my neighbors, who has probably attended more of them than the editors of *Life,* had another name for it. "Well," he said, as he climbed into our car balancing a pot of baked beans wrapped in a paper bag, "here we go to the Chase and Sanborn hour."

It was a fine day for the meeting. About one hundred and twenty-five people turned out, or approximately one-seventh of the population. The hall is old and ugly—one of those Victorian mistakes with a mansard roof. The Masons, I am told, own the top floor, the town owns the rest. Neither can decide whether to tear the thing down or leave it up, but the question is academic because neither could get the consent of the other anyway.

The meeting is held on the first floor, in a room whose walls are sheathed in tin with a decorative tin molding. The windows are curtained with strips of pink and white paper, à la Dennison. Near the door is a wood stove, and at one end, next to the dais, are four voting booths looking perilously like pay toilets. When we arrived the ladies of the church were upstairs preparing lunch. Others were taking their places round the walls on the wooden benches. The men were gathered round the stove, visiting, warming up, talking shop, girding for trouble.

There are lots of people in town whom you see only once a year, at town meeting. They emerge from the back country and put in an appearance early; the meeting is a get-together for the

From *One Man's Meat.*

town the same as Fair day is for the county. The front row of benches was occupied by a delegation from the senior class at the high school who had come to observe government processes in a free country.

This was my first town meeting (I missed last year's) and I was surprised to discover that there was not much discussion on the floor. The warrant contained thirty-eight articles, covering election of town officers and appropriation of town moneys as well as other matters of policy. Most of them aroused no debate. There were questions involving the schools, the roads, the library, public health, yet there was no general discussion of any of these subjects. New Englanders are jealous of their right to govern themselves as they like, but in my town we have learned that town meeting is no place to decide anything. We thrash out our problems well in advance, working in small queues and with a long history of spite as a background. The meeting is just to make everything legal. For the assemblage the meeting virtually was concentrated in the first thirty minutes of bloodletting. It began when one of the citizens, who we all knew was loaded for bear, rose to his feet, walked to the front, drew from his pocket a small but ominous sheet of paper, and in soft pacific tones began:

"Mr. Moderator . . ."

This was when democracy sat up and looked around. This was the spectacle the townfolk had walked miles for. Half way through the speech, when the air was heavy with distilled venom, my neighbor turned to me and whispered: "I get so excited here it makes me sick. I'll commence to shake by and by."

At the conclusion of the barrage the First Selectman rose and returned the fire. Both men held the floor without yielding. There was no motion before the house—this was just pleasure before business. It had the heat and turmoil of the first Continental Congress without its nobility of purpose and purity of design. Old echoes of twenty years ago were awakened, old fires flared up and burned with original heat. At intervals there were bursts of applause when somebody scored a direct hit. At last the Moderator rapped with his gavel. Immediately the meeting settled down to business; cheerfully the taxpayers took up in rapid succession each article in the warrant and without a murmur voted the distribution of the twenty-five thousand dollars that, by dint of much scraping, we had managed to contribute to our community in the form of taxes. We had got our money's worth in the first half hour's skirmish—the rest was routine. You had to have roads and schools; that was all there was to that.

JUNE 19, 1948

TWINS

On a warm, miserable morning last week we went up to the Bronx Zoo to see the moose calf and to break in a new pair of black shoes. We encountered better luck than we had bargained for. The cow moose and her young one were standing near the wall of the deer park below the monkey house, and in order to get a better view we strolled down to the lower end of the park, by the brook. The path there is not much travelled. As we approached the corner where the brook trickles under the wire fence, we noticed a red deer getting to her feet. Beside her, on legs that were just learning their business, was a spotted fawn, as small and perfect as a trinket seen through a reducing glass. They stood there, mother and child, under a gray beech whose trunk was engraved with dozens of hearts and initials. Stretched on the ground was another fawn, and we realized that the doe had just finished twinning. The second fawn was still wet, still unrisen. Here was a scene of rare sylvan splendor, in one of our five favorite boroughs, and we couldn't have asked for more. Even our new shoes seemed to be working out all right and weren't hurting much.

From *The Second Tree from the Corner.*

The doe was only a couple of feet from the wire, and we sat down on a rock at the edge of the footpath to see what sort of start young fawns get in the deep fastnesses of Mittel Bronx. The mother, mildly resentful of our presence and dazed from her labor, raised one forefoot and stamped primly. Then she lowered her head, picked up the afterbirth, and began dutifully to eat it, allowing it to swing crazily from her mouth, as though it were a bunch of withered beet greens. From the monkey house came the loud, insane hooting of some captious primate, filling the whole woodland with a wild hooroar. As we watched, the sun broke weakly through, brightened the rich red of the fawns, and kindled their white spots. Occasionally a sightseer would appear and wander aimlessly by, but of all who passed none was aware that anything extraordinary had occurred. "Looka the kangaroos!" a child cried. And he and his mother stared sullenly at the deer and then walked on.

In a few moments the second twin gathered all his legs and all his ingenuity and arose, to stand for the first time sniffing the mysteries of a park for captive deer. The doe, in recognition of his achievement, quit her other work and began to dry him, running her tongue against the grain and paying particular attention to the key points. Meanwhile the first fawn tiptoed toward the shallow brook, in little stops and goes, and started across. He paused midstream to make a slight contribution, as a child does in bathing. Then, while his mother watched, he continued across, gained the other side, selected a hiding place, and lay down under a skunk-cabbage leaf next to the fence, in perfect concealment, his legs folded neatly under him. Without actually going out of sight, he had managed to disappear completely in the shifting light and shade. From somewhere a long way off a twelve-o'clock whistle sounded. We hung around awhile, but he never budged. Before we left, we crossed the brook ourself, just outside the fence, knelt, reached through the wire, and tested the truth of what we had once heard: that you can scratch a new fawn between the ears without starting him. You can indeed.

FEBRUARY 10, 1945

ABOUT MYSELF

I am a man of medium height. I keep my records in a Weis Folder Re-order Number 8003. The unpaid balance of my estimated tax for the year 1945 is item 3 less the sum of items 4 and 5. My eyes are gray. My Selective Service order number is 10789. The serial number is T1654. I am in Class IV-A, and have been variously in Class 3-A, Class I-A (H), and Class 4-H. My social security number is 067-01-9841. I am married to U.S. Woman Number 067-01-9807. Her eyes are gray. This is not a joint declaration, nor is it made by an agent; therefore it need be signed only by me—and, as I said, I am a man of medium height.

I am the holder of a quit-claim deed recorded in Book 682, Page 501, in the county where I live. I hold Fire Insurance Policy Number 424747, continuing until the 23 day of October in the year nineteen hundred forty-five, at noon, and it is important that the written portions of all policies covering the same property read exactly alike. My cervical spine shows relatively good alignment with evidence of proliferative changes about the bodies consistent with early arthritis. (Essential clinical data: pain in neck radiating to mastoids and occipito-temporal region, not constant, moderately severe; patient in good general health and working.) My operator's license is Number 16200. It expired December 31, 1943, more than a year ago, but I am still carrying it and it appears to be serving the purpose. I shall renew it when I get time. I have made, published, and declared my last will and testament, and it thereby revokes all other wills and codicils at any time heretofore made by me. I hold Basic A Mileage Ration 108950, O.P.A. Form R-525-C. The number of my car is 18-388. Tickets A-14 are valid through March 21st.

I was born in District Number 5903, New York State.

From *The Second Tree from the Corner*.

My birth is registered in Volume 3/58 of the Department of Health. My father was a man of medium height. His telephone number was 484. My mother was a housewife. Her eyes were blue. Neither parent had a social security number and neither was secure socially. They drove to the depot behind an unnumbered horse.

I hold Individual Certificate Number 4320-209 with the Equitable Life Assurance Society, in which a corporation hereinafter called the employer has contracted to insure my life for the sum of two thousand dollars. My left front tire is Number 48KE8846, my right front tire is Number 63T6895. My rear tires are, from left to right, Number 6N4M5384 and Number A26E5806D. I brush my hair with Whiting-Adams Brush Number 010 and comb my hair with Pro-Phy-Lac-Tic Comb Number 1201. My shaving brush is sterilized. I take Pill Number 43934 after each meal and I can get more of them by calling ELdorado 5-6770. I spray my nose with De Vilbiss Atomizer Number 14. Sometimes I stop the pain with Squibb Pill, Control Number 3K49979 (aspirin). My wife (Number 067-01-9807) takes Pill Number 49345.

I hold War Ration Book 40289EW, from which have been torn Airplane Stamps Numbers 1, 2, and 3. I also hold Book 159378CD, from which have been torn Spare Number 2, Spare Number 37, and certain other coupons. My wife holds Book 40288EW and Book 159374CD. In accepting them, she recognized that they remained the property of the United States Government.

I have a black dog with cheeks of tan. Her number is 11032. It is an old number. I shall renew it when I get time. The analysis of her prepared food is guaranteed and is Case Number 1312. The ingredients are: Cereal Flaked feeds (from Corn, Rice, Bran, and Wheat), Meat Meal, Fish Liver and Glandular Meal, Soybean Oil Meal, Wheat Bran, Corn Germ Meal, 5% Kel-Centrate [containing Dried Skim Milk, Dehydrated Cheese, Vitamin B_1 (Thiamin), Flavin Concentrate, Carotene, Yeast,

Vitamin A and D Feeding Oil (containing 3,000 U.S.P. units Vitamin A and 400 U.S.P. units Vitamin D per gram), Diastase (Enzyme), Wheat Germ Meal, Rice Polish Extract], 1½% Calcium Carbonate, .00037% Potassium Iodide, and ¼% Salt. She prefers offal.

When I finish what I am now writing it will be late in the day. It will be about half past five. I will then take up Purchase Order Number 245-9077-B-Final, which I received this morning from the Office of War Information and which covers the use of certain material they want to translate into a foreign language. Attached to the order are Standard Form Number 1034 (white) and three copies of Standard Form Number 1034a (yellow), also "Instructions for Preparation of Voucher by Vendor and Example of Prepared Voucher." The Appropriation Symbol of the Purchase Order is 1153700.001-501. The requisition number is B-827. The allotment is X5-207.1-R2-11. Voucher shall be prepared in ink, indelible pencil, or typewriter. For a while I will be vendor preparing voucher. Later on, when my head gets bad and the pain radiates, I will be voucher preparing vendor. I see that there is a list of twenty-one instructions which I will be following. Number One on the list is: "Name of payor agency as shown in the block 'appropriation symbol and title' in the upper left-hand corner of the Purchase Order." Number Five on the list is: "Vendor's personal account or invoice number," but whether that means Order Number 245-9077-B-Final, or Requisition B-827, or Allotment X5-207.1-R2-11, or Appropriation Symbol 1153700.001-501, I do not know, nor will I know later on in the evening after several hours of meditation, nor will I be able to find out by consulting Woman 067-01-9807, who is no better at filling out forms than I am, nor after taking Pill Number 43934, which tends merely to make me drowsy.

I owe a letter to Corporal 32413654, Hq and Hq Sq., VII AAF S.C., APO 953, c/o PM San Francisco, Calif., thanking him for the necktie he sent me at Christmas. In 1918 I was a private in the Army. My number was 4,345,016. I was a boy of medium height. I had light hair. I had no absences from duty under G.O. 31, 1912, or G.O. 45, 1914. The number of that war was Number One.

DEFINITION

Definition is a matter of wrestling with a term and explaining what you mean when you use a particular word or group of words. But there is more than one wrestling hold. The moronic way is to iterate. "What's an albatross? Why, an albatross is an albatross." The common sense way is to point out or give an example. "You see that large white bird hanging around that sailor's neck? That's an albatross." The methodical way is to place a term in a class (*genus*) and then point out the characteristics (*differentiae*) that set it apart from other members of the class: "Albatross: Any of various large, webfooted sea birds (family *Diomedeidae*), with long, narrow wings and a hooked beak."

A lexicographer, who is concerned with defining thousands of words in a single book, must settle for short definitions. Sometimes a writer may use an equally short one: "A dude, at best, is merely an inexperienced actor in the revival of an old melodrama." White's definition of dude, though not fusty like the one of albatross, is too brief, in itself, to make a composition. But when a student tries to define Pennsylvania Dutch cooking in a letter to a friend in Arizona, he will discover that there are many pages between *apfel kuchen* and *sauerbraten*. Concepts such as *law* or *fascism* also require extended definition to clarify their meaning. Consequently, definition is sometimes a means of developing a composition.

Obviously no writer who seeks to extend the meaning of a key term will fall into moronic iteration, though the trap of circular definition—defining a term with another form of the same word—is a common variant of this obvious error. ("Americanism is doing things the American way.") But the common sense way and the methodical way are equally useful in extending a definition, often doubly useful when they are combined.

Using examples is particularly helpful when the term to be defined identifies an idea drawn from individual experience. Take, for example, "Dudes and Flapsails." White's one-sentence definition of dude is an effective epigram, but what do "inexperienced actor" or "old melodrama" really mean? In "Dudes and Flapsails" an "inexperienced actor" turns out to be a city sailor who refers to a sheet of canvas on a coasting schooner as a "jib flapsail," and "old melodrama" means the revival of windjammers. Thus dude, a term applicable to city sea dogs as well as to the more familiar catered cowboys, is derived from White's experience with a schooner invasion right in his own cove. By giving several examples of this life of "part-time gypsies," White lets the reader share the process by which he arrived at his particular meaning for the term. Reporting the facts in this manner is a way of pointing and saying: "See, that's a dude."

One way of clarifying complex abstractions such as *democracy* is not markedly different from verbal pointing. In 1944, when the smoke of battle obscured the fate of the free world, White was asked to state what democracy meant. Though he responded with understandable emotion, his identifying characteristics such as "the dent in the high hat" and "a song the words of which have not gone bad" compel no agreement. They only reveal metaphorically the many-faceted meaning that the word has for him. But his "literary" definition has a connotative power that no strictly literal statement could provide.

The methodical formula for definition also can be freely adapted to extended discussion, usually by focusing on a detailed consideration of the *differentiae*. This does not mean play with words. In the swirl of language that is modern life, no one can afford to forget that ignorant and evil people use abstractions with powerful connotation to obscure thinking rather than clarify meaning. Anyone can nod his head in agreement when a large abstraction like *justice* or *extremism* is dropped like an olive into an oratorical cocktail, while at the same moment never noticing that he is agreeing with his own meaning of the word, not the speaker's.

Never noticing, that is, unless the mind behind the script, like White's, is fair enough to extend the definition. The extension allows the reader the possibility of agreeing or disagreeing because he then understands the key words. White's "Law and Justice"—combining elements of both common sense and methodical definition—explains a term, in part, by showing what it is not.

The piece on fascism, similar in technique, transforms a slashing cutlass-word into a useful scalpel.

Regardless of the method used, extended definition is a way of quelling a difficulty inherent in language. Specific terms like *albatross* give no trouble that an intelligent question or a quick look at a dictionary cannot solve. But terms like *fascism* pose a problem. When concepts are derived from particular experience or study, only extended definition will help the reader to understand them. Definition can thus become a way of explaining the unknown in terms of the known.

SEPTEMBER   1940

DUDES AND FLAPSAILS

When three coasting schooners, one right after another, tacked into our cove and dropped anchor I knew there must be something wrong. In these days one schooner is news, three in a bunch are almost unheard of. It soon was apparent that the vessels were dude-carriers. Their decks, instead of being loaded with pulp wood, held that most precious freight—men and women on excursion. I rowed out into the cove to see the sights and was invited aboard one of the vessels by an enthusiastic old sea dog who, after three full days of life afloat, was bursting with information of a feverishly nautical character. He kept tying knots in things, and rushed me all over the little ship, above and below, showing off its rude appointments and instructing me in the proper handling of a coasting schooner in fair weather and foul, including the management of a sail which he called the "jib flapsail." The schooners' yawl boats were busy taking passengers ashore for a lobster dinner on the beach, and our usually quiet cove, whose only regular night visitors are myself and a great blue heron, was soon gay with the vagrant screams and cries of persons temporarily removed from their normal environment.

I was told that the schooners were all owned by the same man—he has five or six of them and is buying others as fast as he

From "Sanitation" in *One Man's Meat.*

can find them. Dude business is good. Not much has to be done to the ships—some bunks built into the hold, a toilet installed, a new sail or two, and some paint. They are old boats, most of them, but plenty good enough for summertime cruising, and are competently sailed by Maine captains, who accept the arrival of vacationers on their foredeck with the same stoical reserve with which they accept fog on a flood tide at evening.

The invasion of western ranches and eastern schooners by paying guests who are neither cowboys nor sailors is an American phenomenon that we have grown used to. Some of the ranches have even moved east, to be nearer their cash customers. It's hard to say why the spectacle is saddening to the spirit, but there is no denying the way I feel when I see a coaster that has lost her legitimate deckload and acquired a crew of part-time gypsies. There is nothing wrong about it—anybody who is having a good time can't be wrong—yet the eternal quest for the romantic past that lives in the minds of men and causes them to strike attitudes of hardihood in clothes that don't quite fit them is so obviously a quest for the unattainable. And it ends so abruptly in reality. A dude, at best, is merely an inexperienced actor in the revival of an old melodrama.

MAY 8, 1943

LAW AND JUSTICE

During the great storm that broke following the announcement of the Jap executions of Amercian fliers, two phrases were heard above the crackling fury of everyone's wrath: the Japs had "violated military law" and the Japs would be "brought to justice." Now the storm abates. It is the time, now, for remembering that such phrases are false, such words dangerous when misused. The Japs violated no law and their leaders will never be brought to justice, though they will be brought to something else. Law is, unfortunately, not law unless it is enforceable, and the "laws" of warfare are in their very nature

From *The Wild Flag*.

unenforceable, being a mere set of rules for quarreling, which any country can disregard if it chooses. When war comes, each nation makes its own rules to suit itself. Japan makes hers, which include murdering enemy fliers; we make ours, which include abiding by previous agreements. When at length Japan is punished, as she certainly will be, for having executed American aviators, the act of punishing her will not be "justice," since no court exists that has jurisdiction and no force exists for carrying out such a court's order. To call it justice is to do ourselves a disservice, because it deflects our gaze from the terrible spectacle of a world without law.

This cantankerous attitude which we seem to be striking, this harping on the meaning of words, comes from our belief that there is a sharp need for definitions and that, in the words of Saroyan's barfly, there is "no foundation all the way down the line." Nothing is more frightening than to hear what is not law called law, what is not justice called justice. The recent murders in Japan, which received enormous public attention, were the inevitable extension of certain other Axis murders ten or twelve years ago, which received almost no attention. To speak as though we had law when what we've got is treaties and pacts, to use the word "law" for non-law, is to lessen our chances of ever getting law among peoples, since the first step toward getting it is to realize, with dazzling clearness, that we haven't got it and never have had it.

JULY 3, 1943

DEMOCRACY

We received a letter from the Writers' War Board the other day asking for a statement on "The Meaning of Democracy." It presumably is our duty to comply with such a request, and it is certainly our pleasure.

Surely the Board knows what democracy is. It is the line that forms on the right. It is the don't in Don't Shove. It is the

From *The Wild Flag.*

hole in the stuffed shirt through which the sawdust slowly trickles; it is the dent in the high hat. Democracy is the recurrent suspicion that more than half of the people are right more than half of the time. It is the feeling of privacy in the voting booths, the feeling of communion in the libraries, the feeling of vitality everywhere. Democracy is a letter to the editor. Democracy is the score at the beginning of the ninth. It is an idea that hasn't been disproved yet, a song the words of which have not gone bad. It's the mustard on the hot dog and the cream in the rationed coffee. Democracy is a request from a War Board, in the middle of a morning in the middle of a war, wanting to know what democracy is.

AUGUST 7, 1943

FASCISM

It is already apparent that the word "Fascist" will be one of the hardest-worked words in the Presidential campaign. Henry Wallace called some people Fascists the other day in a speech and next day up jumped Harrison Spangler, the Republican, to remark that if there were any Fascists in this country you would find them in the New Deal's palace guard. It is getting so a Fascist is a man who votes the other way. Persons who vote *your* way, of course, continue to be "right-minded people."

We are sorry to see this misuse of the word "Fascist." If we recall matters, a Fascist is a member of the Fascist party or a believer in Fascist ideals. These are: a nation founded on bloodlines, political expansion by surprise and war, murder or detention of unbelievers, transcendence of state over individual, obedience to one leader, contempt for parliamentary forms, plus some miscellaneous gymnastics for the young and a general feeling of elation. It seems to us that there are many New Deal Democrats who do not subscribe to such a program, also many aspiring Republicans. Other millions of Americans are nonsubscribers.

From *The Wild Flag*.

It's too bad to emasculate the word "Fascist" by using it on persons whose only offense is that they vote the wrong ticket. The word should be saved for use in cases where it applies, as it does to members of our Ku Klux Klan, for instance, whose beliefs and practices are identical with Fascism.

Unfortunately (or perhaps fortunately), there is a certain quality in Fascism which is quite close to a certain quality in nationalism. Fascism is openly against people-in-general, in favor of people-in-particular. Nationalism, although in theory not dedicated to such an idea, actually works against people-in-general because of its preoccupation with people-in-particular. It reminds one of Fascism, also, in its determination to stabilize its own position by whatever haphazard means present themselves —by treaties, policies, balances, agreements, pacts, and the jockeying for position which is summed up in the term "diplomacy." This doesn't make an America Firster a Fascist. It simply makes him, in our opinion, a man who hasn't grown into his pants yet. The persons who have written most persuasively against nationalism are the young soldiers who have got far enough from our shores to see the amazing implications of a planet. Once you see it, you never forget it.

CLASSIFICATION AND DIVISION

Classification and division are ways of thinking that may be effectively adapted to writing. Like definition, classification is a way of coping with general similarities and particular differences. The familiar Dewey Decimal System, which enables librarians to file particular books under general headings so that they may be stored and retrieved efficiently, is a complex application of the principle of classification. Division is the opposite; a way of separating a whole into manageable parts. The value of both is that they aid in the arrangement of things and ideas in writing.

To classify means to group individual members of a collection—of students, for example—in a system of classes. A *class* is a group having common characteristics, as athletes are a class of students who have in common their participation in sports. A *system* is an arrangement of classes from most inclusive to least inclusive: *Student* is an inclusive term while *football players* is a subclass of *athletes.*

A classification, whether of animals, people, or postage stamps, is largely an arbitrary invention of the mind. On a basket-ball court two men, one tall and one short, would be classified by the abstraction "height" as opposites; in a voting booth they might be grouped by "political affiliation" as democrats. It is essential that the inventor apply only one principle at each stage so that the items in each stage do not overlap. A grocer who sorted his produce into bins labelled apples, lemons, and fruit would create confusion. The rule is simple: To be useful a classifi-cation must have a clear purpose and logical stages.

"Divide and conquer" is an adage as useful to writing as to war. The various stages of a division represent progressively finer units of a broad category. White in "Poetry" ignores familiar categories of literary history like "Neo-Classic" or "imagistic" and confines most of his discussion of poetry to the abstraction "poetical obscurity." He divides popular or famous poets into those who are extremely clear and those who are thoroughly opaque. Then, though he mentions only Miss Stein as opaque, he implies that legions of poets may be ranked under the five types of opacity he cites. In simple and efficient fashion, both division and classification provide a way of developing this material.

The chief service of a division (or of a classification) is to provide an outline. White's "Security" shows how a simple outline gives form to an idea. The first paragraph divides men into "air-borne freemen" and "earthbound slaves." The second paragraph develops the idea of freemen; the third, the idea of slaves. The last paragraph is a moment of relief for a reader who has sud-denly seen with startling clarity White's idea of two irreconcilables at war within us.

NOVEMBER   1939

POETRY

"I wish poets could be clearer," shouted my wife angrily from the next room.

From *One Man's Meat.*

Hers is a universal longing. We would all like it if the bards would make themselves plain, or we think we would. The poets, however, are not easily diverted from their high mysterious ways. A poet dares be just so clear and no clearer; he approaches lucid ground warily, like a mariner who is determined not to scrape his bottom on anything solid. A poet's pleasure is to withhold a little of his meaning, to intensify by mystification. He unzips the veil from beauty, but does not remove it. A poet utterly clear is a trifle glaring.

The subject is a fascinating one. I think poetry is the greatest of the arts. It combines music and painting and storytelling and prophecy and the dance. It is religious in tone, scientific in attitude. A true poem contains the seed of wonder; but a bad poem, egg-fashion, stinks. I think there is no such thing as a long poem. If it is long it isn't a poem; it is something else. A book like *John Brown's Body,* for instance, is not a poem—it is a series of poems tied together with cord. Poetry is intensity, and nothing is intense for long.

Some poets are naturally clearer than others. To achieve great popularity or great fame it is of some advantage to be either extremely clear (like Edgar Guest) or thoroughly opaque (like Gertrude Stein). The first poet in the land—if I may use the word loosely—is Edgar Guest. He is the singer who, more than any other, gives to Americans the enjoyment of rhyme and meter. Whether he gives also to any of his satisfied readers that blinding, aching emotion that I get from reading certain verses by other writers is a question that interests me very much. Being democratic, I am content to have the majority rule in everything, it would seem, but literature.

There are many types of poetical obscurity. There is the obscurity that results from the poet's being mad. This is rare. Madness in poets is as uncommon as madness in dogs. A discouraging number of reputable poets are sane beyond recall. There is also the obscurity that is the result of the poet's wishing to appear mad, even if only a little mad. This is rather common and rather dreadful. I know of nothing more distasteful than the work of a poet who has taken leave of his reason deliberately, as a commuter might of his wife.

Then there is the unintentional obscurity or muddiness, that comes from the inability of some writers to express even a simple idea without stirring up the bottom. And there is the obscurity that results when a fairly large thought is crammed into a three- or four-foot line. The function of poetry is to concentrate; but sometimes over-concentration occurs, and there is no more comfort in such a poem than there is in the subway at the peak hour.

Sometimes a poet becomes so completely absorbed in the lyrical possibilities of certain combinations of sounds that he forgets what he started out to say, if anything, and here again a nasty tangle results. This type of obscurity is one that I have great sympathy for: I know that quite frequently in the course of delivering himself of a poem a poet will find himself in possession of a lyric bauble—a line as smooth as velvet to the ear, as pretty as a feather to the eye, yet a line definitely out of plumb with the frame of the poem. What to do with a trinket like this is always troubling to a poet, who is naturally grateful to his Muse for small favors. Usually he just drops the shining object into the body of the poem somewhere and hopes it won't look too giddy. (I sound as though I were contemptuous of poets; the fact is I am jealous of them. I would rather be one than anything.)

My quarrel with poets (who will be surprised to learn that a quarrel is going on) is not that they are unclear but that they are too diligent. Diligence in a poet is the same as dishonesty in a bookkeeper. There are rafts of bards who are writing too much, too diligently, and too slyly. Few poets are willing to wait out their pregnancy—they prefer to have a premature baby and allow it to incubate after being safely laid in Caslon Old Style.

I think Americans, perhaps more than other people, are impressed by what they don't understand, and the poets take advantage of this. Gertrude Stein has had an amazing amount of newspaper space, out of all proportion to the pleasure she has given people by her writings, it seems to me, although I am just guessing. Miss Stein is preoccupied with an experimental sort of writing that she finds diverting and exciting and that is all right by me. Her deep interest in the sound words make is laudable; too little attention is paid by most writers to sound, and too many writers are completely tone-deaf. But on the other hand I am not ready to believe than any writer, except with dogged premeditation, would always work in so elegantly obscure and elliptical a fashion as the author of "A rose is a rose"—never in a more conventional manner. To be one hundred per cent roundabout one must be pure genius—and nobody is that good.

On the whole, I think my wife is right: the poets could be a little clearer and still not get over on to ground which is unsuitably solid. I am surprised that I have gone on this way about them. I too am cursed with diligence. I bite my pencil and stare at a marked calendar.

SEPTEMBER   1938

SECURITY

It was a fine clear day for the Fair this year, and I went up early to see how the Ferris wheel was doing and to take a ride. It pays to check up on Ferris wheels these days: by noting the volume of business one can get some idea which side is ahead in the world—whether the airborne freemen outnumber the earthbound slaves. It was encouraging to discover that there were still quite a few people at the Fair who preferred a feeling of high, breezy insecurity to one of solid support. My friend Healy surprised me by declining to go aloft; he is an unusually cautious man, however—even his hat is insured.

I like to watch the faces of people who are trying to get up their nerve to take to the air. You see them at the ticket booths in amusement parks, in the waiting room at the airport.

From *One Man's Meat*.

Within them two irreconcilables are at war—the desire for safety, the yearning for a dizzy release. My *Britannica* tells nothing about Mr. G. W. G. Ferris, but he belongs with the immortals. From the top of the wheel, seated beside a small boy, windswept and fancy free, I looked down on the Fair and for a moment was alive. Below us the old harness drivers pushed their trotters round the dirt track, old men with their legs still sticking out stiffly round the rumps of horses. And from the cluster of loud speakers atop the judges' stand came the "Indian Love Call," bathing heaven and earth in jumbo tenderness.

This silvery wheel, revolving slowly in the cause of freedom, was only just holding its own, I soon discovered; for farther along in the midway, in a sideshow tent, a tattoo artist was doing a land-office business, not with anchors, flags, and pretty mermaids, but with Social Security Numbers, neatly pricked on your forearm with the electric needle. He had plenty of customers, mild-mannered pale men, asking glumly for the sort of indelible ignominy that was once reserved for prisoners and beef cattle. Drab times these, when the bravado and the exhibitionism are gone from tattooing and it becomes simply a branding operation. I hope the art that produced the bird's eye view of Sydney will not be forever lost in the routine business of putting serial numbers on people who are worried about growing old.

The sight would have depressed me had I not soon won a cane by knocking over three cats with three balls. There is no moment when a man so surely has the world by the tail as when he strolls down the midway swinging a prize cane.

ILLUSTRATION

"Mrs. Wienckus" and "Lime," two examples of the method of development known as illustration, share a common technique: They both employ a vivid individual example to clarify a general idea by representing a class. Illustration is another way of thinking in terms of classes.

The description of the disorderly Mrs. Wienckus—with its ironic nibbling at the notion that material things are in the saddle and riding mankind—is White's oblique way of poking into the "essential disorder" implicit in the "theory of the good life through accumulation of objects." Embodied in an illustration that is both topical and unusual, a commonplace theme here acquires a fresh significance.

"Lime" presents a more extensive use of the principle of illustration. The title may be misleading to some readers, who will expect remarks of a chemical, geological, or agricultural nature. White could have called the piece "New Deal." Someone else, less addicted to brevity, might have written on "The Political Hazards Implicit in the New Deal." But White's choice of a title is right. As a good illustrator, he knows that a vivid particular, chosen wisely to exemplify a broader subject, speaks more clearly than a thousand didactic generalities.

FEBRUARY 17, 1951

MRS. WIENCKUS

The Newark police arrested a very interesting woman the other day—a Mrs. Sophie Wienckus—and she is now on probation after being arraigned as disorderly. Mrs. Wienckus interests us because her "disorderliness" was simply her capacity to live a far more self-contained life than most of us can manage. The police complained that she was asleep in two empty cartons in a hallway. This was her preferred method of bedding down. All the clothes she possessed she had on—several layers of coats and sweaters. On her person were bankbooks showing that she was ahead of the game to the amount of $19,799.09. She was a working woman—a domestic—and, on the evidence, a thrifty one. Her fault, the Court held, was that she lacked a habitation.

"Why didn't you rent a room?" asked the magistrate. But he should have added parenthetically "(and the coat hangers in the closet and the cord that pulls the light and the dish that

From *The Second Tree from the Corner.*

holds the soap and the mirror that conceals the cabinet where lives the aspirin that kills the pain)." Why didn't you rent a room "(with the rug that collects the dirt and the vacuum that sucks the dirt and the man that fixes the vacuum and the fringe that adorns the shade that dims the lamp and the desk that holds the bill for the installment on the television set that tells of the wars)?" We feel that the magistrate oversimplified his question.

Mrs. Wienckus may be disorderly, but one pauses to wonder where the essential disorder really lies. All of us are instructed to seek hallways these days (except school children, who crawl under the desks), and it was in a hallway that they found Mrs. Wienckus, all compact. We read recently that the only hope of avoiding inflation is through ever increasing production of goods. This to us is always a terrifying conception of the social order—a theory of the good life through accumulation of objects. We lean toward the order of Mrs. Wienckus, who has eliminated everything except what she can conveniently carry, whose financial position is solid, and who can smile at Rufus Rastus Johnson Brown. We salute a woman whose affairs are in such excellent order in a world untidy beyond all belief.

NOVEMBER   1940

LIME

Received my allotment of ground limestone from the government last month. They gave me three tons of it, and it cost me nothing save a nominal charge for trucking. I have already spread it on my upper field and harrowed it in. Thus the New Deal comes home to me in powdered form, and I gain a new alkalinity and acquire some fresh doubts and misgivings.

I've been thinking a good bit about this lime, this handout; and it seems to me that it is the principal ingredient of the new form of government which Mr. Roosevelt is introducing, an

From *One Man's Meat*.

ingredient that I must try hard to identify in order to clarify the stew on which I feed and on which the people of America (or Amarrica) are so sharply divided. By applying for and receiving this lime I have become a party to one of the so-called "social gains" that we heard so much about during the political campaign. I don't know whether I like it or not. The lime for my field was a gift to me from all the taxpayers of the United States, a grudging gift on the part of about half of them who disavow the principles of the AAA, a gift in the name of fertility, conservation, and humanity. In so far as it is to the advantage of the nation that the soil of America shall be maintained in all its chemical goodness, the dispensation from Mr. Roosevelt is justifiable. Most farmers need more fertilizer than they can afford to buy; when the government provides it free of charge the land improves. But this of course isn't the whole story.

To be honest I must report that at the time I got the lime I experienced a slight feeling of resentment—a feeling not strong enough to prevent my applying for my share in the booty, but still a recognizable sensation. I seemed to have lost a little of my grip on life. I felt that something inside me, some intangible substance, was leaching away. I also detected a slight sense of being under obligation to somebody, and this, instead of arousing my gratitude, took the form of mild resentment—the characteristic attitude of a person who has had a favor done him whether he liked it or not. All I had to do was spread the lime on a five-acre piece, together with barn dressing; but the Federal government had a harder spreading job than that: the government had to spread the cost of it over the entire citizenry, over not only those who had re-elected Roosevelt but those who had despised him. So much Republican acidity for the lime to sweeten, it must have lost much of its strength before it reached my clay soil.

I don't know. It is something for every man to study over, with the help of his God and his conscience. I do begin to feel the friendly control over me and over my land which an Administration exerts in its eagerness to "adjust" me and to change the soil reaction of my upper field. I believe in this Administration, on the whole; in its vision and in its essential vigor. I even voted for it again. It has been called crackpot, but that doesn't disparage it for me. Genius is more often found in a cracked pot than in a whole one. In the main I prefer to be experimented on by an idealist than allowed to lie fallow through a long dry reactionary season. I believe in this Administration, but I am also trying to make out the implications in a load of limestone.

I think it is an unusually important question, and I wish I could be as sure of it in my mind as the President is in his. (Query: does he ever get any free lime for his Hyde Park place?) The gift of fertilizer is an arbitrary benefit bestowed by thinkers who agree that soil fertility is a national concern—a matter that touches *all* the people and, therefore, that may rightly be charged against all the people. That much is true, I think, even though there are millions of Americans who will never feel any direct gain from the increased alkalinity of my little bit of ground. But I believe it also is true that a government committed to the policy of improving the nation by improving the condition of *some* of the individuals will eventually run into trouble in attempting to distinguish between a national good and a chocolate sundae.

To take an extreme example: through indirect taxation my lime is paid for in part by thousands of young ladies many of whom are nursing a personal want comparable to my want of lime. We will say that they want a permanent wave, to bolster their spirits and improve the chemistry of their nature. Theirs is a real want, however frivolous. Hairdressing, like any other form of top dressing, is a vital need among many people, and the satisfaction of it, in a sense, may be termed a national good. It doesn't come first, as soil does, but it comes eventually at the end of a long line of reasoning or unreasoning. I think that one hazard of the "benefit" form of government is the likelihood that there will be an indefinite extension of benefits, each new one establishing an easy precedent for the next.

Another hazard is that by placing large numbers of

people under obligation to their government there will develop a self-perpetuating party capable of supplying itself with a safe majority. I notice that a few days after my lime had come I received a letter from my county agent that started, "To Members of the H— County Agricultural Conservation Association. Dear Member . . ." You see, already I was a paid-up Democrat, before ever the lime had begun to dissolve.

Well, I'm not trying to take sides. I'm just a man who got a few bags of lime for nuthin', and whose cup runneth over, troubling his dreams.

COMPARISON AND CONTRAST

Under a wan winter sun a cat will crouch on a board rather than on the ground. A physicist can explain the various heat gathering and reflecting properties of bare ground versus dressed lumber. Both mammals thus exhibit the ability to compare. In ordinary language *compare* is a verb meaning to examine for the purpose of discovering likenesses and differences. In rhetoric, comparison means clarifying a subject by means of systematic arrangement of points of likeness; contrast is its opposite. (Because the two processes commonly work in tandem, it is convenient, as in this discussion, to name both with one word.) The physicist has the fun of using progressively more complex refinements of his natural ability as a way not only of searching for understanding but of expressing it in writing.

Systematic comparison depends on the alertness, observation, and imaginative understanding stimulated by the curiosity and playfulness natural to man. One form of comparison occurs in figurative language and is the imaginative perception of similar aspects in dissimilar things. Metaphor, simile, and analogy are simple comparisons, but of progressively greater length. When White describes Dr. Townsend as "a skinny, bespectacled, little savior, with a big jaw, like the Tin Woodman," his flash of identify brings out the Wizard of Oz quality in this famed zealot of the 1930s. But the best of such capsule comparisons, vividly useful as they may be, often do more to reveal a writer's attitude than to clarify the nature of the subject. Systematic comparison, on the other hand, draws heavily on the techniques, already considered, of thinking in terms of classes.

The essential aspect of a systematic comparison is that those things being compared belong to the same class. A class, however, is usually an arbitrary arrangement to meet some specific end. White's comparison in "Education" of his son's experiences in city and country schools obviously treats the class of "school experiences." But the intriguing ironies of "Beside the Shalimar" rise like a genie from the unexpected juxtaposition of the black hands of the mechanic and the pale hands that exist only in a song on the radio.

Three general purposes may guide a writer. A comparison or contrast may be arbitrarily set up to explain the unknown in terms of the known (as in definition); to explore the nature of two or more members of a class in terms of their relationships to each other (classification); or to illuminate general principles by examining particular examples (illustration). The second of these is probably most frequently used, because contrast is such an effective tool of evaluation. In "Camp Meeting" the striking contrast between Dr. Townsend firing and Dr. Townsend under fire brilliantly explores the gap between ideal and reality without injustice to a sincere crusader.

There are two basic ways of presenting a systematic comparison. One is to divide the subject into a number of points, each of which becomes the focus of a comparison; the other is to give all the necessary points about the first half of the comparison and then present, in the same order, the complementary points about the second part. As an example, note "Beside the Shalimar," which follows the first pattern. With some variations, White develops his experience in a garage using such ironic contrasts as the sound of music with that of tinkering, the pale hands of the dream with the greasy but capable ones of the mechanic, and life in the oasis of love with life in a car with a smooth-running engine. The organization of "Camp Meeting" and "Education" is quite different. White develops his comment on Townsendism not with contrasts like "sounds" and "hands" but with the more vivid contrast of "Dr. Townsend before" and "Dr. Townsend after"—the two halves of his subject. Within this frame he first portrays the confident crusader and then, in the orderly but free way appropriate to narrative, he portrays the nervous defender of a dubious doctrine. In like manner, but in a systematic order which lends itself more to exposition, "Education" presents first the aspects— dress, transportation, teaching, recreation—of a "city school" and then, in the same order, those of a "country school."

These two patterns apply both to the organization of a single paragraph by comparison and to the formation of the whole composition. The last paragraph of "Education" contrasts the family apprehensions on the first morning of country school with the curiosity of the adults a year later and the boy's relaxed acceptance of days that go "just like lightning." Conceivably White could have used a point by point comparison, perhaps in alternating sentences, but he chose instead to use the second pattern of development. Thus not only is "Education" divided into the two halves of the subject, but the final paragraph itself has the same form as the whole piece. "Beloved Barriers," on the other hand, is an effective comparison without strictly conforming to either method.

Although the two methods may be varied or combined to meet particular needs, the objective is always a special clarity that comes from comparison and contrast. The first pattern is advantageous for a long and complex comparison because the points can be presented one at a time and thereby be developed fully and clearly. As "Education" demonstrates, the second pattern works well for a short comparison. On some occasions a writer may choose to combine the two in a single piece. The central problem is always how to achieve continuity between the organization of the specific comparison and that of the whole composition.

MARCH   1939

EDUCATION

I have an increasing admiration for the teacher in the country school where we have a third-grade scholar in attendance. She not only undertakes to instruct her charges in all the subjects of the first three grades, but she manages to function

From *One Man's Meat*.

quietly and effectively as a guardian of their health, their clothes, their habits, their mothers, and their snowball engagements. She has been doing this sort of Augean task for twenty years, and is both kind and wise. She cooks for the children on the stove that heats the room, and she can cool their passions or warm their soup with equal competence. She conceives their costumes, cleans up their messes, and shares their confidences. My boy already regards his teacher as his great friend, and I think tells her a great deal more than he tells us.

The shift from city school to country school was something we worried about quietly all last summer. I have always rather favored public school over private school, if only because in public school you meet a greater variety of children. This bias of mine, I suspect, is partly an attempt to justify my own past (I never knew anything but public schools) and partly an involuntary defense against getting kicked in the shins by a young ceramist on his way to the kiln. My wife was unacquainted with public schools, never having been exposed (in her early life) to anything more public than the washroom of Miss Winsor's. Regardless of our backgrounds, we both knew that the change in schools was something that concerned not us but the scholar himself. We hoped it would work out all right. In New York our son went to a medium-priced private institution with semi-progressive ideas of education, and modern plumbing. He learned fast, kept well, and we were satisfied. It was an electric, colorful, regimented existence with moments of pleasurable pause and giddy incident. The day the Christmas angel fainted and had to be carried out by one of the Wise Men was educational in the highest sense of the term. Our scholar gave imitations of it around the house for weeks afterwards, and I doubt if it ever goes completely out of his mind.

His days were rich in formal experience. Wearing overalls and an old sweater (the accepted uniform of the private seminary), he sallied forth at morn accompanied by a nurse or a parent and walked (or was pulled) two blocks to a corner where the school bus made a flag stop. This flashy vehicle was as punctual as death: seeing us waiting at the cold curb, it would sweep to a halt, open its mouth, suck the boy in, and spring away with an angry growl. It was a good deal like a train picking up a bag of mail. At school the scholar was worked on for six or seven hours by half a dozen teachers and a nurse, and was revived on orange juice in midmorning. In a cinder court he played games supervised by an athletic instructor, and in a cafeteria he ate lunch worked out by a dietitian. He soon learned to read with gratifying facility and discernment and to make Indian weapons of a semi-deadly nature. Whenever one of his classmates fell low of a fever the news was put on the wires and there were breathless phone calls to physicians, discussing periods of incubation and allied magic.

In the country all one can say is that the situation is different, and somehow more casual. Dressed in corduroys, sweatshirt, and short rubber boots, and carrying a tin dinner-pail, our scholar departs at crack of dawn for the village school, two and a half miles down the road, next to the cemetery. When the road is open and the car will start, he makes the journey by motor, courtesy of his old man. When the snow is deep or the motor is dead or both, he makes it on hoof. In the afternoons he walks or hitches all or part of the way home in fair weather, gets transported in foul. The schoolhouse is a two-room frame building, bungalow type, shingles stained a burnt brown with weather-resistant stain. It has a chemical toilet in the basement and two teachers above stairs. One takes the first three grades, the other the fourth, fifth, and sixth. They have little or no time for individual instruction, and no time at all for the esoteric. They teach what they know themselves, just as fast and as hard as they can manage. The pupils sit still at their desks in class, and do their milling around outdoors during recess.

There is no supervised play. They play cops and robbers (only they call it "Jail") and throw things at one another—snowballs in winter, rose hips in fall. It seems to satisfy them. They also construct darts, pinwheels, and "pick-up sticks" (jackstraws), and the school itself does a brisk trade in penny candy, which is for sale right in the classroom and which contains "surprises." The most highly prized surprise is a fake cigarette, made of cardboard, fiendishly lifelike.

The memory of how apprehensive we were at the beginning is still strong. The boy was nervous about the change too. The tension, on that first fair morning in September when we drove him to school, almost blew the windows out of the sedan. And when later we picked him up on the road, wandering along with his little blue lunch-pail, and got his laconic report "All right" in answer to our inquiry about how the day had gone, our relief was vast. Now, after almost a year of it, the only difference we can discover in the two school experiences is that in the country he sleeps better at night—and *that* probably is more the air than the education. When grilled on the subject of school-in-country *vs.* school-in-city, he replied that the chief difference is that the day seems to go so much quicker in the country. "Just like lightning," he reported.

JANUARY 1940

BESIDE THE SHALIMAR

They keep the radio going low at the village garage. You can sit on a bench by the stove and listen while the mechanic tinkers with your car. The car is brought in and the doors are rolled shut behind it to keep out the cold, and everything is sort of cozy and quiet in there, with the music faintly in your ears and the re-treads suspended above your head from the rafters and the inner tubes arranged in boxes on the shelf. The radio singer (a baritone) is singing "Pale Hands I Loved Beside the Shalimar." Love oozes in a ribbon from the cabinet—genuine, passionate, romantic love, yet quiet and restful because it is turned down low. I don't know where the Shalimar is. Perhaps Persia. Love, riding the waves of warmth from the stove, takes posses-

From "Fro-Joy" in *One Man's Meat*.

sion of me. I see a girl of breathtaking loveliness; her hands are Persian and pale. The mechanic, adjusting the points on my distributor, has hands that are not pale. They are almost black and they know what they're doing. The mechanic has never seen the Shalimar, never seen the inside of a radio studio where love originates, but he knows everything there is to know about a motor. The stove and the music create a moment of total contentment of mind and body as the singer ends with the haunting question: "Where are you now? Where are you now?" In twenty minutes they give me back my car and I pass through the doorway into the crisp world, away from the oasis of love and dreams of fair women—a man with a smooth-running engine, beside the Shalimar.

AUGUST   1939

CAMP MEETING

Over in the next county the Methodists have a camp ground, in a clump of woods near East Machias. They were in session there for about a week, and I went over on Saturday for the *pièce de résistance*—Dr. Francis E. Townsend (himself) of California. I had long wanted to see the author of America's favorite plan, and there he was, plain as day, right under the GOD IS LOVE sign.

It was a peaceful spot, though it gave one a sultry, hemmed-in feeling, as hardwood dingles often do. There was a ticket booth, where I paid my quarter; and beyond was a lane opening out into the *al fresco* temple where about six hundred people were gathered to hear the good news. They were Methodist farmers and small-town merchants and their Methodist wives and children and dogs, Townsendites from Townsend Club Number One of East Machias, pilgrims from all over the State, honest, hopeful folks, their faces grooved with the extra lines that come from leading godly, toilsome lives. The men sat

From *One Man's Meat.*

stiffly in the dark-blue suits that had carried them through weddings, funerals, and Fair days. In a big circle surrounding the temple were the cottages (seventy or eighty of them), little two-storey frame shacks, set ten or a dozen feet apart, each with its front porch, its stuffy upstairs bedroom, and its smell from the kitchen. Beyond, in a nobler circle, were the backhouses, at the end of the tiny trails. The whole place, even with hymns rising through the leafy boughs, had the faintly disreputable air that pervades any woodland rendezvous where the buildings stand unoccupied for most of the year, attracting woodpeckers, sneak thieves, and lovers in season.

On the dais, behind some field flowers, sat the Doctor, patiently awaiting his time—a skinny, bespectacled little savior, with a big jaw, like the Tin Woodman. He had arrived by plane the night before at the Bangor airport a hundred miles away, and had driven over that morning for the meeting. As I sat down a voice was lifted in prayer, heads were bowed. The voice came from a loudspeaker suspended from the branch of an elm, and the speaker was talking pointedly of milk and honey. When he quit, Dr. Townsend's henchman, a baldish fellow with a businesslike manner, took the stand and introduced the man who needed no introduction, Dr. Francis E. Townsend, of California, the world's greatest humanitarian. We all rose and clapped. Children danced on the outskirts, dogs barked, and faces appeared in the windows of some of the nearest cottages. The Doctor held out his hands for silence. He stood quietly, looking round over the assemblage. And then, to the old folks with their troubled, expectant faces, he said, simply:

"I like you people very much."

It was like a handclasp, a friendly arm placed round the shoulder. Instantly his listeners warmed, and smiled, and wriggled with sudden newfound comfort.

"I have come nearly four thousand miles to see you," continued the Doctor. "You look like good Methodists, and I like that. I was raised in a Methodist family, so I know what it means."

He spoke calmly, without any platform tricks, and he sounded as though this was the first time he had ever expounded Townsendism. In words of one syllable he unfolded the plan he had conceived, the plan he knew would work, the plan he promised to see enacted into law, so that all people might enjoy equally the good things of this life.

"The retirement of the elders is a matter of concern to the entire population." Grizzly heads nodded assent. Old eyes shone with new light.

"In a nation possessed of our natural resources, with great masses of gold and money at our command, it is unthinkable that conditions such as exist today should be tolerated. There is something radically wrong with any political philosophy that permits this to exist. Now, then, how did it come about?"

Dr. Townsend explained how it had come about. Flies buzzed in the clearing. The sun pierced the branches overhead, struck down on the folding music stands of the musicians, gleamed on the bare thighs of young girls in shorts, strolling with their fellows outside the pale of economics. The world, on this hot Saturday afternoon, seemed very old and sad, very much in need of something. Maybe this Plan was it. I never heard a milder-mannered economist, nor one more fully convinced of the right and wisdom of his proposal. I looked at the audience, at the faces. They were the faces of men and women reared on trouble, and now they wanted a few years of comfort on earth, and then to be received into the lap of the Lord. I think Dr. Townsend wanted this for them: I'm sure *I* did.

"Business is stymied," murmured the Doctor. "Almost half the population is in dire want. Sixty millions of people cannot buy the products of industry." The Doctor's statistics were staggering and loose-jointed, but his tone was quietly authoritative. There could be small room for doubt.

He spoke disparagingly of the New Deal, and knocked all the alphabetical schemes for employing idle men. "Do you want to be taxed for these useless and futile activities?"

His audience shook their heads.

And all the while he spoke, the plan itself was unfolding—simply, logically. A child could have understood it. Levy a two per cent tax on the gross business of the country and divide the revenue among persons over sixty years of age, with the one stipulation that they spend the money ($200 a month) within a certain number of days.

"And mind you," said the Doctor, with a good-natured grin, "we don't care a rap what you spend it for!"

The old folks clapped their hands and winked at one another. They were already buying pretty things, these Methodists, were already paying off old cankerous debts.

"We want you to have new homes, new furniture, new shoes and clothes. We want you to travel and go places. You old folks have earned the right to loaf, and you're going to do it luxuriously in the near future. The effect on business, when all this money is put into circulation, will be tremendous. Just let us have two billion dollars to distribute this month, and see what happens!"

The sound of the huge sum titivated the group; two billion dollars flashed across the clearing like a comet, trailing a wispy trail of excitement, longing, hope.

"It may even be three," said the Doctor, thoughtfully, as though the possibility had just occurred to him. "America has the facilities, all we need is the sense to use them."

He said he was reminded of a story in the old McGuffey's Reader. The one about the ship flying a distress signal, and another ship came to its assistance. "Get us water!" shouted the captain. "We are perishing of thirst."

"Dip up and drink, you fools!" answered the captain of the other ship. "You're in the mouth of the Amazon River."

"Friends," said the good Doctor, "we are in the mouth of the Amazon River of Abundance. But we haven't the sense to dip up and drink."

It was a nice story, and went well.

Suddenly the Doctor switched from words of promise to words of threat. Lightly, with bony fingers, he strummed the strings of terror. If we're going to save this democracy of ours (he said), we shall have to begin soon. You've read about strikes in the great industrial centers; in a very brief time you will read of riots. And when rioting starts, it will be an easy matter for someone to seize the armed forces of the country and put them to his own use. This has happened in Europe. It can happen here.

The glade darkened ominously. Trees trembled in all their limbs. The ground, hard-packed under the Methodist heel, swam in the vile twilight of Fascist doom. Still the little Doctor's voice droned on—calm, full of humility, devoid of theatrics. Just the simple facts, simply told.

And then the vexatious question of money to carry on with. The audience shifted, got a new grip on their seats with their behinds. The ancient ceremony of plate-passing was a familiar and holy rite that had to be gone through with. The Doctor carefully disclaimed any personal ambitions, financial or political. "I don't want a fortune," he said, confidentially. "I mean that. I don't seek wealth. For one thing, it might ruin my fine son. But it does take money to educate people to a new idea. Give us a penny a day and we'll educate the next Congress."

A joke or two, to restore amiability; another poke at Uncle Sam; another mention of the need for funds to carry on with; and the speech was over.

It had been an impressive performance. Most speeches lack the sincerity the Doctor had given his; not many speeches are so simply made and pleasantly composed. It had been more like a conversation with an old friend. I had listened, sitting there near the musicians, with all the sympathy that within me lay, and (I trust) with an open mind. Even a middle-aged hack has his moments of wanting to see the world get along. After all, this was no time for cynicism; most of what Dr. Townsend had said, God knows, was true enough. If anybody could devise a system for distributing wealth more evenly, more power to him. One man's guess was as good as another's. Well, pretty nearly as good. I pocketed the few scribbled notes I had made and gave myself over to a mood of summer afternoon despondency and world decay.

The chairman rose and announced that the meeting would be thrown open to questions, but that the time was short, so please speak right up. It was at this point that Dr. Francis E. Townsend (of California) began quietly to come apart, like an inexpensive toy. The questions came slowly, and they were neither very numerous nor very penetrating. Nor was there any heckling spirit in the audience: people were with him, not against him. But in the face of inquiry, the Doctor's whole manner changed. He had apparently been through this sort of thing before and was as wary as a squirrel. It spoiled his afternoon to be asked anything. Details of Townsendism were irksome in the extreme—he wanted to keep the Plan simple and beautiful, like young love before sex has reared its head. And now he was going to have to answer a lot of nasty old questions.

"How much would it cost to administer?" inquired a thrifty grandmother, rising to her feet.

The Doctor frowned. "Why, er," he said. (This was the first "er" of the afternoon.) "Why, not a great deal. There's nothing about it, that is, there's no reason why it needs to cost much." He then explained that it was just a matter of the Secretary of the Treasury making out forty-eight checks each month, one to each State. Surely that wouldn't take much of the Secretary's time. Then these big checks would be broken up by the individual State administrators, who would pay out the money to the people over sixty years of age who qualified. "We're not going to have any administrative problems to speak of, at all," said the Doctor, swallowing his spit. The little grandmother nodded and sat down.

"Can a person get the pension if they hold property?" inquired an old fellow who had suddenly remembered his home, and his field of potatoes.

"Yes, certainly," replied the Doctor, shifting from one foot to the other. "But we *do* have a stipulation; I mean, in our plan we are going to say that the money shall not go to anybody who has a gainful pursuit." An uneasy look crossed the farmer's face: very likely he was wondering whether his field of potatoes was gainful. Maybe his potato bugs would stand him in good stead at last. Things already didn't look so simple.

"How much bookkeeping would it mean for a business man?" asked a weary capitalist.

"Bookkeeping?" repeated the Doctor vaguely. "Oh, I don't think there will be any trouble about bookkeeping. It is so simple. Every business man just states what his gross is for the thirty-day period, and two per cent of it goes to pay the old people. In the Hawaiian Islands they already have a plan much like mine in operation. It works beautifully, and I was amazed, when I was there, at how few people it took to administer it. No, there'll be no difficulty about bookkeeping."

"How will the Townsend Plan affect foreign trade?" asked an elderly thinker on Large Affairs.

Doctor Townsend gave him a queer look—not exactly hateful, but the kind of look a parent sometimes gives a child on an off day.

"Foreign trade?" he replied, somewhat weakly. "Foreign trade? Why should we concern ourselves with foreign trade?" He stopped. But then he thought maybe he had given short measure on that one, so he told a story of a corn-flakes factory, and all the corn came from some foreign country. What kind of way was that—buying corn from foreigners?

Next question: "Would a person receiving the pension be allowed to use it to pay off a mortgage?"

Answer: "Yes. Pay your debts. Let's set our government a good example!" (Applause.)

And now a gentleman down front—an apple-cheeked old customer with a twinkle: "Doctor, would buying a drink count as spending your money?"

"A drink?" echoed the Doctor. Then he put on a hearty manner. "Why, if anybody came to me and wanted to drink himself into an early grave with money from the fund, I'd say,

'Go to it, old boy!'" There was a crackle of laughter, but the Doctor knew he was on slippery footing. "Don't misunderstand me," he put in. "Let's not put too many restrictions on morality. The way to bring about temperance in this world is to bring up our young sons and daughters decently, and teach them the evils of abuse. (Applause.) And now, friends, I must go. It has been a most happy afternoon."

The meeting broke up. Townsendites rose and started down the aisles to shake hands reverently with their chief. The chairman announced a take of eighty dollars and three cents. Life began to settle into its stride again. Pilgrims filed out of the pews and subsided in rocking chairs on the porches of the little houses. Red and white paper streamers, festooning the trees, trembled in the fitful air; and soft drinks began to flow at the booth beyond the Inner Circle. The Doctor, waylaid by a group of amateur photographers, posed in front of an American flag, and then departed in a Dodge sedan for the airport—a cloud-draped Messiah, his dream packed away in a brief case for the next performance. On the porch of a cottage called "Nest o'Rest" three old ladies rocked and rocked and rocked. And from a score of rusty stovepipes in the woods rose the first thick coils of smoke from the kitchen fires, where America's housewives, never quite giving up, were laboriously preparing one more meal in the long, long procession. The vision of milk and honey, it comes and goes. But the odor of cooking goes on forever.

DECEMBER 1941

BELOVED BARRIERS

Clubs, fraternities, nations—these are the beloved barriers in the way of a workable world, these will have to surrender some of their rights and some of their ribs. A "fraternity" is the antithesis of *fraternity*. The first (that is, the order or organiza-

From "Intimations" in *One Man's Meat*.

tion) is predicated on the idea of exclusion; the second (that is, the abstract thing) is based on a feeling of total equality. Anyone who remembers back to his fraternity days at college recalls the enthusiasts in his group, the rabid members, both old and young, who were obsessed with the mystical charm of membership in their particular order. They were usually men who were incapable of genuine brotherhood, or at least unaware of its implications. Fraternity begins when the exclusion formula is found to be distasteful. The effect of any organization of a social and brotherly nature is to strengthen rather than diminish the lines which divide people into classes; the effect of states and nations is the same, and eventually these lines will have to be softened, these powers will have to be generalized. It is written on the wall that this is so. I'm not inventing it, I'm just copying it off the wall.

ANALYSIS

The object of analysis is the special understanding that begins with separating or distinguishing component parts of something. Whether the thing analyzed is an old type of steel or a new type of poem, a process or a situation, the method is to separate the whole into its parts in some logical fashion.

An advanced civilization rests not upon steel and concrete but upon the ability to analyze. Remove the forms but retain the power of analysis, with human institutions to support it, and the forms of modern civilization will rise again. Because this skill is so important, students are required to do many analytical papers and reports. Those students whose strongest loyalty is to the arts sometimes feel uneasy before analysis, like a child meeting a new stepmother. Nevertheless, the house of intellect is erected on the foundation of analysis.

Since each discipline has its own specialized logic for loosening the whole into its parts, generalizations about analysis are perilous and usually incomplete. A student is better advised here to study logic or mathematics than rhetoric. To write an analysis is but to tidy up a trail blazed by a logical mind at work on a specific problem. But a few guidelines can alert the student to some common problems.

Though most exposition is a form of analysis, there is an important difference between analysis and ways of development such as definition or classification: An analysis is always of a structure. The subject may be as tangible as a steel bridge or as subtle as a sonnet, but the purpose is to examine the parts so as to understand the structure.

In the simplest analysis the writer merely enumerates the parts. Such technical description differs from literary description because its purpose is to convey information, not to share experience. A simple example would be an objective description of an automobile that will identify it for a buyer. But to explain the relationship between the gasoline at one end the the mysterious mechanical noises at the other requires a more intricate form of analysis.

One way of understanding the relationship of parts is to analyze a process—that is, a series of stages that occur in time and constitute a purposeful structure. The step-by-step directions for assembling a plastic toy make up a simple process, usually presented in what is called expository narration. In "A Shepherd's Life" White's remarks on the behavior of a ewe when giving birth to her young involve a more complex process. White uses narrative to present three instinctive acts of the mother that take place in a single time sequence and make probable the success of the birth. The narrative clarifies the general and typical details of birth, not the particular and individual.

Another way of understanding the relationship of parts is through cause-and-effect analysis. This makes greater demands on the capacity for logical reasoning. There are two basic problems. First, a reader wants to understand not the apparent causes but the real ones and to strike at the root of the matter. That two cats are colored yellow is not an explanation of why they are fighting; that they are males may have more to do with the fur that is flying. Second, a reader wants some assurance that he is dealing with the typical. In "The Shape of the U.N." White addresses himself not to particular instances of aggression but to the problems that stem from the failure to define this word in the United Nations Charter. Aggression is even discussed as a type of "joker" in the structure of the U.N. In a literate analysis he makes the trenchant point that you have to keep your words straight if you are going to give your world a shape.

DECEMBER 15, 1956

THE SHAPE OF THE U.N.

Turtle Bay, December 1, 1956

My most distinguished neighbor in Turtle Bay, as well as my most peculiar one, is the U.N., over on the East River. Its fame has soared in the past month, on the wings of its spectacular deeds, and its peculiarities have become more and more apparent. Furthermore, the peculiarities have taken on an added importance, because of President Eisenhower's determination to make United States foreign policy jibe with the U.N. Charter. In many respects, I would feel easier if he would just make it jibe with the Classified Telephone Directory, which is clear and pithy.

The Charter was a very difficult document to draft and get accepted. The nations were still at war and the founding fathers were doubtful about whether a world organization could be made to work at all, so they inserted a clause or two to cover themselves in case it didn't. Every member went in with his fingers crossed, and the Charter reflects this. It derives a little from the Ten Commandments, a little from the Covenant of the League of Nations, and a little from the fine print on a bill of lading. It is high in purpose, low in calories. Portions of it are sheer double-talk and, as a result, support double-dealing, but membership in a league is an exercise in double-dealing anyway, because the stern fact is that each sovereign nation has one foot in, one foot out. When the United States, for example, found itself up to its neck in the Middle East dilemma, it subscribed to

A "Letter from the East" in *The Points of My Compass.*

the Charter's pledge to suppress aggression in the common interest; it also issued an order to the commander of the 6th Fleet: "Take no guff from anyone!" You won't find such words in the Charter, but they are implicit in the Charter, and that is one of its peculiarities.

In shape the U.N. is like one of the very early flying machines—a breath-taking sight as it takes to the air, but full of bugs. It is obviously in the experimental stage, which is natural. Since many readers have probably never examined the Charter, I will give a quick rundown, covering merely the Preamble and Chapter One, where the gist of the political structure is to be found.

The Preamble awards honorable mention to the following: human rights, equal rights, justice, respect for treaties (the Charter itself is a treaty, so it is just whistling to keep up its courage here), tolerance, peace, neighborliness, economic and social advancement. The Preamble is *against*: war, and the use of armed force except in the common interest.

Chapter One deals with (1) Purposes, (2) Principles. The *purposes* are, in summarized form: to maintain peace; to suppress aggression; to develop friendly relations among nations on the principle of equal rights and self-determination (which I presume includes cannibalism); to cooperate; to harmonize actions of nations. The *principles* are: sovereign equality; members shall fulfill obligations in good faith; settle disputes by peaceful means; refrain from the threat or use of force against the territorial integrity or political independence of any state; cooperate; and never, never intervene in matters that are essentially within the domestic jurisdiction of any state.

As you can see, the thing has bugs. There are some truly comical ones, like Chapter I, Article 2, Paragraph 5, which, if I interpret it correctly, commands a member to help deliver a public whipping to himself. But I shall not dwell on the funny ones. Let us just stare for a few moments at two of the more serious bugs.

One: In a fluid world, the Charter affirms the *status quo*.

By its use of the word "aggression" and by other devices it makes the *status quo* the test of proper international conduct.

Two: Aimed at building a moral community, of peace, order, and justice, the Charter fails to lay down rules of conduct as a condition of membership. Any nation can enjoy the sanctuary of the Charter while violating its spirit and letter. A member, for example, is not required to allow the organization to examine its internal activities. Mr. Shepilov can come to Turtle Bay, but can Mr. Hammarskjöld go to Budapest? The world waits to see. Even if he makes it, he will arrive awfully late.

Despite its faults, the U.N. has just emerged from a great month in world history, and emerged all in one piece. It pulled England and France out of a shooting war and sent the constabulary to replace them in Egypt. It failed in Hungary, but in the General Assembly the Soviet Union took a rhetorical shellacking that really counted. The U.N. is our most useful international device, but it is built on old-fashioned ideas. The Charter is an extremely tricky treaty. Its trickiness is dangerous to the world because, for one thing, it leads idealistic nations like ours into situations that suddenly become sticky and queer. This very thing happened when, in order to "condemn aggression" in the Middle East, in conformity with our Charter obligations, we deserted England and France and took up with the dictator of the Arab world and his associate the Soviet Union.

Some people, perhaps most people, think words are not really important, but I am a word man and I attach the very highest importance to words. I even think it was dishonest to call the world organization the "United Nations," when everybody knew the name was a euphemism. Why start on a note of phonyness, or wistfulness? The newspapers, with their sloppy proofreading, sometimes call the world organization the United Notions, sometimes the Untied Nations. Neither of these typos would make a serviceable title, but curiously enough, both are pat. Dr. Luns, of the Netherlands, recently described the U.N. Charter as "the expression of an attitude of mind." He said some countries used it merely as a juke box—they put in their nickel and the box would light up and play. That is about it. The Charter is an accommodating box and can produce a remarkable variety of tunes.

When Hungary erupted, the world was shocked beyond measure at what was taking place. But under the Charter of the United Nations the Hungarian government was in a position to put up just as noisy an argument as the oppressed people who were in rebellion. "Nothing contained in the present Charter shall authorize the United Nations to intervene in matters which are essentially within the domestic jurisdiction of any state." (Chapter I, Article 2, Paragraph 7.) And when the U.N. wanted to send observers in, it received a polite no. This is palpably ridiculous, and it boils down to a deficiency in the Charter, a deficiency that is in the nature of an eleven-year-old appeasement. The Charter says that a member shall encourage "respect for human rights." That is laudable but fluffy. One way a Charter can advance human rights is to insist that the rights themselves (such as they are) remain visible to the naked eye, remain open to inspection. One of the preconditions of membership in the United Nations should be that the member himself not shut his door in the face of the Club. If the member won't agree to that, let him look elsewhere, join some other club.

Many will argue that if you are dealing with Iron Curtain countries, you have to take them on their own terms or you don't get them at all. That may be true. But who agreed to that amount of appeasement in the first place? And were they right? The appeasement was agreed to eleven years ago by charter writers who were trying to put together a world organization while a world war was still in progress. Their eye was not always on the ball, and they were looking back more than ahead. They were playing with century-old ideas: nonaggression (which is undefinable), self-determination (which includes the determination to send people to the salt mines), sovereign equality (which means that all nations are equal in the sight of God but the big ones are equal in the Security Council). The Charter bravely tries to keep these threadbare ideas alive, but they will not stay alive in the modern world of hydrogen and horror, and unless the Charter is brought up to date, it may fail us.

Much has happened in eleven years. Almost everything that has happened indicates that the United Nations should never have admitted the Communist nations on *their* terms; that is, freedom to operate behind a wall. If nations are to cooperate, the first condition must be that they have social and political intercourse. The Soviet Union held out for cooperation without intercourse, which is a contradiction in terms and which is as unworkable for nations as for spouses. A marriage can be annulled on the ground of denial of intercourse. A world organization can blow up on account of it.

The subtlest joker in the Charter is the word "aggression." There are other jokers, but none so far-reaching. When the United States was confronted with the Middle East crisis, it was surprised and bewildered to discover itself backing Nasser and Russia against France and England. One reason for this queer turn of events was that Britain and France had "aggressed," and therefore had violated the Charter of the United Nations. Actually, our government did not take its stand solely, or even principally, on the basis of its U.N. membership, but it did use its U.N. membership to justify its decision and lend it a high moral tone.

The word "aggression" pops up right at the very beginning of the Charter: Chapter I, Article 1, Paragraph 1. Aggression is the keystone of the Charter. It is what every member is pledged to suppress. It is also what nobody has been able to define. In 1945, the founding fathers agreed among themselves that it would be unwise to include a definition of aggression in the Charter, on the score that somebody would surely find a loophole in it. But in 1954 a special U.N. committee was appointed to see if it could arrive at a definition of aggression. The committee was called the United Nations Special Committee on the Question of Defining Aggression. It huffed and it puffed, but it did not come up with a definition, and around the first of last month it adjourned. So one of the great peculiarities of the

Charter is that all nations are pledged to oppose what no nation is willing to have defined. I think it can fairly be said that the one subject the seventy-nine members of the United Nations are in silent agreement on is aggression: they are agreed that each nation shall reserve the right to its own interpretation, when the time comes.

This isn't surprising. To define aggression, it is necessary to get into the realm of right and wrong, and the Charter of the United Nations studiously avoids this delicate area. It is also necessary to go back a way. Webster says of aggression, "A first or unprovoked attack." And that, you see, raises the old, old question of which came first, the hen or the egg. What, we must ask, came first in the Middle East clash between Arab and Jew? You could go back two thousand years, if you wanted to. You could certainly go back beyond October 29, 1956, when the Israelis came streaming across the Sinai desert.

Not only has no member, in eleven years, accepted a definition of aggression, no member has admitted that it has committed an aggressive act, although many members have used arms to get their way and at least one member, the U.S.S.R., employs the threat of force as a continuing instrument of national policy. The Charter of the U.N. is a treaty signed by sovereign nations, and the effect of a treaty written around the concept of aggression is to equate the use of arms with wrongdoing and to assume that the world is static, when, of course, that is not so—the world is fluid and (certainly at this point in history) riddled with revolutionary currents at work everywhere. The tendency of any document founded on the idea of nonaggression is to freeze the world in its present mold and command it to stand still.

The world has seen a lot happen lately; it hasn't been standing still. And you will get as many definitions of aggression as there are parties to the event. Ask the delegate of the Soviet Union what happened in Hungary and he will say, "Remnants of Fascist bands aggressed." And he will cite Chapter I, Article 2, Paragraph 4: "All members shall refrain . . . from the threat or use of force against the territorial integrity or political independence of any state." Ask a citizen of Budapest what happened and he will say, "We couldn't take it any longer. We threw stones." And he will cite the Preamble on fundamental human rights and the dignity and worth of the human person. Under the Charter, it is possible to condemn both these aggressive acts—you just take your choice. Is the aggressor the man who throws stones at a tank, or is the aggressor the man who drives the tank into the angry crowd? The world was quick to form an opinion about this, but it got little help from the Charter. The Charter affirms the integrity of Hungary as a political entity, and officially designates both the Hungarian government and the Soviet government as "peace-loving." But that's not the way it looked to most of the world.

When the Israelis were asked what had happened, Eban replied, "The Israeli forces took security measures in the Sinai Peninsula in the exercise of Israel's inherent right of self-defense" (Chapter VII, Article 51). When the Arabs were asked what had happened, the heads of the Arab League issued a statement applauding Egypt's "glorious defense of the safety of her territories and sovereignty" (same chapter, same verse).

Neither England nor France has admitted to an aggression, although the two nations mounted an assault and carried it out—two permanent members of the Security Council shooting their way into Egypt before breakfast. It is, in fact, inconceivable that any nation will ever admit to having aggressed.

In the *Herald Tribune* the other morning, Walter Lippmann wrote, "In the past few days, the U.N. has been pushed into a position where its main function seems to be that of restoring conditions as they were before the explosion." That is certainly true, and one reason for it is that the Charter condemns aggression, sight unseen, and then turns over to the forum the task of studying the events leading up to the tragedy and the atmosphere in which it occurred. To condemn aggression is to decide *in advance of an event* the merits of the dispute. Since this is absurd, the subject of aggression should not be made part of a charter. The business of a charter is not to decide arguments in advance, it is to diagram the conditions under which it may be possible, with luck, to settle the argument when it arises. Surely one of those conditions is the right to observe at close hand.

Another peculiarity of the U.N. is its police. These are now famous, and rightly so. A couple of weeks ago, ninety-five Danish and Norwegian riflemen, wearing emergency blue, dropped out of the sky to keep the peace of the world. They were the advance unit of the United Nations Emergency Force. The men were reported looking "tired," and I should think they might. One editorial writer described them as "symbolic soldiers"; the label is enough in itself to tire a man. The *Times* correspondent in Abu Suweir, where the troops landed, described the policemen's task as "most delicate."

Their task is more than merely delicate; it is primeval. This force (it now numbers about two thousand) is the true dawn patrol, and these Scandinavian riflemen are dawn men. They are the police who are charged with enforcing the laws that do not yet exist. They are clothed with our universal good intentions, armed with the hopes and fears of all the years. They have been turned loose in a trouble spot with the instructions "Enforce the absence of law! Keep us all safe!" Behind them is the authority of the United Nations, all of whose members are "peace-loving" and some of whose members have just engaged in war. It is a confusing scene to a young policeman. It is confusing for people everywhere. One of the first things that happened on the arrival of UNEF was that General Burns, the commander, had to fly back to First Avenue to find out what the Chief of Police had in mind. Another thing that happened was that the Secretary General of the U.N. had to fly to Cairo to get permission from the Egyptian government to let the world be policed in its bailiwick.

It is confusing, but it is not hopeless. Police (so-called) have sometimes been known to antedate the laws that they enforce. It is again a case of the egg and the hen—law enforcers preceding law itself, like the vigilantes of our frontier West.

The U.N. has from the very start stirred people's imaginations and hopes. There seems little doubt that the very existence of a world organization is a help. I read in the *Times* magazine section the other day a good analysis of the U.N. by Ambassador Henry Cabot Lodge, who praised it because it "mobilizes world opinion" and because it shows "midnight courage." All this is certainly true. The U.N. is the shaky shape of the world's desire for order. If it is to establish order, though, it will have to muster the right words as well as the midnight courage. The words of the Charter are soft and punky. The Charter makes "aggression" synonymous with "wrongdoing" but drops the matter there, as though everyone understood the nature of sin. Yet it would appear from recent events that the users of force rarely think they are aggressing, and never admit they are. To simplify an idea this way is bad writing.

A league of sovereign nations—some of them much sovereigner than others—is not in a good position to keep order by disciplining a member in the middle of a fracas. Discipline can mean war itself, as we saw in Korea, and the U.N. is physically puny. But a league *is* in a position to do other things. One thing it can do is lay down conditions of membership. In its own house the U.N. has unlimited power and authority. Its bylaws should not appease anybody or make life easy for bad actors. The U.N. swings very little weight in Moscow or in Budapest, but it swings a lot of weight in Turtle Bay, and that's where it should start to bear down. Whether the U.N. could have been effective in Hungary is anybody's guess, but certainly its chances of operating effectively, for human rights and humankind, were diminished by the softness of the Charter and the eleven-year-old accommodation to the Communists, who from the very start showed that they intended to eat their forum and have it, too. Munich has nothing on San Francisco in this matter.

Ambassador Lodge, in his article, pointed out that the U.N., contrary to what a few Americans hope and a few Americans fear, is not a world government. He wrote, "As for the future, a world government which free men could accept is as far off as a worldwide common sense of justice—without which world government would be world tyranny."

True enough. And the world is a long way from a common sense of justice. But the way to cut down the distance is to get on the right track, use the right words. Our Bill of Rights doesn't praise free speech, it forbids Congress to make any law abridging it. The U.N. could profit from that kind of tight writing. The Charter sings the praises of the dignity of man, but what it lacks is a clause saying, "A member shall make no move abridging the right of the Secretary General to stop by for a drink at any hour of the day or night."

APRIL 1940

A SHEPHERD'S LIFE

This is a day of high winds and extravagant promises, a day of bright skies and the sun on the white painted south sides of buildings, of lambs on the warm slope of the barnyard, their forelegs folded neatly and on their miniature faces a look of grave miniature content. Beneath the winter cover of spruce boughs the tulip thrusts its spear. A white hen is chaperoning thirteen little black chicks all over the place, showing them the world's fair with its lagoons and small worms. The wind is northwest and the bay is on the march. Even on the surface of the watering fountain in the hen-yard quite a sea is running. My goose will lay her seventh egg today, in the nest she made for herself alongside the feed rack in the sheep shed, and on cold nights the lambs will lie on the eggs to keep them from freezing until such time as the goose decides to sit. It is an arrangement they have worked out among themselves—the lambs enjoying the comfort of the straw nest in return for a certain amount of body heat delivered to the eggs—not enough to start the germ but enough to keep the frost out. Things work out if you leave

From *One Man's Meat*.

them alone. At first, when I found lambs sitting on goose eggs I decided that my farm venture had got out of hand and that I better quit before any more abortive combinations developed. "At least," I thought, "you'll have to break up that nest and shift the goose." But I am calmer than I used to be, and I kept clear of the situation. As I say, things work out. This is a day of the supremacy of warmth over cold, of God over the devil, of peace over war. There is still a little snow along the fence rows, but it looks unreal, like the icing of a store cake. I am conducting my own peace these days. It's like having a little business of my own. People have quit calling me an escapist since learning what long hours I put in.

Lambs come in March, traditionally and actually. My ewes started dropping their lambs in February, were at their peak of production in March, and now are dribbling into April. At the moment of writing, thirteen have lambed, two still await their hour. From the thirteen sheep I have eighteen live lambs— six sets of twins and six single lambs. April is the big docking and castrating month, and since I have named all my lambs for friends, I wield the emasculatome with a somewhat finer flourish than most husbandrymen. Tails come off best with a dull ax— the lambs bleed less than with a sharp instrument. I never would have discovered that in a hundred years, but a neighbor tipped me off. He also told me about black ash tea, without which nobody should try to raise lambs. You peel some bark from a black ash, steep it, and keep it handy in a bottle. Then when your lambs come up from the pasture at night frothing at the mouth, poisoned from a too sudden rush of springtime to the first, second, and third stomach, you just put the tea to them. It makes them drunk, but it saves their lives.

That peerless organ of British pastoral life, *The Country-man,* published at Idbury, recently printed a list of ancient Celtic sheep-counting numerals. I was so moved by this evidence of Britain's incomparable poise during her dark crisis that I gave the antique names to my fifteen modern ewes. They are called Yain, Tain, Eddero, Peddero, Pitts, Tayter, Later, Overro, Covvero, Dix, Yain-dix, Tain-dix, Eddero-dix, Peddero-dix, and

Bumfitt. I think Yain is rather a pretty name. And I like Later too and Pitts. Bumfitt is a touch on the A. A. Milne side, but I guess it means fifteen all right. As a matter of fact, giving numerals for names is a handy system; I have named the ewes in the order of their lambing, and it helps me keep my records straight. Peddero-dix and Bumfitt are still fighting it out for last place.

When I invested in a band of sheep last fall (they cost seven dollars apiece) I had no notion of what I was letting myself in for in the way of emotional involvements. I knew there would be lambs in spring, but they seemed remote. Lambing, I felt, would take place automatically and would be the sheep's business, not mine. I forgot that sheep come up in late fall and join the family circle. At first they visit the barn rather cautiously, eat some hay, and depart. But after one or two driving storms they abandon the pasture altogether, draw up chairs around the fire, and settle down for the winter. They become as much a part of your group as your dog, or your Aunt Maudie. Our house and barn are connected by a woodshed, like the Grand Central Station and the Yale Club; and without stepping out of doors you can reach any animal on the place, including the pig. This makes for greater intimacy than obtains in a layout where each farm building is a separate structure. We don't encourage animals to come into the house, but they get in once in a while, particularly the cosset lamb, who trotted through this living room not five minutes ago looking for an eight-ounce bottle. Anyway, in circumstances such as ours you find yourself growing close to sheep. You give them names not for whimsy but for convenience. And when one of them approaches her confinement you get almost as restless as she does.

The birth of a mammal was once a closed book to me. Except for the famous "Birth of a Baby" picture and a couple of old receipted bills from an obstetrician, I was unacquainted with the more vivid aspects of birth. All that is changed. For the past six weeks I have been delivering babies with great frequency, moderate abandon, and no little success. Eighteen lambs from thirteen sheep isn't bad. I lost one pair of twins—they were dropped the first week of February, before I expected them, and they chilled. I also lost a single lamb, born dead.

A newcomer to the realm of parturition is inclined to err on the side of being too helpful. I have no doubt my early ministrations were as distasteful to the ewe as those of the average night nurse are to an expectant mother. Sheep differ greatly in their ability to have a lamb and to care for it. They also differ in their attitude toward the shepherd. Some sheep enjoy having you mincing around, arranging flowers and adjusting the window. Others are annoyed beyond words. The latter, except in critical cases, should be left to work out their problem by themselves. They usually get along. If you've trimmed the wool around their udders the day before with a pair of desk shears, the chances are ten to one they will feed their lambs all right when they arrive.

At first, birth strikes one as the supreme example of bad planning—a thoroughly mismanaged and ill-advised functional process, something thought up by a dirty-minded fiend. It appears cluttery, haphazard. But after you have been mixed up with it for a while, have spent nights squatting beneath a smoky lantern in a cold horse stall helping a weak lamb whose mother fails to own it; after you have grown accustomed to the odd trappings and by-products of mammalian reproduction and seen how marvelously they contribute to the finished product; after you've broken down an animal's reserve and have identified yourself with her and no longer pull your punches, then this strange phenomenon of birth becomes an absorbingly lustrous occasion, full of subdued emotion, like a great play, an occasion for which you unthinkingly give up any other occupation that might be demanding your attention. I've never before in my life put in such a month as this past month has been—a period of pure creation, vicarious in its nature, but extraordinarily moving.

I presume that everything a female does in connection with birthing her young is largely instinctive, not rational. A sheep makes a hundred vital movements and performs a dozen indispensable and difficult tasks, blissfully oblivious of her role. Everything is important, but nothing is intelligent. Before the lamb is born she paws petulantly at the bedding. Even this is functional, for she manages to construct a sort of nest into which the lamb drops, somewhat to the lamb's advantage. Then comes the next miraculous reflex. In the first instant after a lamb is dropped, the ewe takes one step ahead, turns, and lowers her head to sniff eagerly at her little tomato surprise. This step ahead that she takes is a seemingly trivial thing, but I have been thinking about it and I guess it is not trivial at all. If she were to take one step backward it would be a different story—she would step on her lamb, and perhaps damage it. I have often seen a ewe step backward while laboring, but I never remember seeing one take a backward step after her lamb has arrived on the ground. This is the second instinctive incident.

The third is more important than either of the others. A lamb, newly born, is in a state of considerable disrepair; it arrives weak and breathless, with its nose plugged with phlegm or covered with a sac. It sprawls, suffocated, on the ground, and after giving one convulsive shake, is to all appearances dead. Only quick action, well-directed, will save it and start it ticking. The ewe takes this action, does the next important thing, which is to open the lamb's nostrils. She goes for its nose with unerring aim and starts tearing off the cellophane. I can't believe that she is intelligently unstoppering these air passages for her child; she just naturally feels like licking a lamb on the nose. You wonder (or I do, anyway) what strange directional force impels her to begin at the nose, rather than at the other end. A lamb has two ends, all right, and before the ewe gets through she has attended to both of them; but she always begins with the nose, and with almost frenzied haste. I suppose Darwin is right, and that a long process of hereditary elimination finally produced sheep that began cleaning the forward end of a lamb, not the after end. It is an impressive sight, no matter what is responsible for it. It is literally life-giving, and you can see life take hold with the first in-draught of air in the freed nostril. The lamb twitches and utters a cry, as though from a long way off. The ewe answers with a stifled grunt, her sides still contracting with the spasms of birth; and in this answering cry the silver cord is complete and takes the place of the umbilicus, which has parted, its work done.

These are only the beginnings of the instinctive events in the maternal program. The ewe goes on to dry her lamb and boost it to its feet. She keeps it moving so that it doesn't lodge and chill. She finally works it into position so that it locates, in an almost impenetrable jungle of wool, the indispensable fountain and the early laxative. One gulp of this fluid (which seems to have a liberal share of brandy in it) and the lamb is launched. Its little tail wiggles and satisfaction is written all over it, and your heart leaps up.

Even your own technique begins to grow more instinctive. When I was a novice I used to work hard to make a lamb suck by forcing its mouth to the teat. Now I just tickle it on the base of its tail.

A SUITABLE DESIGN

Explicit in White's comments on writing is the belief that a particular piece, like a particular style, "takes its final shape more from attitudes of mind than from principles of composition." Judging one's main intention and considering the different ways of developing a subject are important aspects of writing, to be sure; but how the writer sees the world, what constitutes his vision of reality, is the ultimate question of composition. A literary mechanic may manipulate stock responses with success, but the result is as disposable as a daily paper. By contrast, "Bedfellows" lingers tenaciously in memory because of the highly personal quality of its extended definition of democracy. So does "Death of a Pig," a simple narrative where White takes a fresh look at the mutability of all life.

Like all imaginative work, writing requires the alertness of a hunter:

Writing is, for most, laborious and slow. The mind travels faster than the pen; consequently, writing becomes a question of learning to make occasional wing shots, bringing down the bird of thought as it flashes by.*

* See p. 16.

The rarest game to stalk is the insight, however tiny, that transforms reality; thus the very act of hunting precludes any arrival at a point of static truth. Though the writer is responsible for seeing the world afresh like Miranda, he must also institutionalize his insight by freezing it in form. Locked in lonely wrestling with the opposed demands of vision and form, the writer acts out a human dilemma. On the side of form is the solace of security and the lucidity of craftsman-like statement, which evokes many old familiar emotions; on the side of vision is art, which, even in spite of skill or technique, remains ambiguous and offers temptation. F. Scott Fitzgerald's test of a first-rate intelligence defines the problem: "the ability to hold two opposed ideas in the mind at the same time and still retain the ability to function." Confined in the breast of an alert writer are two little men, one an absolutist who is secure within the set bounds of a known, stable universe, and the other a hardy venturer among what William James called "uncertified possibilities." If a writer forgets the mechanic, he will be incomprehensible; if he ignores the hardy venturer, he will be dead. His resolution of the problem will shape his vision of reality.

Once the writer learns to gauge himself and "the nature and extent of the enterprise," his next step, according to White, in *The Elements of Style,* is to "choose a suitable design and hold to it."

> A basic structural design underlies every kind of writing. The writer will in part follow this design, in part deviate from it, according to his skill, his needs, and the unexpected events that accompany the act of composition. Writing, to be effective, must follow closely the thoughts of the writer, but not necessarily in the order in which those thoughts occur. This calls for a scheme of procedure. In some cases the best design is no design, as with a love letter, which is simply an outpouring, or with a casual essay, which is a ramble. But in most cases, planning must be a deliberate prelude to writing. The first principle of composition, therefore, is to foresee or determine the shape of what is to come and pursue that shape.

White's basic design is sometimes simple, as in the division between earth-bound slaves and air-borne freemen in "Security" or the point-by-point analysis in "The Shape of the U.N." But the basic designs of the following two pieces are more subtle.

"Bedfellows" is a teasing tangle of remarks on prayer and Fred, a long dead dachshund, as well as references to such illustrious names in public print as Truman, Stevenson, Acheson, and Eisenhower—with passing attention to starlings and imaginary eagles carrying imaginary babies. What at first glance might look like a nightmare ramble through a haggis pudding takes on the indirections of a poetically sensitive definition of democracy: a religious faith in "a society in which the unbeliever feels undisturbed and at home." The ghost of Fred ("half vigilante, half dissenter," White later called him) quells any urge in the writer to pontificate, or any feeling in the reader that *serious matters are under discussion,* while allowing White a symbolic way of saying that criticism in a democratic society can somehow, in the process of tearing us apart, hold us together. Fred in life, like freedom of speech, "tended to knock down, rather than build up," and, after death, his memory suggested the danger that lurks in liberty in the possible "insidious encroachment by men of zeal." Alive or ghostly the dog's "rich, aromatic heresy" nourished the faith of the family he joined. At the end the starlings and the eagles, Fred and the Democrats, Eisenhower and White on liberty, somehow come together in an envelope large enough to encompass dissent in a definition of democracy.

By contrast, "Death of a Pig" is a simple narrative covering the three or four nights of a pig's dying, plus the time necessary to receive condolences. But White states the dénouement of the barnyard tragedy in the first few paragraphs. This device, as with Greek dramatists using familiar plots, shifts his emphasis from suspense to illumination. The pig's suffering rather than his death becomes the subject of the narrative, and that suffering becomes "the embodiment of all earthly wretchedness." The routine of the farm calls for feeding a pig from "blossomtime" till butchering. White's experience, however, brought something other than the ceremonial ending of "smoked bacon and ham"; it evoked concern for a creature in pain and the resultant insecurity of a tidy world gone awry. Cropping up throughout the piece is Fred, lugubrious and arthritic, but with a corrosive grin. Equally corrosive is White's perception of the irony of a nursery that turns into a slaughterhouse. Of all the structural designs possible with such material, White elected a narrative form that briskly states the fact of the pig's death; then in three basic steps—noticing something wrong, calling the veterinary, facing the death—his narrative presents his reluctant journey from solace in the "classic course of raised pigs" to the pain of perception on flagless memorial days.

Whether the designs of these two essays were deliberately chosen only White could say, but a growing number of his readers find them suitable. White's facts are eloquent and his style is clear. Fred has the capacity to "blow things up to proportions that satisfied his imagination" and turn a starling into an eagle carrying a baby, his soft brown eyes alight all the while with secret-agent zeal. The pig receives castor oil in the pink corrugated area of his throat. While such details are memorable, the writer's views are not strident. Beneath a surface clarity is not dogmatic certainty but a sensitive intelligence groping amidst the pain and darkness of the world. In "Bedfellows," a ramble in which disparate parts teasingly coalesce at the end, White holds in mind the paradox that dissent binds democracy together. In "Death of a Pig," where a clear stream of narrative reflects the turbid depths of human experience, White has the ability to hold in mind two opposed glimpses of his own nature. The ambiguities and ironies of this essay cast a faint glow over one man's attitudes of mind and over a life poised between the security of ritual forms and the perception of the ceaseless surge of strange tides.

FEBRUARY 18, 1956

BEDFELLOWS

Turtle Bay, February 6, 1956

I am lying here in my private sick bay on the east side of town between Second and Third avenues, watching starlings from the vantage point of bed. Three Democrats are in bed with me: Harry Truman (in a stale copy of the *Times*), Adlai

A "Letter from the East" in *The Points of My Compass*.

Stevenson (in *Harper's*), and Dean Acheson (in a book called *A Democrat Looks at His Party.*) I take Democrats to bed with me for lack of a dachshund, although as a matter of fact on occasions like this I am almost certain to be visited by the ghost of Fred, my dash-hound everlasting, dead these many years. In life, Fred always attended the sick, climbing right into bed with the patient like some lecherous old physician, and making a bad situation worse. All this dark morning I have reluctantly entertained him upon the rumpled blanket, felt his oppressive weight, and heard his fraudulent report. He was an uncomfortable bedmate when alive; death has worked little improvement—I still feel crowded, still wonder why I put up with his natural rudeness and his pretensions.

The only thing I used to find agreeable about him in bed was his smell, which for some reason was nonirritating to my nose and evocative to my mind, somewhat in the way that a sudden whiff of the cow barn or of bone meal on a lawn in springtime carries sensations of the richness of earth and of experience. Fred's aroma has not deserted him; it wafts over me now, as though I had just removed the stopper from a vial of cheap perfume. His aroma has not deserted the last collar he wore, either. I ran across this great, studded strap not long ago when I was rummaging in a cabinet. I raised it cautiously toward my nose, fearing a quill stab from his last porcupine. The collar was extremely high—had lost hardly ten percent of its potency.

Fred was sold to me for a dachshund, but I was in a buying mood and would have bought the puppy if the store-keeper had said he was an Irish Wolfschmidt. He was only a few weeks old when I closed the deal, and he was in real trouble. In no time at all, his troubles cleared up and mine began. Thirteen years later he died, and by rights *my* troubles should have cleared up. But I can't say they have. Here I am, seven years after his death, still sharing a fever bed with him and, what is infinitely more burdensome, still feeling the compulsion to write about him. I sometimes suspect that subconsciously I'm trying to revenge myself by turning him to account, and thus recompensing myself for the time and money he cost me.

He was red and low-posted and long-bodied like a dachshund, and when you glanced casually at him he certainly gave the quick impression of being a dachshund. But if you went at him with a tape measure, and forced him onto scales, the dachshund theory collapsed. The papers that came with him were produced hurriedly and in an illicit atmosphere in a back room of the pet shop, and are most unconvincing. However, I have no reason to unsettle the Kennel Club; the fraud, if indeed it was a fraud, was ended in 1948, at the time of his death. So much of his life was given to shady practices, it is only fitting that his pedigree should have been (as I believe it was) a forgery.

I have been languishing here, looking out at the lovely branches of the plane tree in the sky above our city back yard. Only starlings and house sparrows are in view at this season, but soon other birds will show up. (Why, by the way, doesn't the *Times* publish an "Arrival of Birds" column, similar to its famous "Arrival of Buyers"?) Fred was a window gazer and bird watcher, particularly during his later years, when hardened arteries slowed him up and made it necessary for him to substitute sedentary pleasures for active sport. I think of him as he used to look on our bed in Maine—an old four-poster, too high from the floor for him to reach unassisted. Whenever the bed was occupied during the daylight hours, whether because one of us was sick or was napping, Fred would appear in the doorway and enter without knocking. On his big gray face would be a look of quiet amusement (at having caught somebody in bed during the daytime) coupled with his usual look of fake respectability. Whoever occupied the bed would reach down, seize him by the loose folds of his thick neck, and haul him painfully up. He dreaded this maneuver, and so did the occupant of the bed. There was far too much dead weight involved for anybody's comfort. But Fred was always willing to put up with being hoisted in order to gain the happy heights, as, indeed, he was willing to put up with far greater discomforts—such as a mouthful of porcupine quills—when there was some prize at the end.

Once up, he settled into his pose of bird-watching,

propped luxuriously against a pillow, as close as he could get to the window, his great soft brown eyes alight with expectation and scientific knowledge. He seemed never to tire of his work. He watched steadily and managed to give the impression that he was a secret agent of the Department of Justice. Spotting a flicker or a starling on the wing, he would turn and make a quick report.

"I just saw an eagle go by," he would say. "It was carrying a baby."

This was not precisely a lie. Fred was like a child in many ways, and sought always to blow things up to proportions that satisfied his imagination and his love of adventure. He was the Cecil B. deMille of dogs. He was also a zealot, and I have just been reminded of him by a quote from one of the Democrats sharing my bed—Acheson quoting Brandeis. "The greatest dangers to liberty," said Mr. Brandeis, "lurk in insidious encroachment by men of zeal, well-meaning but without understanding." Fred saw in every bird, every squirrel, every housefly, every rat, every skunk, every porcupine, a security risk and a present danger to his republic. He had a dossier on almost every living creature, as well as on several inanimate objects, including my son's football.

Although birds fascinated him, his real hope as he watched the big shade trees outside the window was that a red squirrel would show up. When he sighted a squirrel, Fred would straighten up from his pillow, tense his frame, and then, in a moment or two, begin to tremble. The knuckles of his big forelegs, unstable from old age, would seem to go into spasm, and he would sit there with his eyes glued on the squirrel and his front legs alternately collapsing under him and bearing his weight again.

I find it difficult to convey the peculiar character of this ignoble old vigilante, my late and sometimes lamented companion. What was there about him so different from the many other dogs I've owned that he keeps recurring and does not, in fact, seem really dead at all? My wife used to claim that Fred was deeply devoted to me, and in a certain sense he was, but his was the devotion of an opportunist. He knew that on the farm I took the over-all view and travelled pluckily from one trouble spot to the next. He dearly loved this type of work. It was not his habit to tag along faithfully behind me, as a collie might, giving moral support and sometimes real support. He ran a trouble-shooting business of his own and was usually at the scene ahead of me, compounding the trouble and shooting in the air. The word "faithful" is an adjective I simply never thought of in connection with Fred. He differed from most dogs in that he tended to knock down, rather than build up, the master's ego. Once he had outgrown the capers of puppyhood, he never again caressed me or anybody else during his life. The only time he was ever discovered in an attitude that suggested affection was when I was in the driver's seat of our car and he would lay his heavy head on my right knee. This, I soon perceived, was not affection, it was nausea. Drooling always followed, and the whole thing was extremely inconvenient, because the weight of his head made me press too hard on the accelerator.

Fred devoted his life to deflating me and succeeded admirably. His attachment to our establishment, though un-tinged with affection, was strong nevertheless, and vibrant. It was simply that he found in our persons, in our activities, the sort of complex, disorderly society that fired his imagination and satisfied his need for tumult and his quest for truth. After he had subdued six or seven porcupines, we realized that his private war against porcupines was an expensive bore, so we took to tying him, making him fast to any tree or wheel or post or log that was at hand, to keep him from sneaking off into the woods. I think of him as always at the end of some outsize piece of rope. Fred's disgust at these confinements was great, but he improved his time, nonetheless, in a thousand small diversions. He never just lay and rested. Within the range of his tether, he continued to explore, dissect, botanize, conduct post-mortems, excavate, ex-periment, expropriate, savor, masticate, regurgitate. He had no contemplative life, but he held as a steady gleam the belief that under the commonplace stone and behind the unlikely piece of driftwood lay the stuff of high adventure and the opportunity to save the nation.

But to return to my other bedfellows, these quick Democrats. They are big, solid men, every one of them, and they have been busy writing and speaking, and sniffing out the truth. I did not deliberately pack my counterpane with members of a single political faith; they converged on me by the slick device of getting into print. All three turn up saying things that interest me, so I make bed space for them.

Mr. Truman, reminiscing in a recent issue of the *Times,* says the press sold out in 1948 to "the special interests," was ninety percent hostile to his candidacy, distorted facts, caused his low popularity rating at that period, and tried to prevent him from reaching the people with his message in the campaign. This bold, implausible statement engages my fancy because it is a half-truth, and all half-truths excite me. An attractive half-truth in bed with a man can disturb him as deeply as a cracker crumb. Being a second-string member of the press myself, and working, as I do, for the special interests, I tend to think there is a large dollop of pure irascibility in Mr. Truman's gloomy report. In 1948, Mr. Truman made a spirited whistle-stop trip and worked five times as hard as his rival. The "Republican-controlled press and radio" reported practically everything he said, and also gave vent to frequent horselaughs in their editorials and commentaries. Millions of studious, worried Americans heard and read what he said; then they checked it against the editorials; then they walked silently into the voting booths and returned him to office. Then they listened to Kaltenborn. Then they listened to Truman doing Kaltenborn. The criticism of the opposition in 1948 was neither a bad thing nor a destructive thing. It was healthy and (in our sort of society) necessary. Without the press, radio, and TV, President Truman couldn't have got through to the people in anything like the volume he achieved. Some of the published news was distorted, but distortion is inherent in partisan journalism, the same as it is in political rallies. I have yet to see a piece of writing, political or nonpolitical, that doesn't have a slant. All writing slants the way a writer leans, and no man is born perpendicular, although many men are born upright. The beauty of the American free press is that the slants and the twists and the distortions come from so many directions, and the special interests are so numerous, the reader must sift and sort and check and countercheck in order to find out what the score is. This he does. It is only when a press gets its twist from a single source, as in the case of government-controlled press systems, that the reader is licked.

Democrats do a lot of bellyaching about the press being preponderantly Republican, which it is. But they don't do the one thing that could correct the situation: they don't go into the publishing business. Democrats say they haven't got that kind of money, but I'm afraid they haven't got that kind of temperament or, perhaps, nerve.

Adlai Stevenson takes a view of criticism almost opposite to Harry Truman's. Writing in *Harper's,* Stevenson says, ". . . I very well know that in many minds 'criticism' has today become an ugly word. It has become almost *lèse majesté.* It conjures up pictures of insidious radicals hacking away at the very foundations of the American way of life. It suggests nonconformity and nonconformity suggests disloyalty and disloyalty suggests treason, and before we know where we are, this process has all but identified the critic with the saboteur and turned political criticism into an un-American activity instead of democracy's greatest safeguard."

The above interests me because I agree with it and everyone is fascinated by what he agrees with. Especially when he is sick in bed.

Mr. Acheson, in his passionately partisan yet temperate book, writes at some length about the loyalty-security procedures that were started under the Democrats in 1947 and have modified our lives ever since. This theme interests me because I believe, with the author, that security declines as security machinery expands. The machinery calls for a secret police. At first, this device is used solely to protect us from unsuitable servants in sensitive positions. Then it broadens rapidly and permeates non-sensitive areas, and, finally, business and industry. It is in the portfolios of the secret police that nonconformity makes the subtle change into disloyalty. A secret-police system first unsettles, then desiccates, then calcifies a free society. I think the recent loyalty investigation of the press by the Eastland subcommittee was a disquieting event. It seemed to assume for Congress the right to poke about in newspaper offices and instruct the management as to which employees were O.K. and which were not. That sort of procedure opens wonderfully attractive vistas to legislators. If it becomes an accepted practice, it will lead to great abuses. Under extreme conditions, it could destroy the free press.

The loyalty theme also relates to Fred, who presses ever more heavily against me this morning. Fred was intensely loyal to himself, as every strong individualist must be. He held unshakable convictions, like Harry Truman. He was absolutely sure that he was in possession of the truth. Because he was loyal to himself, I found his eccentricities supportable. Actually, he contributed greatly to the general health and security of the household. Nothing has been quite the same since he departed. His views were largely of a dissenting nature. Yet in tearing us apart he somehow held us together. In obstructing, he strengthened us. In criticizing, he informed. In his rich, aromatic heresy, he nourished our faith. He was also a plain damned nuisance, I must not forget that.

The matter of "faith" has been in the papers again lately. President Eisenhower (I will now move over and welcome a Republican into bed, along with my other visitors) has come out for prayer and has emphasized that most Americans are motivated (as they surely are) by religious faith. The *Herald Tribune* headed the story, "PRESIDENT SAYS PRAYER IS PART OF DEMOCRACY." The implication in such a pronouncement, emanating from the seat of government, is that religious faith is a *condition,* or even a *precondition,* of the democratic life. This is just wrong. A President should pray whenever and wherever he feels like it (most Presidents have prayed hard and long, and some of them in desperation and in agony), but I don't think a President should advertise prayer. That is a different thing. Democracy, if I understand it at all, is a society in which the unbeliever feels undisturbed and at home. If there were only half a dozen unbelievers in America, their well-being would be a test of our democracy, their tranquillity would be its proof. The repeated suggestion by the present administration that religious faith is a precondition of the American way of life is disturbing to me and, I am willing to bet, to a good many other citizens. President Eisenhower spoke of the tremendous favorable mail he received in response to his inaugural prayer in 1953. What he perhaps did not realize is that the persons who felt fidgety or disquieted about the matter were not likely to write in about it, lest they appear irreverent, irreligious, unfaithful, or even un-American. I remember the prayer very well. I didn't mind it, although I have never been able to pray electronically and doubt that I ever will be. Still, I was able to perceive that the President was sincere and was doing what came naturally, and anybody who is acting in a natural way is all right by me. I believe that our political leaders should live by faith and should, by deeds and sometimes by prayer, demonstrate faith, but I doubt that they should *advocate* faith, if only because such advocacy renders a few people uncomfortable. The concern of a democracy is that no honest man shall feel uncomfortable, I don't care who he is, or how nutty he is.

I hope that Belief never is made to appear mandatory. One of our founders, in 1787, said, "Even the diseases of the people should be represented." Those were strange, noble words, and they have endured. They were on television yesterday. I distrust the slightest hint of a standard for political rectitude, knowing that it will open the way for persons in authority to set arbitrary standards of human behavior.

Fred was an unbeliever. He worshiped no personal God, no Supreme Being. He certainly did not worship *me*. If he had suddenly taken to worshiping me, I think I would have felt as queer as God must have felt the other day when a minister in California, pronouncing the invocation for a meeting of Democrats, said, "We believe Adlai Stevenson to be Thy choice for President of the United States. Amen."

I respected this quirk in Fred, this inability to conform to conventional canine standards of religious feeling. And in the miniature democracy that was, and is, our household he lived undisturbed and at peace with his conscience. I hope my country will never become an uncomfortable place for the unbeliever, as it could easily become if prayer was made one of the requirements of the accredited citizen. My wife, a spiritual but not a prayerful woman, read Mr. Eisenhower's call to prayer in the *Tribune* and said something I shall never forget. "Maybe it's all right," she said. "But for the first time in my life I'm beginning to feel like an outsider in my own land."

Democracy is itself a religious faith. For some it comes close to being the only formal religion they have. And so when I see the first faint shadow of orthodoxy sweep across the sky, feel the first cold whiff of its blinding fog steal in from sea, I tremble all over, as though I had just seen an eagle go by, carrying a baby.

Anyway, it's pleasant here in bed with all these friendly Democrats and Republicans, every one of them a dedicated man, with all these magazine and newspaper clippings, with Fred, watching the starlings against the wintry sky, and the prospect of another Presidential year, with all its passions and its distortions and its dissents and its excesses and special interests. Fred died from a life of excesses, and I don't mind if I do, too. I love to read all these words—most of them sober, thoughtful words— from the steadily growing book of democracy: Acheson on security, Truman on the press, Eisenhower on faith, Stevenson on criticism, all writing away like sixty, all working to improve and save and maintain in good repair what was so marvelously constructed to begin with. This is the real thing. This is bedlam in bed. As Mr. Stevenson puts it: ". . . no civilization has ever had so haunting a sense of an ultimate order of goodness and rationality which can be known and achieved." It makes me eager to rise and meet the new day, as Fred used to rise to his, with the complete conviction that through vigilance and good works all porcupines, all cats, all skunks, all squirrels, all houseflies, all footballs, all evil birds in the sky could be successfully brought to account and the scene made safe and pleasant for the sensible individual—namely, him. However distorted was his crazy vision of the beautiful world, however perverse his scheme for establishing an order of goodness by murdering every creature that seemed to him bad, I had to hand him this: he really worked at it.

JANUARY   1948

DEATH OF A PIG

I spent several days and nights in mid-September with an ailing pig and I feel driven to account for this stretch of time, more particularly since the pig died at last, and I lived, and things might easily have gone the other way round and none left to do the accounting. Even now, so close to the event, I cannot recall the hours sharply and am not ready to say whether death came on the third night or the fourth night. This uncertainty afflicts me with a sense of personal deterioration; if I were in decent health I would know how many nights I had sat up with a pig.

The scheme of buying a spring pig in blossomtime, feeding it through summer and fall, and butchering it when the solid cold weather arrives, is a familiar scheme to me and follows an antique pattern. It is a tragedy enacted on most farms with perfect fidelity to the original script. The murder, being premeditated, is in the first degree but is quick and skillful, and the smoked bacon and ham provide a ceremonial ending whose fitness is seldom questioned.

From *The Second Tree from the Corner.*

Once in a while something slips—one of the actors goes up in his lines and the whole performance stumbles and halts. My pig simply failed to show up for a meal. The alarm spread rapidly. The classic outline of the tragedy· was lost. I found myself cast suddenly in the role of pig's friend and physician—a farcical character with an enema bag for a prop. I had a presentiment, the very first afternoon, that the play would never regain its balance and that my sympathies were now wholly with the pig. This was slapstick—the sort of dramatic treatment that instantly appealed to my old dachshund, Fred, who joined the vigil, held the bag, and, when all was over, presided at the interment. When we slid the body into the grave, we both were shaken to the core. The loss we felt was not the loss of ham but the loss of pig. He had evidently become precious to me, not that he represented a distant nourishment in a hungry time, but that he had suffered in a suffering world. But I'm running ahead of my story and shall have to go back.

My pigpen is at the bottom of an old orchard below the house. The pigs I have raised have lived in a faded building that once was an icehouse. There is a pleasant yard to move about in, shaded by an apple tree that overhangs the low rail fence. A pig couldn't ask for anything better—or none has, at any rate. The sawdust in the icehouse makes a comfortable bottom in which to root, and a warm bed. This sawdust, however, came under suspicion when the pig took sick. One of my neighbors said he thought the pig would have done better on new ground—the same principle that applies in planting potatoes. He said there might be something unhealthy about that sawdust, that he never thought well of sawdust.

It was about four o'clock in the afternoon when I first noticed that there was something wrong with the pig. He failed to appear at the trough for his supper, and when a pig (or a child) refuses supper a chill wave of fear runs through any household, or ice-household. After examining my pig, who was stretched out in the sawdust inside the building, I went to the phone and cranked it four times. Mr. Dameron answered. "What's good for a sick pig?" I asked. (There is never any identification needed on a country phone; the person on the other end knows who is talking by the sound of the voice and by the character of the question.)

"I don't know, I never had a sick pig," said Mr. Dameron, "but I can find out quick enough. You hang up and I'll call Henry."

Mr. Dameron was back on the line again in five minutes. "Henry says roll him over on his back and give him two ounces of castor oil or sweet oil, and if that doesn't do the trick give him an injection of soapy water. He says he's almost sure the pig's plugged up, and even if he's wrong, it can't do any harm."

I thanked Mr. Dameron. I didn't go right down to the pig, though. I sank into a chair and sat still for a few minutes to think about my troubles, and then I got up and went to the barn, catching up on some odds and ends that needed tending to. Unconsciously I held off, for an hour, the deed by which I would officially recognize the collapse of the performance of raising a pig; I wanted no interruption in the regularity of feeding, the steadiness of growth, the even succession of days. I wanted no interruption, wanted no oil, no deviation. I just wanted to keep on raising a pig, full meal after full meal, spring into summer into fall. I didn't even know whether there were two ounces of castor oil on the place.

Shortly after five o'clock I remembered that we had been invited out to dinner that night and realized that if I were to dose a pig there was no time to lose. The dinner date seemed a familiar conflict: I move in a desultory society and often a week or two will roll by without my going to anybody's house to dinner or anyone's coming to mine, but when an occasion does arise, and I am summoned, something usually turns up (an hour or two in advance) to make all human intercourse seem vastly inappropriate. I have come to believe that there is in hostesses a special power of divination, and that they deliberately arrange dinners to coincide with pig failure or some other sort of failure. At any rate, it was after five o'clock and I knew I could put off no longer the evil hour.

When my son and I arrived at the pigyard, armed with a

small bottle of castor oil and a length of clothesline, the pig had emerged from his house and was standing in the middle of his yard, listlessly. He gave us a slim greeting. I could see that he felt uncomfortable and uncertain. I had brought the clothesline thinking I'd have to tie him (the pig weighed more than a hundred pounds) but we never used it. My son reached down, grabbed both front legs, upset him quickly, and when he opened his mouth to scream I turned the oil into his throat—a pink, corrugated area I had never seen before. I had just time to read the label while the neck of the bottle was in his mouth. It said Puretest. The screams, slightly muffled by oil, were pitched in the hysterically high range of pig-sound, as though torture were being carried out, but they didn't last long: it was all over rather suddenly, and, his legs released, the pig righted himself.

In the upset position the corners of his mouth had been turned down, giving him a frowning expression. Back on his feet again, he regained the set smile that a pig wears even in sickness. He stood his ground, sucking slightly at the residue of oil; a few drops leaked out of his lips while his wicked eyes, shaded by their coy little lashes, turned on me in disgust and hatred. I scratched him gently with oily fingers and he remained quiet, as though trying to recall the satisfaction of being scratched when in health, and seeming to rehearse in his mind the indignity to which he had just been subjected. I noticed, as I stood there, four or five small dark spots on his back near the tail end, reddish brown in color, each about the size of a housefly. I could not make out what they were. They did not look troublesome but at the same time they did not look like mere surface bruises or chafe marks. Rather they seemed blemishes of internal origin. His stiff white bristles almost completely hid them and I had to part the bristles with my fingers to get a good look.

Several hours later, a few minutes before midnight, having dined well and at someone else's expense, I returned to the pighouse with a flashlight. The patient was asleep. Kneeling, I felt his ears (as you might put your hand on the forehead of a child) and they seemed cool, and then with the light made a careful examination of the yard and the house for sign that the oil had worked. I found none and went to bed.

We had been having an unseasonable spell of weather—hot, close days, with the fog shutting in every night, scaling for a few hours in midday, then creeping back again at dark, drifting in first over the trees on the point, then suddenly blowing across the fields, blotting out the world and taking possession of houses, men, and animals. Everyone kept hoping for a break, but the break failed to come. Next day was another hot one. I visited the pig before breakfast and tried to tempt him with a little milk in his trough. He just stared at it, while I made a sucking sound through my teeth to remind him of past pleasures of the feast. With very small, timid pigs, weanlings, this ruse is often quite successful and will encourage them to eat; but with a large, sick pig the ruse is senseless and the sound I made must have made him feel, if anything, more miserable. He not only did not crave food, he felt a positive revulsion to it. I found a place under the apple tree where he had vomited in the night.

At this point, although a depression had settled over me, I didn't suppose that I was going to lose my pig. From the lustiness of a healthy pig a man derives a feeling of personal lustiness; the stuff that goes into the trough and is received with such enthusiasm is an earnest of some later feast of his own, and when this suddenly comes to an end and the food lies stale and untouched, souring in the sun, the pig's imbalance becomes the man's, vicariously, and life seems insecure, displaced, transitory.

As my own spirits declined, along with the pig's, the spirits of my vile old dachshund rose. The frequency of our trips down the footpath through the orchard to the pigyard delighted him, although he suffers greatly from arthritis, moves with difficulty, and would be bedridden if he could find anyone willing to serve him meals on a tray.

He never missed a chance to visit the pig with me, and he made many professional calls on his own. You could see him down there at all hours, his white face parting the grass along the fence as he wobbled and stumbled about, his stethoscope dangling—a happy quack, writing his villainous prescriptions and grinning his corrosive grin. When the enema bag appeared, and the bucket of warm suds, his happiness was complete, and he managed to squeeze his enormous body between the two lowest rails of the yard and then assumed full charge of the irrigation. Once, when I lowered the bag to check the flow, he reached in and hurriedly drank a few mouthfuls of the suds to test their potency. I have noticed that Fred will feverishly consume any substance that is associated with trouble—the bitter flavor is to his liking. When the bag was above reach, he concentrated on the pig and was everywhere at once, a tower of strength and inconvenience. The pig, curiously enough, stood rather quietly through this colonic carnival, and the enema, though ineffective, was not as difficult as I had anticipated.

I discovered, though, that once having given a pig an enema there is no turning back, no chance of resuming one of life's more stereotyped roles. The pig's lot and mine were inextricably bound now, as though the rubber tube were the silver cord. From then until the time of his death I held the pig steadily in the bowl of my mind; the task of trying to deliver him from his misery became a strong obsession. His suffering soon became the embodiment of all earthly wretchedness. Along toward the end of the afternoon, defeated in physicking, I phoned the veterinary twenty miles away and placed the case formally in his hands. He was full of questions, and when I casually mentioned the dark spots on the pig's back, his voice changed its tone.

"I don't want to scare you," he said, "but when there are spots, erysipelas has to be considered."

Together we considered erysipelas, with frequent interruptions from the telephone operator, who wasn't sure the connection had been established.

"If a pig has erysipelas can he give it to a person?" I asked.

"Yes, he can," replied the vet.

"Have they answered?" asked the operator.

"Yes, they have," I said. Then I addressed the vet again. "You better come over here and examine this pig right away."

"I can't come myself," said the vet, "but McFarland can come this evening if that's all right. Mac knows more about pigs than I do anyway. You needn't worry too much about the spots. To indicate erysipelas they would have to be deep hemorrhagic infarcts."

"Deep hemorrhagic what?" I asked.

"Infarcts," said the vet.

"Have they answered?" asked the operator.

"Well," I said, "I don't know what you'd call these spots, except they're about the size of a housefly. If the pig has erysipelas I guess I have it, too, by this time, because we've been very close lately."

"McFarland will be over," said the vet.

I hung up. My throat felt dry and I went to the cupboard and got a bottle of whiskey. Deep hemorrhagic infarcts—the phrase began fastening its hooks in my head. I had assumed that there could be nothing much wrong with a pig during the months it was being groomed for murder; my confidence in the essential health and endurance of pigs had been strong and deep, particularly in the health of pigs that belonged to me and that were part of my proud scheme. The awakening had been violent and I minded it all the more because I knew that what could be true of my pig could be true also of the rest of my tidy world. I tried to put this distasteful idea from me, but it kept recurring. I took a short drink of the whiskey and then, although I wanted to go down to the yard and look for fresh signs, I was scared to. I was certain I had erysipelas.

It was long after dark and the supper dishes had been put away when a car drove in and McFarland got out. He had a girl with him. I could just make her out in the darkness—she seemed young and pretty. "This is Miss Owen," he said. "We've been having a picnic supper on the shore, that's why I'm late."

McFarland stood in the driveway and stripped off his

jacket, then his shirt. His stocky arms and capable hands showed up in my flashlight's gleam as I helped him find his coverall and get zipped up. The rear seat of his car contained an astonishing amount of paraphernalia, which he soon overhauled, selecting a chain, a syringe, a bottle of oil, a rubber tube, and some other things I couldn't identify. Miss Owen said she'd go along with us and see the pig. I led the way down the warm slope of the orchard, my light picking out the path for them, and we all three climbed the fence, entered the pighouse, and squatted by the pig while McFarland took a rectal reading. My flashlight picked up the glitter of an engagement ring on the girl's hand.

"No elevation," said McFarland, twisting the thermometer in the light. "You needn't worry about erysipelas." He ran his hand slowly over the pig's stomach and at one point the pig cried out in pain.

"Poor piggledy-wiggledy!" said Miss Owen.

The treatment I had been giving the pig for two days was then repeated, somewhat more expertly, by the doctor, Miss Owen and I handing him things as he needed them—holding the chain that he had looped around the pig's upper jaw, holding the syringe, holding the bottle stopper, the end of the tube, all of us working in darkness and in comfort, working with the instinctive teamwork induced by emergency conditions, the pig unprotesting, the house shadowy, protecting, intimate. I went to bed tired but with a feeling of relief that I had turned over part of the responsibility of the case to a licensed doctor. I was beginning to think, though, that the pig was not going to live.

He died twenty-four hours later, or it might have been forty-eight—there is a blur in time here, and I may have lost or picked up a day in the telling and the pig one in the dying. At intervals during the last day I took cool fresh water down to him and at such times as he found the strength to get to his feet he would stand with head in the pail and snuffle his snout around. He drank a few sips but no more; yet it seemed to comfort him to dip his nose in water and bobble it about, sucking in and blowing out through his teeth. Much of the time, now, he lay indoors half buried in sawdust. Once, near the last, while I was attending him I saw him try to make a bed for himself but he lacked the strength, and when he set his snout into the dust he was unable to plow even the little furrow he needed to lie down in.

He came out of the house to die. When I went down, before going to bed, he lay stretched in the yard a few feet from the door. I knelt, saw that he was dead, and left him there: his face had a mild look, expressive neither of deep peace nor of deep suffering, although I think he had suffered a good deal. I went back up to the house and to bed, and cried internally—deep hemorrhagic intears. I didn't wake till nearly eight the next morning, and when I looked out the open window the grave was already being dug, down beyond the dump under a wild apple. I could hear the spade strike against the small rocks that blocked the way. Never send to know for whom the grave is dug, I said to myself, it's dug for thee. Fred, I well knew, was supervising the work of digging, so I ate breakfast slowly.

It was a Saturday morning. The thicket in which I found the gravediggers at work was dark and warm, the sky overcast. Here, among alders and young hackmatacks, at the foot of the apple tree, Lennie had dug a beautiful hole, five feet long, three feet wide, three feet deep. He was standing in it, removing the last spadefuls of earth while Fred patrolled the brink in simple but impressive circles, disturbing the loose earth of the mound so that it trickled back in. There had been no rain in weeks and the soil, even three feet down, was dry and powdery. As I stood and stared, an enormous earthworm which had been partially exposed by the spade at the bottom dug itself deeper and made a slow withdrawal, seeking even remoter moistures at even lonelier depths. And just as Lennie stepped out and rested his spade against the tree and lit a cigarette, a small green apple separated itself from a branch overhead and fell into the hole. Everything about this last scene seemed overwritten—the dismal sky, the shabby woods, the imminence of rain, the worm (legendary bedfellow of the dead), the apple (conventional garnish of a pig).

But even so, there was a directness and dispatch about

animal burial, I thought, that made it a more decent affair than human burial: there was no stopover in the undertaker's foul parlor, no wreath nor spray; and when we hitched a line to the pig's hind legs and dragged him swiftly from his yard, throwing our weight into the harness and leaving a wake of crushed grass and smoothed rubble over the dump, ours was a businesslike procession, with Fred, the dishonorable pallbearer, staggering along in the rear, his perverse bereavement showing in every seam in his face; and the post mortem performed handily and swiftly right at the edge of the grave, so that the inwards that had caused the pig's death preceded him into the ground and he lay at last resting squarely on the cause of his own undoing.

I threw in the first shovelful, and then we worked rapidly and without talk, until the job was complete. I picked up the rope, made it fast to Fred's collar (he is a notorious ghoul), and we all three filed back up the path to the house, Fred bringing up the rear and holding back every inch of the way, feigning unusual stiffness. I noticed that although he weighed far less than the pig, he was harder to drag, being possessed of the vital spark.

The news of the death of my pig travelled fast and far, and I received many expressions of sympathy from friends and neighbors, for no one took the event lightly and the premature expiration of a pig is, I soon discovered, a departure which the community marks solemnly on its calendar, a sorrow in which it feels fully involved. I have written this account in penitence and in grief, as a man who failed to raise his pig, and to explain my deviation from the classic course of so many raised pigs. The grave in the woods is unmarked, but Fred can direct the mourner to it unerringly and with immense good will, and I know he and I shall often revisit it, singly and together, in seasons of reflection and despair, on flagless memorial days of our own choosing.

ONE MAN'S WORLD

*"Before you can be an
internationalist you have first to
be a naturalist and feel the
ground under you making a
whole circle."*

In the first two parts of this book the selections illustrate problems in usage and rhetoric that confront every writer, whether he is an undergraduate amateur or an experienced professional. The editorial comments have been primarily concerned with those problems and with one writer's ways of solving them. It would be impossible, however, to limit the discussion to White's manner and pay no attention to his matter. Because form and content are two halves of a single whole, the familiar distinctions of textbook and classroom cannot divide them precisely. The same is true of the arbitrary division between life and letters. ("So much for Shelley the man; now what can be said of Shelley the poet?") The useful critical method that reduces a writer to an anonymous stranger has little relevance to E. B. White, whose way and view of life are characteristically revealed at first hand in the personal essay. Any perceptive reader of the selections in parts one and two has inevitably formed a picture of the man who wrote them.

It is the main purpose of this third part to expand that picture by shifting the emphasis from the technical problems facing the writer to the reactions of the writer facing himself and his world. In its gross anatomy a writer's world is Everyman's—eyed by the same sun, regulated by the same seasons, colored by the same basic emotions, threatened by the same plagues and bombs. At times the world of E. B. White may seem strangely like that of William Wordsworth, Henry David Thoreau, Robert Frost, or Don Marquis. But White's world remains peculiarly his own, not only because no one else has lived through the same experiences, but because, like any original writer, he has observed them with an acute private vision and re-created them with an art that defies exact imitation or complete analysis. To share that world vicariously is the privilege of the sensitive reader.

The prose selections here are grouped to represent White looking directly at himself ("Self-Portraits"); at other people he has known ("Portraits"); at the vicarious experience of reading ("Book Country"); at the environments where he has lived and worked ("Habitats"); and at the disturbing vision of a "civilization" that contrives to dehumanize and threatens to destroy mankind ("Shadow of the Future"). The "Song Trio" is included to remind the reader that White cannot be categorically dismissed as a "prose writer": His world is always accompanied by music.

To say that these divisions are arbitrary—that "Don Marquis," for example, could be located in "Book Country" or that "Walden" is properly a habitat—is only to admit that the careful forms of art and pedagogy are never identical. Nor can the careless shape of any man's life be divided in symmetrical segments like a pie. Any human wayfarer is, like Tennyson's Ulysses, "a part of all that [he has] known." Awareness of things present or future can never be isolated from remembrance of things past; all human experiences spin together in an endless ring of time. The essays in the "Epilogue" realize this truth.

SELF-PORTRAITS

The self-portraits in the following section have been arranged in the chronological order of their events. In "First World War" the protagonist is the romantic adolescent of the troubled years between 1914 and 1918. The four short essays that follow—dated 1938 to 1942—are a part of White's personal journal of the era of World War II. Like all the pieces of *One Man's Meat*, they were composed at his salt water farm in Maine, where he was, according to his own testimony, "engaged in trivial, peaceable pursuits, knowing all the time that the world hadn't arranged any true peace or granted anyone the privilege of indulging himself for long in trivialities." In "The Sea and the Wind that Blows" an old boy in his sixties confesses to a lifetime love affair with boats.

These essays might have been grouped to represent varying dimensions of autobiography in accordance with the size of the lens. The four miniatures from *One Man's Meat* show how an informal essayist can throw a sharp pinpoint of light on his own personality by focusing on a single moment, a commonplace dilemma in life: the winnowing of moving, the chaotic organization of a desk, the payment of a tax, the completion of a questionnaire. None of these are the standard areas of inspiration for the writer of deathless prose. In "First World War" the lens is opened wider to film both the high and the low moments of a confusing era. In "The Sea and the Wind that Blows" a whole lifetime of moments coalesces in the affectionate picture of an avocation.

After visiting this small gallery of self-portraits—and examining others, both direct and indirect, throughout the book ("Two Letters, Both Open," "About Myself," "A Shepherd's Life," "Death of a Pig," "Once More to the Lake")—the student can easily see that there is no formula for "An Autobiographical Theme." Unless the teacher prescribes a particular method, it is left to the writer to portray himself directly or indirectly; in the first, second, or third person; through narrative, description, or exposition; by focusing on a moment of time or a whole era; by caricaturing one eccentric aspect of his personality or attempting a full-length character sketch. What matters is that he adjust his lens to his choice of subject so that, whether from a glimpsing candid snapshot or a panoramic time exposure, a human being comes to life.

OCTOBER   1939

FIRST WORLD WAR

I keep forgetting that soldiers are so young. I keep thinking of them as my age, or Hitler's age. (Hitler and I are about the same age.) Actually, soldiers are often quite young. They haven't finished school, many of them, and their heads are full of the fragile theme of love, and underneath their bluster and swagger everything in life is coated with that strange beautiful importance that you almost forget about because it dates back so far. The other day some French soldiers on the western front sent a request to a German broadcasting studio asking the orchestra to play *"Parlez moi d'amour."* The station was glad to oblige, and all along the Maginot Line and the Siegfried Line the young men were listening to the propaganda of their own desire instead of attending to the fight. So few people speak to the young men of love any more, except the song writers and scenarists. The leaders speak always of raw materials and *Lebensraum*. But the young men in uniforms do not care much for raw materials (except tobacco) and they are thinking of *Liebestraum*, and are resolving their dream as best they can. I am trying hard to remember what it is like to be as young as a soldier.

When war was getting under way in 1914, I was in high school. I was translating Cæsar, studying ancient history, working with algebraic equations, and drawing pictures of the bean, which is a dicotyledonous seed, and of the frog, an amphibian. In those days I kept a journal. My life and activities and thoughts were dear to me, and I took the trouble to set them down. I still have this journal, and the outbreak of the present war has started

From *One Man's Meat*.

me going through its pages to refresh my memory. The entries are disappointingly lacking in solid facts. Much of the stuff is sickening to read, but I have a strong stomach and a deep regard for the young man that was I. Everyone, I believe, has this tolerance and respect if he is worth anything, and much of life is unconsciously an attempt to preserve and perpetuate this youth, this strange laudable young man. Though my journal is a mass of horrid little essays, moral in tone and definitely on the pretty side, I cannot bring myself to throw it away. Just now I like to consult it to rediscover what the impact of a world war meant to one young fellow in the 1914–1918 period—how important each step seemed, what preposterous notions I held, how uncertain and groping and unscathed I was.

At first, before the United States entered the fray, the War seemed to mean mighty little. In those years, war was remote, implausible—a distant noise or threat, something that was ahead perhaps, like college or marriage or earning one's living, but not near enough to be of any immediate concern. In the early pages of my journal I was thinking and writing about keeping pigeons, about going skating, about the comings and goings of people on the same block with us. After a couple of years of it the War begins to take shape and I begin swelling with large thoughts. On March 16, 1917, carefully described as a "rainy Saturday," I pasted into my journal an editorial from the *Globe* on the emancipation of Russia, which spoke of the sunlight of freedom shining over the Russian steppes. "Father thinks it will be an important factor in the ultimate results of the war," I wrote. "I have always wondered what the purpose—in the bigger sense—of the war was. Perhaps this is it."

Russian freedom probably occupied my mind upward of ten minutes. The next entry in the journal was concerned with plans for a canoe trip down the Housatonic (which I never took) and with the rehearsals of a Pinero farce in which I acted the part of an English servant.

On Palm Sunday, 1917, with a bad cold in the head, I reported the advent of springtime, and the flags flying from houses all along the block. "War and springtime are being heralded with one breath and the thoughts of the people are in confusion." My own thoughts, however, were not in any particular confusion. They came to an orderly, if not monumental, focus in the composition, on the same page, of a love poem of twenty-four lines, celebrating an attachment to a girl I had met on an ice pond.

On April 3rd, with America still three days away from war, I speculated on the possibility of another canoe trip, for August—a journey on which I proposed to carry "a modified form of miner's tent." Apparently I was spending more time reading sporting goods catalogues and dreaming of the woods than studying news accounts of hostilities in Europe. I was also considering the chances of getting a summer job. Next fall I was to enter college.

Springtime and wartime! Of the two, springtime clearly took precedence. I was in love. Not so much actively as retrospectively. The memory of winter twilights when the air grew still and the pond cracked and creaked under our skates, was enough to sustain me; and the way the trails of ice led off into the woods, and the little fires burning along the shore. It was enough, that spring, to remember what a girl's hand felt like, suddenly ungloved in winter. I never tried to pursue the acquaintanceship off the pond. Without ice and skates, there seemed no reason for her existence. Lying on my back on the settee in the hall, I listened to Liszt on the pianola.

I wrote half a dozen nature poems, got a haircut, read *Raymond* by Sir Oliver Lodge, and heard one of Billy Sunday's workers in church on the text: "Follow me and I will make you fishers of men." One of my friends enlisted in the Naval Reserve. Another became wireless operator on a mosquito boat. Dimly, dimly I became aware that something was going on.

April 26, 1917. I suppose this little Journal ought to be filled with war talk, because that is what people are all thinking about now. It is believed that there will be a shortage of food soon, and so the State is supervising a "Farm Cadet" movement.

I joined the cadets that July, and served in Hempstead, L. I. It never seemed to me that the farmers were particularly pleased with the arrangement.

May 14, 1917. Yesterday I heard Billy Sunday deliver his booze sermon.

May 27, 1917. I don't know what to do this summer. The country is at war and I think I ought to serve. Strange that the greatest war in the history of the world is now going on, and it is hard to get men to enlist.

June 3, 1917. I'm feeling extraordinarily patriotic tonight, after having read the papers. I think tomorrow I shall buy a Liberty Bond and get a job on a farm. The struggle in Europe isn't over by any means, and so much history is being made every minute that it's up to every last one of us to see that it's the right kind of history. It is my firm conviction that only the unstinted giving of time, money, and resources of the American people can save this world from its most terrible doom.

June 7, 1917. I guess there is no place in the world for me. I've been trying to get a job since Monday, and have failed. Yesterday afternoon I applied at G———'s School of Popular Music for a job playing piano at a summer hotel in the Catskills. This was in answer to an ad that I had seen in the paper. When I got there, I couldn't play the kind of music he gave me, so I started for the door, but not before he had handed me a circular showing how, by his method, ragtime piano playing might be taught in 20 lessons. However, when I arrived home, I discovered that the little town in the Catskills was not on the map. I don't weigh enough to join the Army, and a job on a farm would probably be hard on my hay fever. I want to join the American Ambulance Corps, but I'm not eighteen and I've never had any experience driving a car, and Mother doesn't think I ought to go to France. So here I am, quite hopeless, and undeniably jobless. I think either I must be very stupid or else I lack faith in myself and in everything else.

My morale at this point had sunk so low that I pasted into the journal a clipping called "Foolishness of Worry," a reprint from *The White Road to Verdun,* by Kathleen Burke.

> June 10, 1917. Tomorrow I am going to the city to find out facts concerning the American Ambulance Corps. Somewhere in Europe there must be a place for me, and I would rather save men than destroy them. Father and L—— have just come back from the city where they went in a fruitless attempt to hear Billy Sunday.
>
> July 5, 1917. I can think of nothing else to do but to run away. My utter dependence galls me, and I am living the life of a slacker, gorging my belly with food which others need. I wish I were old enough to be drafted.
>
> July 11, 1917. My birthday! Eighteen, and still no future! I'd be more contented in prison, for there at least I would know precisely what I had to look forward to.
>
> September 4, 1917. Tonight I have been reading about aviation tests—I think I would like to fly, but as with everything else I have thought of, I lack the necessary qualifications.

Leaving the war behind, I packed my suitcase and went off to college, itself no small adventure. I took along the strip of bicycle tape that she and I used to hang onto in our interminable circuit of the pond the winter before. I was homesick. After the football games on Saturday afternoons I would walk down the long streets into the town shuffling through the dry leaves in the gutters, past children making bonfires of the piles of leaves, and the spirals of sweet, strong smoke. It was a golden fall that year, and I pursued October to the uttermost hill.

> October 13, 1917. My English prof said the other day that bashfulness was a form of vanity, the only difference being that vanity is the tendency to overestimate your worth, and bashfulness to underestimate it; both arising from the

overindulgence of self-consciousness. The days are getting colder.

November 10, 1917. The war still continues in this its third autumn. [I couldn't even count—it was the *fourth* autumn.] Our troops are in the trenches on a relatively quiet sector of the west front. Just the other day I read that the first American Sammy had been killed. More are being trained by experienced officers in back of the line, and still more are in this country training in the several cantonments for the National Draft Army. It is a wonderful thing. The Russians have again overthrown their new-born republic and are showing themselves incapable of meeting the crises that are being put in their way. The Italian Army has been out-guessed by the combined Austro-German forces and has retreated to the Piave River. The French and English lines show little change. Now, after more than three years of intensive warfare, Germany stands, solidly defying three-fourths of the countries of the world. They all look to us as the only hope of salvation, and I firmly believe that, slow as we are to foresee danger and loath as we seem to be to give up our pleasures and amusements, once in the struggle for fair we will live up to the examples set by our sturdy fore-fathers and will shed the last drop of blood for the great cause for which the whole world is now shedding blood.

November 21, 1917. I've been feeling sick for the past week and I think I must have consumption. If I have, I will leave college and travel for my health.

December 25, 1917. I have just finished *Over the Top* by Arthur Guy Empey. On the last page of his narra-tive he confirms what I have always sensed as truth, that strength comes surely at the critical hour, that anticipation far exceeds the realization of the utmost trial; and that man, despite his recent gentle breeding and flabby ways, when called, is not found wanting, nor untrue when facing death.

December 31, 1917. I find myself thinking the same thoughts and wishing the same wishes that I thought and wished this night a year ago. I'm wondering if I'm any nearer my ultimate goal—certainly still a long way off inasmuch as the goal itself is an unknown quantity.

February 18, 1918. The talk is of Universal Peace

after the war—everlasting peace through the medium of an international council. Nations will be ruled by brotherly love and divine principle, arms will be laid down forever and man will return to the ploughshare. Bosh!

March 26, 1918. Sunday was the beginning of the immense German offensive along a 50-mile front which is threatening the civilized world and which is paralyzing the stoutest of hearts in the enormity of its plan and the apparent success of its execution. The grimness of impending danger is settling slowly over the American people. I had begun to think that perhaps I would not be called to war, but now I am not so sure. In fact, it seems almost inevitable that I will go. Things are happening on a tremendous scale.

April 13, 1918. I heard ex-President Taft speak in Bailey Hall this morning. He spoke on the war—nothing else is spoken of in these days. Now the question is, shall I set out, at the close of this academic year, to fit myself for some branch of the service so that at the age of 21 I will be trained in military or war work, or shall I wait still longer in the hope that peace will come?

On April 25th I inscribed a short nature poem, celebrating spring. On May 11th, while other freshmen were burning their caps, I recorded the belief that the greatest period of my life was past and gone. The school year was drawing to a close and again I was left stranded for the summer. "I don't even know that I'll return in the fall. I ought to want to, but I'm not sure that I do. I am never sure of anything."

I settled this feeling of uncertainty by buying a second-hand Oldsmobile and taking a job in my father's store, in the credit department. But I could feel the War in my bowels now.

July 14, 1918. I have been thinking of a sentence I read somewhere: "Destiny makes no mistakes."

Armed with a copy of *Marcus Aurelius,* I accompanied my family to Bellport, Long Island, for the month of August. There was a noticeable dearth of young men at the summer resort. The sea washed over me, the sun struck down, the wind

blew at me, in an attempt to dispel the fearful mists of inde-
cision. On the first of September we returned to the cicada-laden
streets of our suburb; the month in Bellport had become a
memory of sea and sky and doubt. On August 31st I wrote a
poem strongly advising myself to get killed in action. On September 12th, with thirteen million other Americans, I registered
for the draft.

> September 21, 1918. My serial number is 3751 and
> I don't understand what it means, except that I can remember
> the days when I didn't used to have a number. The harvest
> moon is full tonight . . . and looking through the window
> 3751 enjoys the splendor.

The War, and my own travail, were both drawing to a
close. I returned to Ithaca and enlisted in the Army. The enemy
turned out to be an epidemic of flu—which I met stoically with a
bag of licorice drops. I can't remember who told me that licorice
fended off flu germs, but he was right.

> November 12, 1918. Yesterday was one of the great-
> est days in the history of the world. The war came to an end
> at 2:15 o'clock in the morning. At half-past five a hand
> pushed against me in the darkness and a voice whispered
> "The whole town of Ithaca must be on fire—listen to the
> bells!" I sat up in bed. Just at that moment the chimes in the
> library tower rang out "The Star Spangled Banner" and
> someone down below yelled "The war is over!" . . . The
> terms are little less than unconditional surrender. Germany
> is brought to her knees, and is no longer in a position to
> menace the safety of other European nations. Peace with
> victory has been established, to the everlasting glory of all
> the allied countries who stood side by side in the greatest
> conflict of history.

For another month we had to go on drilling as though
nothing had happened. As a parting blessing, the War Department vaccinated all of us for smallpox, shot us with a triple dose

of typhus serum, and confined us to barracks. It was dark when I walked out of the Army, and the lights were beginning to twinkle in the valley. I strode away from the mess hall in a mantle of serenity.

December 25, 1918. Christmas Day. I argued with father for about an hour and a half after breakfast, and just as is always the case we came to no agreement. He believes that the plans now being formulated for a League of Nations will be the means of preventing war in the future for all time. I cannot believe that that is so. He believes that a new era has dawned, that our President and his associate representatives of other nations have a great vision, that all the countries of the world will be united by a bond so strong that there can be no war. Father did most of the talking.

December 28, 1918.

The pines hang dark by a little pond
Where the ice has formed in the night
And the light in the west fades slowly out
Like a bird in silent flight.
The memory of the sun that's gone
Is just the glow in the sky,
And in the dusk beyond the trees
A figure is skating by.

I was still in love. The great world war had come and gone. *Parlez moi d'amour*.

JULY   1938

REMOVAL

Several months ago, finding myself in possession of one hundred and seventeen chairs divided about evenly between a city house and a country house, and desiring to simplify my life,

From *One Man's Meat.*

I sold half my worldly goods, evacuated the city house, gave up my employment, and came to live in New England. The difficulty of getting rid of even one half of one's possessions is considerable, even at removal prices. And after the standard items are disposed of—china, rugs, furniture, books—the surface is merely scratched: you open a closet door and there in the half-dark sit a catcher's mitt and an old biology notebook.

I recall a moment of peculiar desperation over a gold mirror that, in spite of all our attempts to shake it off, hung steadfastly on till within an hour or so of our scheduled departure. This mirror, which was a large but fairly unattractive one, rapidly came to be a sort of symbol of what I was trying to escape from, and its tenacity frightened me. I was quite prepared simply to abandon it (I knew a man once who, tiring of an automobile, walked away from it on the street and never saw it again), but my wife wouldn't consent to abandon anything. It seems there are rules, even to the sort of catharsis to which we were committed: I could give the mirror away or sell it, but I was not privileged to leave it in the house, which (she said) had to be stripped clean.

So I walked out the door hatless and in my shirtsleeves and went round the corner to a junk shop on Second Avenue—a place that displayed a thoroughly miserable assortment of bruised and castoff miscellany. The proprietor stood in the doorway.

"Do you want . . ." I began. But at that instant an El train joined us and I had to start again and shout.

"*Do you want to buy a gold mirror?*"

The man shook his head.

"It's *gold!*" I yelled. "*A beautiful thing!*"

Two kibitzers stopped, to attend the deal, and the El train went off down the block, chuckling.

"Nuh," said the proprietor coldly. "Nuh."

"I'm giving it away," I teased.

"I'm nut taking it," said the proprietor, who, for all I know, may have been trying to simplify his own life.

A few minutes later, after a quick trip back to the house,

I slipped the mirror guiltily in a doorway, a bastard child with not even a note asking the finder to treat it kindly. I took a last look at myself in it and I thought I looked tired.

AUGUST   1938

INCOMING BASKET

It seemed to me that I should have to have a desk, even though I had no real need for a desk. I was afraid that if I had no desk in my room my life would seem too haphazard.

The desk looked incomplete when I got it set up, so I found a wire basket and put that on it, and threw a few things in it. This basket, however, gave me a lot of trouble for the first couple of weeks. I had always had *two* baskets in New York. One said IN, and the other OUT. At intervals a distribution boy would sneak into the room, deposit something in IN, remove the contents of OUT. Here, with only one basket, my problem was to decide whether it was IN or OUT, a decision that a person of some character could have made promptly and reasonably but that I fooled round with for days—tentative, hesitant, trying first one idea then another, first a day when it would be IN, then a day when it would be OUT, then, somewhat desperately, trying to combine the best features of both and using it as a catch-all for migratory papers no matter which way they were headed. This last was disastrous. I found a supposedly out-going letter buried for a week under some broadsides from the local movie house. The basket is now IN. I discovered by test that fully ninety per cent of whatever was on my desk at any given moment were IN things. Only ten per cent were OUT things—almost too few to warrant a special container. This, in general, must be true of other people's lives too. It is the reason lives get so cluttered up—so many things (except money) filtering in, so few things (except strength) draining out. The phenomenon is difficult for

From *One Man's Meat.*

me to understand and has not been explained, to my knowledge, by physicists: how it is that, with a continuous interchange of goods or "things" between people, everybody can have more coming in (except money) than going out (except strength).

My inability to make a simple decision concerning a desk basket is an indication of some curious nervous weakness. Psychiatrists know about it, I don't doubt, and have plenty of theories about its cause and cure. Question: Does a psychiatrist have an IN basket?

JANUARY   1940

FIGURES

I was thinking as I prepared to pay my tax how lucky I am about figures. Figures mean little to me, and on that account use up very little of my time. To some people figures are the most vivid signs there are. Some people can look at the notation 5/23/29 and it means something to them, calls up some sort of image. I can't do that. I can see lust in a pig's eye, but I can't see a day in a number. I remember days, if at all, by the dent they made on me, not by the dent they made on the calendar.

When figures refer to sums of money it all depends on what scale they're in whether they register with me or not. To me all sums under a dollar seem vital and important. Sums under a dollar seem to me to have an enormous quantitative variation. I think of fifty cents as the devil of a lot more than a quarter. The sum of ninety cents seems a lot to spend for anything, no matter what. But when I get up into gustier amounts, among sums like fifty dollars, or a hundred and thirty-two dollars, or three hundred and seven dollars, they all sound pretty much alike. If I have the money at all I can spend two hundred and thirty dollars with the same painless ease with which I might spend one hundred and fifteen. They seem virtually the same

From "Fro-Joy" in *One Man's Meat*.

thing. Probably the importance that I attach to sums less than a dollar is a hangover from the days when practically every transaction in life was for something under a dollar, and was breathtaking.

One reason I bother to set down these remarks is because I think department stores should be informed that, to at least one customer, a dollar seems less money than ninety-eight cents. Stores are frittering away their time when they mark down something in the hope of luring me to buy. Another reason is that I think my government should be told that a vast amount of fuss could be avoided if, in taxing my income, it would explain clearly what is expected of me in the way of a payment and then, if it feared this might not supply enough revenue, simply wind up its instructions for computing the tax with the brisk remark: "Double it." I could double my tax and not bat an eye. It's only when I double the time spent translating Form 1040, or when I pay a lawyer to do it for me, that I feel the pinch. I doubt that there is any such complexity in the financial aspects of my life as is implied by the Treasury Department's searching inquiry. In many ways my life *is* complex. I keep sheep, and there is nothing simple about being a part-time shepherd. But neither the profit nor the loss from my association with ruminants need bother my country overmuch. There is nothing in it, one way or another, for the United States. I have my own little system for making and spending money. I am honest and I am willing. It shouldn't require a lawyer to set me at peace with my country.

MAY 1942

QUESTIONNAIRE

The mail this morning brought my occupational questionnaire from Selective Service headquarters. I have been working on it off and on all day, trying to give my country some

From *One Man's Meat*.

notion of what sort of life I lead—which I take to be what it is
after. Since my life is cluttered with dozens of pursuits, some of
which seem wholly unrelated to the others, the form has proved
hard to fill out. Explaining oneself by inserting words in little
boxes and squares is like getting an idea over to a jury when you
are limited to answering the questions of the attorneys.

I was rather surprised, but not alarmed, to discover that
"writing" is not recognized in selective service, either as professional work or as an "occupation." Nothing is said in the questionnaire about a writer. In the lengthy list of pursuits and
professions the name of writer does not anywhere appear. Scarf-
ers, riggers, glass blowers, architects, historians, metallurgists—
all are mentioned in the long alphabet of American life. But not
writers. This, I feel, is as it should be, and shows that the
selective service system is more perceptive than one might
suppose. Writing is not an occupation nor is it a profession. (Bad
writing can be, and often is, an occupation; but I rather agree
with the government that writing in the pure sense and in
noblest form is neither an occupation nor a profession.) It is
more of an affliction, or just punishment. It is something that
raises up on you, as a welt. Or you might say that it is a by-
product of many occupations and professions, which the writer
pursues (or is pursued by) recklessly or necessarily. A really pure
writer is a man like Conrad, who is first of all a mariner; or
Isadora Duncan, a dancer; or Ben Franklin, an inventor and
statesman; or Hitler, a scamp. The intellectual who simply says
"I am a writer," and forthwith closets himself with a sharp pencil
and a dull Muse, may well turn out to be no artist at all but
merely an ambitious and perhaps misguided person. I think the
best writing is often done by persons who are snatching the time
from something else—from an occupation, or from a profession,
or from a jail term—something that is either burning them up,
as religion, or love, or politics, or that is boring them to tears, as
prison, or a brokerage house, or an advertising firm. A great
violinist must begin fairly early in life to play the violin; but I
think a literary artist has a better chance of producing something

great if he spends the first forty years of his life doing something else—grinding a lens or surveying a wilderness. There are of course notable exceptions. Shakespeare was one. He was a writing fool, apparently. And I have often suspected that some of his noblest passages were written with his tongue at least halfway in his cheek. "Boy," you can hear him mutter, "will that panic 'em!"

Since I now lead a dual existence—half farmer, half literary gent—I found difficulty making myself sound like anything but a flibbertigibbet. The initial disappointment at not finding my life's work listed among the selected occupations, professions, and sciences was greatly relieved, however, when after a careful study of the list I found, under the "f's":

> Farmer, dairy
> Farmer, other

I'm not getting a cow till next year, but it is something in this life to be Farmer Other. Not Farmer Brown or Farmer White but Farmer Other. I liked the name very much, and immediately wrote the words "4 years" in front of Farmer Other. When I consider that most of my neighbors have been carrying pails for half a century, four years is a mere apprenticeship, I know; but nevertheless, it is a beginning, and in the greatest occupation of all.

I imagine that my local draft board, like any group of registrars, prefers to have lives fall into conventional patterns and will not take kindly to a citizen who is so far out of line as to be both farmer and writer. It doesn't have a clean-cut sound. It is Jekyll and Hyde stuff, lacks an honest ring. In war it is better to be a clean-cut man: a hammersmith plain, a riveter simple, a born upholsterer, an inveterate loftsman, a single-hearted multipurpose machine operator. To be farmer and writer suggests a fickleness of character out of key with the war effort. To produce, in a single week, seventy dozen table eggs and a twenty-six-hundred-word article, sounds confused, immature, and smacks of divided loyalty.

Question 20 is called "Duties of Your Present Job." Three lines are allotted for the answer, space for about forty words of crowded confession. I got myself into thirty-seven, by taking thought and by following closely the sample reply given above, starting "I clean, adjust, and repair watches and clocks. I take them apart . . . etc." I could almost have followed the sample exactly, changing only a word or two: "I clean, adjust, and repair manuscripts and farm machinery. I take them apart and examine the parts through an eyepiece to find which parts need repair. I repair or replace parts. Sometimes I make a new part, using a jackplane or an infinitive. I clean the parts and put them back together again."

Under JOB FOR WHICH YOU ARE BEST FITTED I wrote "Editor and writer." Under JOB FOR WHICH YOU ARE NEXT BEST FITTED I wrote "Poultryman and farmer." But I realized that it was not so much fitness that I was thinking about as returns. What I meant was JOB BY WHICH YOU MAKE THE MOST MONEY. And NEXT MOST. It is hard to tell about fitness. Physically I am better fitted for writing than for farming, because farming takes great strength and great endurance. Intellectually I am better fitted for farming than for writing.

JUNE   1963

THE SEA AND THE WIND THAT BLOWS

Waking or sleeping, I dream of boats—usually of rather small boats under a slight press of sail. When I think how great a part of my life has been spent dreaming the hours away and how much of this total dream life has concerned small craft, I wonder about the state of my health, for I am told that it is not a good sign to be always voyaging into unreality, driven by imaginary breezes.

I have noticed that most men, when they enter a barber shop and must wait their turn, drop into a chair and pick up a

From *Ford Times*, June, 1963.

magazine. I simply sit down and pick up the thread of my sea wandering, which began more than fifty years ago and is not quite ended. There is hardly a waiting room in the East that has not served as my cockpit, whether I was waiting to board a train or to see a dentist. And I am usually still trimming sheets when the train starts or the drill begins to whine.

If a man must be obsessed by something, I suppose a boat is as good as anything, perhaps a bit better than most. A small sailing craft is not only beautiful, it is seductive and full of strange promise and the hint of trouble. If it happens to be an auxiliary cruising boat, it is without question the most compact and ingenious arrangement for living ever devised by the restless mind of man—a home that is stable without being stationary, shaped less like a box than like a fish or a bird or a girl, and in which the homeowner can remove his daily affairs as far from shore as he has the nerve to take them, close-hauled or running free—parlor, bedroom, and bath, suspended and alive.

Men who ache all over for tidiness and compactness in their lives often find relief for their pain in the cabin of a thirty-foot sailboat at anchor in a sheltered cove. Here the sprawling panoply of The Home is compressed in orderly miniature and liquid delirium, suspended between the bottom of the sea and the top of the sky, ready to move on in the morning by the miracle of canvas and the witchcraft of rope. It is small wonder that men hold boats in the secret place of their mind, almost from the cradle to the grave.

Along with my dream of boats has gone the ownership of boats, a long succession of them upon the surface of the sea, many of them makeshift and crank. Since childhood I have managed to have some sort of sailing craft and to raise a sail in fear. Now, in my sixties, I still own a boat, still raise my sail in fear in answer to the summons of the unforgiving sea. Why does the sea attract me in the way it does? Whence comes this compulsion to hoist a sail, actually or in dream? My first encounter with the sea was a case of hate at first sight. I was taken, at the age of four, to a bathing beach in New Rochelle. Everything about the experience frightened and repelled me: the taste of salt in my mouth, the foul chill of the wooden bathhouse, the littered sand, the stench of the tide flats. I came away hating and fearing the sea. Later, I found that what I had feared and hated, I now feared and loved.

I returned to the sea of necessity, because it would support a boat; and although I knew little of boats, I could not get them out of my thoughts. I became a pelagic boy. The sea became my unspoken challenge: the wind, the tide, the fog, the ledge, the bell, the gull that cried help, the never-ending threat and bluff of weather. Once having permitted the wind to enter the belly of my sail, I was not able to quit the helm; it was as though I had seized hold of a high-tension wire and could not let go.

I liked to sail alone. The sea was the same as a girl to me—I did not want anyone else along. Lacking instruction, I invented ways of getting things done, and usually ended by doing them in a rather queer fashion, and so did not learn to sail properly, and still cannot sail well, although I have been at it all my life. I was twenty before I discovered that charts existed; all my navigating up to that time was done with the wariness and the ignorance of the early explorers. I was thirty before I learned to hang a coiled halyard on its cleat as it should be done. Until then I simply coiled it down on deck and dumped the coil. I was always in trouble and always returned, seeking more trouble. Sailing became a compulsion: there lay the boat, swinging to her mooring, there blew the wind; I had no choice but to go. My earliest boats were so small that when the wind failed, or when I failed, I could switch to manual control—I could paddle or row home. But then I graduated to boats that only the wind was strong enough to move. When I first dropped off my mooring in such a boat, I was an hour getting up the nerve to cast off the pennant. Even now, with a thousand little voyages notched in my belt, I still feel a memorial chill on casting off, as the gulls jeer and the empty mainsail claps.

Of late years, I have noticed that my sailing has increasingly become a compulsive activity rather than a source of pleasure. There lies the boat, there blows the morning breeze—it is a point of honor, now, to go. I am like an alcoholic who cannot put his bottle out of his life. With me, I cannot not sail. Yet I know well enough that I have lost touch with the wind and, in fact, do not like the wind any more. It jiggles me up, the wind does, and what I really love are windless days, when all is peace. There is a great question in my mind whether a man who is against wind should longer try to sail a boat. But this is an intellectual response—the old yearning is still in me, belonging to the past, to youth, and so I am torn between past and present, a common disease of later life.

When does a man quit the sea? How dizzy, how bumbling must he be? Does he quit while he's ahead, or wait till he makes some major mistake, like falling overboard or being flattened by an accidental jibe? This past winter I spent hours arguing the question with myself. Finally, deciding that I had come to the end of the road, I wrote a note to the boatyard, putting my boat up for sale. I said I was "coming off the water." But as I typed the sentence, I doubted that I meant a word of it.

If no buyer turns up, I know what will happen: I will instruct the yard to put her in again—"just till somebody comes along." And then there will be the old uneasiness, the old uncertainty, as the mild southeast breeze ruffles the cove, a gentle, steady, morning breeze, bringing the taint of the distant wet world, the smell that takes a man back to the very beginning of time, linking him to all that has gone before. There will lie the sloop, there will blow the wind, once more I will get under way. And as I reach across to the black can off the Point, dodging the trap buoys and toggles, the shags gathered on the ledge will note my passage. "There goes the old boy again," they will say. "One more rounding of his little Horn, one more conquest of his Roaring Forties." And with the tiller in my hand, I'll feel again the wind imparting life to a boat, will smell again the old menace, the one that imparts life to me: the cruel beauty of the salt world, the barnacle's tiny knives, the sharp spine of the urchin, the stinger of the sun jelly, the claw of the crab.

PORTRAITS

Though E. B. White is neither novelist, nor playwright, nor formal biographer, his miniatures reflect many of the problems and techniques of characterization that are associated with the larger literary forms. In the group selected here, his Maine neighbor, Charles Dameron, is sketched from first-hand observation: Dameron the lobsterman viewed within the frame of his daily occupation; and Charles, a fellow shepherd, portrayed mostly through dialogue as he plays his part in a small drama. The affectionate portrait of Will Strunk in action is a blend of long-remembered personal experience and inferences drawn from the written record of a single book. In the tribute to Don Marquis one word man salutes another in the context of a bygone era (a miniature "life and times"); there is some synopsis of vital statistics, but, the focus, as in literary biography, is on the man at his work.

White's sympathy for his fellow men is broad and deep, and he writes about them, not as statistics or stereotypes or faceless wanderers in a lonely crowd, but as unique human individuals. In a nation where the search for status leads people to conform to small concentric circles, many of White's subjects would qualify as eccentrics. But though they may not listen to the loudest drummer, they are never completely isolated from the parade. He portrays each individual not as an island but as a part of the main. His people may be pictured against a background limited by place and time—Maine in the 1940s, Manhattan in the 1920s; but they are typically associated with a universal human concern: freedom, ambition, the search for order and simplicity in language or life. And White is seldom the detached, anonymous observer. Whether he is in the picture or outside of it, his own attitude is conspicuously clear. His characteristic portrait is a partial self-portrait.

SEPTEMBER   1939

OLD DAMERON

Six days a week, eight months of the year, in war or in peace, Dameron goes down the bay in the morning and hauls his

From "Second World War" in *One Man's Meat*.

traps. He gets back about noon, his white riding-sail showing up first around the point, then the hull, then the sound of the engine idling and picking up again as he pulls his last two traps. Sometimes, if the sun is right, we can see pinwheels of light as he hurls crabs back into the sea, spinning them high in air. And sometimes, if he has had a good catch of lobsters, we can hear him singing as he picks up his mooring. It is a song of victory, the words of which I've never made out; but from this distance it sounds like a hymn being clowned.

He is as regular as a milk train, and his comings and goings give the day a positive quality that is steadying in a rattle-brained world. In fog we can't see him but we can hear his motor, homebound in the white jungle; and then the creak of oar in lock, tracing the final leg of his journey, from mooring to wharf. He has no watch, yet we can set ours by his return. (We could set it by his departure too if we were up—but he leaves at six o'clock.)

I went with him in his boat the other day, to see what it was like, tending seventy traps. He told me he's been lobstering twenty-five or six years. Before that he worked in yachts—in the days when there were yachts—and before that in coasting schooners. "I liked coasting fine," he said, "but I had to get out of yachting." A look of honest reminiscent fright came into his face. "Yachting didn't agree with me. Hell, I was mad the whole time."

"You know," he explained, pushing a wooden plug into a lobster's claw, "there's a lot o' them yacht owners who haven't much use for the common man. That's one thing about lobstering—it gives you a hell of an independent feeling."

I nodded. Dameron's whole boat smelled of independence —a rich blend of independence and herring bait. When you have your own boat you have your own world, and the sea is anybody's front yard. Old Dameron, pulling his living out of the bay at the end of twelve fathoms of rope, was a crusty symbol of self-sufficiency. He cared for nobody, no not he, and nobody cared for him. Later in the fall he would haul his boat out on his own beach, with his own tackle. He would pull the engine out, take it up through the field to his woodshed, smear it with oil, and put it to bed in a carton from the grocer's. On winter evenings he would catch up on his reading, knit his bait pockets, and mend his traps. On a nasty raw day in spring he would get the tar bucket out and tar his gear and hang it all over the place on bushes, like the Monday wash. Then he would pay the State a dollar for a license and seventy-five cents for an official measuring stick and be ready for another season of fishing, another cycle of days of fog, wind, rain, calm, and storm.

Freedom is a household word now, but it's only once in a while that you see a man who is actively, almost belligerently free. It struck me as we worked our way homeward up the rough bay with our catch of lobsters and a fresh breeze in our teeth that this was what the fight was all about. This was it. Either we would continue to have it or we wouldn't, this right to speak our own minds, haul our own traps, mind our own business, and wallow in the wide, wide sea.

NOVEMBER   1939

THE FLOCKS WE WATCH BY NIGHT

On the afternoon of the day after the first killing frost, I was coming around the barn carrying a sack of straw when I saw Charles turn in from the road and start down toward my pasture. He had on his gray fedora hat with the low crown and the turned-up brim, and his arms overflowed with turnip tops to bring the sheep in with. He had a rope, too. Charles had just shaved and was bleeding freely around the chin. One arm encircled the greens; with his free hand he mopped away at the blood. I thought, "I guess Charles has come to get that ewe with the cough." (Maybe I should explain that Charles has his sheep in with mine—I let him use my pasture and he lets me use his,

From *One Man's Meat*.

and we alternate the sheep back and forth because they get better feed that way.)

It was cold, clear weather, and the wind had a bite to it. The darkness comes early these afternoons. I put my sack down and set out across the field toward the stile, the dachshund following, expectant, full of an instinctive notion that something might be up and that it might involve sheep. Charles was calling them. "Knaac, knaac," he said, and the tame ewe came bobbling up from the cedars, tolling the others in. Charles handed out greens all round. The sheep surrounded him, ate thankfully. When I was halfway to the stile I saw him let the greens fall to the ground; his left arm went out and took one of the ewes suddenly by the wool at the base of her neck. She ducked, backed away madly; Charles was jerked forward and flung himself on her shoulders, tackling her hard, his jacket riding up around his neck and his hat slipping back off his forehead. It was a big ewe, and she took Charles with her, plunging and slipping among the rocks. I walked on, climbed the stile, picked up the rope that Charles had dropped, and walked over to where the two of them had fallen after the last spasm. Charles's chin was buried in the ewe, the blood showing red in the dirty gray wool. Gathering her strength, she bolted. I took a quick hold on her rear end and went along with them. As she dropped I threw my leg over her back and we came to rest, with Charles breathing heavily on account of his asthma. The dachshund tested out one of her legs, going in cautiously, nipping, then withdrawing quickly. We all three, the ewe, Charles, and myself, lay there a second, breathing.

"I found out what was the matter with that engine," said Charles.

"The magneto?" I asked.

"Yes," he said. "Bert was down this afternoon tinkering with it. . . . This gets my wind awfully." His wind was almost done. He rested his head on the sheep and closed his eyes, as though he would soon sleep.

I passed Charles the rope, which had a knot near one end so that when he made a noose it wouldn't draw tight. Charles tied it around the ewe's neck and I made up the coil.

"Miss Templeton was over to my house earlier," said Charles. "That woman has had everything the matter with her a woman can."

"I better take the dog up," I replied.

"Wait till we get her over the stile. She must weigh nearly two hundred." Charles pushed her eyelid back with his big fingers, exposing the eyeball with tiny veins of blood. "That's a good ewe—look at that blood," he said.

The dachshund, almost insane with the kill, withdrew and went forward to finish off at the throat. His mouth clogged with wool. Charles heaved on one side and I pushed from behind, but it was hard work. It was mostly a case of waiting till she wanted to go. The ewe backed against me, then jumped furiously ahead toward the stile. The rope caught in Charles's foot and he was down, against a rock; the dachshund quickly transferred to him and danced about him while I grabbed the line and held. We eased the ewe up the first step of the stile and she crumpled. Charles's breath was coming short and we had to rest. I had one knee on the stile, one hand under the ewe's tail to keep her from sliding back. We didn't want to lose what we had gained. The ewe went limp on us and was dead weight.

"Will you have to take the magneto to town?"

"Yes," he said, "I can't do anything with it. Let's give her one more, but watch when she goes over the other side she doesn't jam you." He took out a dirty handkerchief and held it against his chin. "I can't seem to stop bleeding once I start."

"Why don't you get a styptic pencil?" I asked.

"I got one," said Charles.

We both lifted together and the ewe stumbled to her feet on the stile, fell forward on the other side, and plunged down. Charles made it up over in time, wheezing, with the rope, and snubbed her as she bolted for the bushes along the fence. The dachshund was under her, fighting his way up through wool.

"Why don't you use it?" I asked.

"Doesn't do any good. I rubbed it on these cuts, but it doesn't stop. I always bleed a lot."

"You heard her cough lately?" I asked.

"No. But it might be the worms. You can tell—if they brace themselves with their front feet planted forward when they cough, it's more likely it's worms than a cold. If it's worms, we want her out of here anyway. It might just be a cold. She's a damn good ewe."

I got hold of the dachshund's tail and pulled hard. He came out whimpering and I took him in my arms.

"I'll put him in the house," I said. "We'll get along better." As I walked up to the house my boy came out and ran toward us, catching up a switch as he came. I went on with the dog and shut him in the kitchen, breaking his heart for the millionth time. When I got back the boy was prodding and Charles would pay the line out while the ewe ran, and then jump along at the end of the rope in long, impossible strides. His hat was on with the bow on the right-hand side, and it was twisted slightly. The ewe was always either running hard or at a dead stop.

"I'll take the rope," I said, "if running gets your wind." Charles handed it over.

"The ram ought to be here this week, hadn't he?" Charles asked.

"Yes. It's a yearling. Do you think a yearling can handle this size flock?"

"Sure," said Charles. "That's a lot of nonsense about not breeding too much. Frank Bickford had a thoroughbred Jersey bull and he wouldn't let it breed only twice a week. Damn bull died of loneliness."

At the end of a long run the ewe veered off the road in front of McEachern's house, which is just this side of Charles's place, went down on her knees, then sank. The boy and I went down with her, hanging on. Charles caught up with us, walking. His breath was coming better. He knelt down beside the ewe. Her eyes were closed with weariness and grief. The boy stroked her tenderly. The sun had gone, and the car that came along had its parking lights on, showing clear and clean-cut in the dusk, with no glare. "She's dead," said the boy. "Her eyes are closed."

The McEacherns' little girl came out of the house and stood watching. "Is that sheep dead?" she asked.

"Yes," said the boy.

"Can you go after the ram with your truck when he comes?" asked Charles.

"Yes," I said. We pushed the ewe and she went on and turned into Charles' yard. I held her while he went and got a pinch bar to tether her to.

"Come in, won't you?" said Charles when the ewe was tied. "I'll show you my new cat."

It was good and dark now. My toe caught on the edge of the linoleum rug.

"This place smells like a monkey cage," Charles said, "but I never do anything about it when Sarah's away. She'll be back Tuesday. I had a letter."

The boy and I groped along, and Charles struck a match and lit a lamp. I sat down in an old rocker by the stove and the boy stood beside me, his arm around me. Charles put the black kitten in my lap and it settled there.

"What's the iron pipe out back?" I asked.

"I'm going to pipe water into the house," said Charles. "Sarah wants it and I guess she ought to have it. I got a pump from Sears a year ago, but I never put the pipe in. I don't like to get things *too* handy around here."

He took down from the mantelpiece, one by one, the photographs of his four grown children and showed them to me. They were high-school graduation pictures, by a studio photographer. He had shown them to me before, but he took them down again. "I haven't anything else to be proud of," he said, "but I *am* proud of them. They're good kids. A couple of them are married now."

I studied their faces gravely.

"That son's my favorite, I guess," he said.

"He looks fine," I said.

"This war's a terrible thing."

"Yes, it is."

"What do you think's going to happen?"

"I don't know," I said.

The kitchen was warming up. We lit cigarettes and sat and smoked. My boy stroked the cat. Charles put the photographs back on the mantelpiece under the picture of the ship. He had got his breath back. I felt pleasantly tired and comfortable, and hated to go, but it was suppertime. I got up to leave.

"Those lambs will be cunning, in the Spring," Charles said.

"They sure will."

As we walked back along the road, the boy and I, I noticed that the ewe was grazing quietly at her tether. Overhead the stars were bright in the sky. It looked like a good day tomorrow.

"What did he mean when he asked you what was going to happen?"

"He meant about the war."

"Does anybody know what's going to happen?"

"No."

"Do you?"

"No."

"Do people have to fight whether they want to or not?"

"Some of them."

When we got near our house we could look down and see the sheep in the pasture below us, grazing spread out, under the stars.

"I can hardly wait to see the lambs," said the boy.

JULY 27, 1957

WILL STRUNK

Turtle Bay, July 15, 1957

Mosquitoes have arrived with the warm nights, and our bedchamber is their theater under the stars. I have been up and down all night, swinging at them with a face towel dampened at

A "Letter from the East" in *The Points of My Compass.*

one end to give it authority. This morning I suffer from the lightheadedness that comes from no sleep—a sort of drunkenness, very good for writing because all sense of responsibility for what the words say is gone. Yesterday evening my wife showed up with a few yards of netting, and together we knelt and covered the fireplace with an illusion veil. It looks like a bride. (One of our many theories is that mosquitoes come down chimneys.) I bought a couple of adjustable screens at the hardware store on Third Avenue and they are in place in the windows; but the window sashes in this building are so old and irregular that any mosquito except one suffering from elephantiasis has no difficulty walking into the room through the space between sash and screen. (And then there is the even larger opening between upper sash and lower sash when the lower sash is raised to receive the screen—a space that hardly ever occurs to an apartment dweller but must occur to all mosquitoes.) I also bought a very old air-conditioning machine for twenty-five dollars, a great bargain, and I like this machine. It has almost no effect on the atmosphere of the room, merely chipping the edge off the heat, and it makes a loud grinding noise reminiscent of the subway, so that I can snap off the lights, close my eyes, holding the damp towel at the ready, and imagine, with the first stab, that I am riding in the underground and being pricked by pins wielded by angry girls.

Another theory of mine about the Turtle Bay mosquito is that he is swept into one's bedroom through the air conditioner, riding the cool indraft as an eagle rides a warm updraft. It is a feeble theory, but a man has to entertain theories if he is to while away the hours of sleeplessness. I wanted to buy some old-fashioned bug spray, and went to the store for that purpose, but when I asked the clerk for a Flit gun and some Flit, he gave me a queer look, as though wondering where I had been keeping myself all these years. "We got something a lot stronger than that," he said, producing a can of stuff that contained chlordane and several other unmentionable chemicals. I told him I couldn't use it because I was hypersensitive to chlordane. "Gets me right in the liver," I said, throwing a wild glance at him.

The mornings are the pleasantest times in the apartment, exhaustion having set in, the sated mosquitoes at rest on ceiling and walls, sleeping it off, the room a swirl of tortured bedclothes and abandoned garments, the vines in their full leafiness filtering the hard light of day, the air conditioner silent at last, like the mosquitoes. From Third Avenue comes the sound of the mad builders—American cicadas, out in the noonday sun. In the garden the sparrow chants—a desultory second courtship, a subdued passion, in keeping with the great heat, love in summertime, relaxed and languorous. I shall miss this apartment when it is gone; we are quitting it come fall, to turn ourselves out to pasture. Every so often I make an attempt to simplify my life, burning my books behind me, selling the occasional chair, discarding the accumulated miscellany. I have noticed, though, that these purifications of mine—to which my wife submits with cautious grace—have usually led to even greater complexity in the long pull, and I have no doubt this one will, too, for I don't trust myself in a situation of this sort and suspect that my first act as an old horse will be to set to work improving the pasture. I may even join a pasture-improvement society. The last time I tried to purify myself by fire, I managed to acquire a zoo in the process and am still supporting it and carrying heavy pails of water to the animals, a task that is sometimes beyond my strength.

A book I have decided not to get rid of is a small one that arrived in the mail not long ago, a gift from a friend in Ithaca. It is *The Elements of Style,* by the late William Strunk, Jr., and it was known on the Cornell campus in my day as "the little book," with the stress on the word "little." I must have once owned a copy, for I took English 8 under Professor Strunk in 1919 and the book was required reading, but my copy presumably failed to survive an early purge. I'd not laid eyes on it in thirty-eight years. Am now delighted to study it again and rediscover its rich deposits of gold.

The Elements of Style was Will Strunk's *parvum opus,* his attempt to cut the vast tangle of English rhetoric down to size and write its rules and principles on the head of a pin. Will himself hung the title "little" on the book: he referred to it sardonically and with secret pride as "the *little* book," always giving the word "little" a special twist, as though he were putting a spin on a ball. The title page reveals that the book was privately printed (Ithaca, N.Y.) and that it was copyrighted in 1918 by the author. It is a forty-three-page summation of the case for cleanliness, accuracy, and brevity in the use of English. Its vigor is unimpaired, and for sheer pith I think it probably sets a record that is not likely to be broken. The Cornell University Library has one copy. It had two, but my friend pried one loose and mailed it to me.

The book consists of a short introduction, eight rules of usage, ten principles of composition, a few matters of form, a list of words and expressions commonly misused, a list of words commonly misspelled. That's all there is. The rules and principles are in the form of direct commands, Sergeant Strunk snapping orders to his platoon. "Do not join independent clauses with a comma." (Rule 5.) "Do not break sentences in two." (Rule 6.) "Use the active voice." (Rule 11.) "Omit needless words." (Rule 13.) "Avoid a succession of loose sentences." (Rule 14.) "In summaries, keep to one tense." (Rule 17.) Each rule or principle is followed by a short hortatory essay, and the exhortation is followed by, or interlarded with, examples in parallel columns—the true vs. the false, the right vs. the wrong, the timid vs. the bold, the ragged vs. the trim. From every line there peers out at me the puckish face of my professor, his short hair parted neatly in the middle and combed down over his forehead, his eyes blinking incessantly behind steel-rimmed spectacles as though he had just emerged into strong light, his lips nibbling each other like nervous horses, his smile shuttling to and fro in a carefully edged mustache.

"Omit needless words!" cries the author on page 21, and into that imperative Will Strunk really put his heart and soul. In the days when I was sitting in his class, he omitted so many needless words, and omitted them so forcibly and with such eagerness and obvious relish, that he often seemed in the position of having short-changed himself, a man left with nothing more to say yet with time to fill, a radio prophet who had outdistanced the clock. Will Strunk got out of this predicament by a simple trick: he uttered every sentence three times. When he delivered his oration on brevity to the class, he leaned forward over his desk, grasped his coat lapels in his hands, and in a husky, conspiratorial voice said, "Rule Thirteen. Omit needless words! Omit needless words! Omit needless words!"

He was a memorable man, friendly and funny. Under the remembered sting of his kindly lash, I have been trying to omit needless words since 1919, and although there are still many words that cry for omission and the huge task will never be accomplished, it is exciting to me to reread the masterly Strunkian elaboration of this noble theme. It goes:

> Vigorous writing is concise. A sentence should contain no unnecessary words, a paragraph no unnecessary sentences, for the same reason that a drawing should have no unnecessary lines and a machine no unnecessary parts. This requires not that the writer make all his sentences short, or that he avoid all detail and treat his subjects only in outline, but that every word tell.

There you have a short, valuable essay on the nature and beauty of brevity—sixty-three words that could change the world. Having recovered from his adventure in prolixity (sixty-three words were a lot of words in the tight world of William Strunk, Jr.), the Professor proceeds to give a few quick lessons in pruning. The student learns to cut the deadwood from "This is a subject which . . . ," reducing it to "This subject . . . ," a gain of three words. He learns to trim ". . . used for fuel purposes" down to "used for fuel." He learns that he is being a chatterbox when he says "The question as to whether" and that he should just say "Whether"—a gain of four words out of a possible five.

The Professor devotes a special paragraph to the vile expression "the fact that," a phrase that causes him to quiver with revulsion. The expression, he says, should be "revised out of every sentence in which it occurs." But a shadow of gloom seems to hang over the page, and you feel that he knows how hopeless his cause is. I suppose I have written "the fact that" a thousand times in the heat of composition, revised it out maybe five hundred times in the cool aftermath. To be batting only .500 this late in the season, to fail half the time to connect with this fat pitch, saddens me, for it seems a betrayal of the man who showed me how to swing at it and made the swinging seem worth while.

I treasure *The Elements of Style* for its sharp advice, but I treasure it even more for the audacity and self-confidence of its author. Will knew where he stood. He was so sure of where he stood, and made his position so clear and so plausible, that his peculiar stance has continued to invigorate me—and, I am sure, thousands of other ex-students—during the years that have intervened since our first encounter. He had a number of likes and dislikes that were almost as whimsical as the choice of a necktie, yet he made them seem utterly convincing. He disliked the word "forceful" and advised us to use "forcible" instead. He felt that the word "clever" was greatly overused; "it is best restricted to ingenuity displayed in small matters." He despised the expression "student body," which he termed gruesome, and made a special trip downtown to the *Alumni News* office one day to protest the expression and suggest that "studentry" be substituted, a coinage of his own which he felt was similar to "citizenry." I am told that the *News* editor was so charmed by the visit, if not by the word, that he ordered the student body buried, never to rise again. "Studentry" has taken its place. It's not much of an improvement, but it does sound less cadaverous, and it made Will Strunk quite happy.

A few weeks ago I noticed a headline in the *Times* about Bonnie Prince Charlie: "CHARLES' TONSILS OUT." Immediately Rule 1 leapt to mind.

     1. Form the possessive singular of nouns with 's. Fol-
low this rule whatever the final consonant. Thus write,
          Charles's friend
          Burns's poems
          the witch's malice.

Clearly Will Strunk had foreseen, as far back as 1918, the dangerous tonsillectomy of a Prince, in which the surgeon removes the tonsils and the *Times* copy desk removes the final "s." He started his book with it. I commend Rule 1 to the *Times* and I trust that Charles's throat, not Charles' throat, is mended.

    Style rules of this sort are, of course, somewhat a matter of individual preference, and even the established rules of grammar are open to challenge. Professor Strunk, although one of the most inflexible and choosy of men, was quick to acknowledge the fallacy of inflexibility and the danger of doctrine.

    "It is an old observation," he wrote, "that the best writers sometimes disregard the rules of rhetoric. When they do so, however, the reader will usually find in the sentence some compensating merit, attained at the cost of the violation. Unless he is certain of doing as well, he will probably do best to follow the rules."

    It is encouraging to see how perfectly a book, even a dusty rulebook, perpetuates and extends the spirit of a man. Will Strunk loved the clear, the brief, the bold, and his book is clear, brief, bold. Boldness is perhaps its chief distinguishing mark. On page 24, explaining one of his parallels, he says, "The left-hand version gives the impression that the writer is undecided or timid; he seems unable or afraid to choose one form of expression and hold to it." And his Rule 12 is "Make definite assertions." That was Will all over. He scorned the vague, the tame, the colorless, the irresolute. He felt it was worse to be irresolute than to be wrong. I remember a day in class when he leaned far forward in his characteristic pose—the pose of a man about to impart a secret—and croaked, "If you don't know how to pronounce a word, say it loud! If you don't know how to pronounce a word, say it loud!" This comical piece of advice struck me as sound at the time, and I still respect it. Why compound ignorance with inaudibility? Why run and hide?

All through *The Elements of Style* one finds evidences of the author's deep sympathy for the reader. Will felt that the reader was in serious trouble most of the time, a man floundering in a swamp, and that it was the duty of anyone attempting to write English to drain this swamp quickly and get his man up on dry ground, or at least throw him a rope.

"The little book" has long since passed into disuse. Will died in 1946, and he had retired from teaching several years before that. Longer, lower textbooks are in use in English classes nowadays, I daresay—books with upswept tail fins and automatic verbs. I hope some of them manage to compress as much wisdom into as small a space, manage to come to the point as quickly and illuminate it as amusingly. I think, though, that if I suddenly found myself in the, to me, unthinkable position of facing a class in English usage and style, I would simply lean far out over the desk, clutch my lapels, blink my eyes, and say, "Get the *little* book! Get the *little* book! Get the *little* book!"

1950

DON MARQUIS

Among books of humor by American authors, there are only a handful that rest solidly on the shelf. This book about Archy and Mehitabel, hammered out at such awful cost by the bug hurling himself at the keys, is one of those books. It is funny, it is wise; it goes right on selling, year after year. The sales do not astound me; only the author astounds me, for I know (or think I do) at what cost Don Marquis produced these gaudy and irreverent tales. He was the sort of poet who does not create easily; he was left unsatisfied and gloomy by what he produced;

From *The Second Tree from the Corner*.

day and night he felt the juices squeezed out of him by the merciless demands of daily newspaper work; he was never quite certified by intellectuals and serious critics of belles lettres. He ended in an exhausted condition—his money gone, his strength gone. Describing the coming of Archy in the Sun Dial column of the New York *Sun* one afternoon in 1916, he wrote: "After about an hour of this frightfully difficult literary labor he fell to the floor exhausted, and we saw him creep feebly into a nest of the poems which are always there in profusion." In that sentence Don Marquis was writing his own obituary notice. After about a lifetime of frightfully difficult literary labor keeping newspapers supplied with copy, he fell exhausted.

I feel obliged, before going any further, to dispose of one troublesome matter. The reader will have perhaps noticed that I am capitalizing the name Archy and the name Mehitabel. I mention this because the capitalization of Archy is considered the unforgivable sin by a whole raft of old Sun Dial fans who have somehow nursed the illogical idea that because Don Marquis's cockroach was incapable of operating the shift key of a typewriter, nobody else could operate it. This is preposterous. Archy himself wished to be capitalized—he was no e. e. cummings. In fact he once flirted with the idea of writing the story of his life all in capital letters, if he could get somebody to lock the shift key for him. Furthermore, I capitalize Archy on the highest authority: wherever in his columns Don Marquis referred to his hero, Archy was capitalized by the boss himself. What higher authority can you ask?

The device of having a cockroach leave messages in his typewriter in the *Sun* office was a lucky accident and a happy solution for an acute problem. Marquis did not have the patience to adjust himself easily and comfortably to the rigors of daily columning, and he did not go about it in the steady, conscientious way that (for example) his contemporary Franklin P. Adams did. Consequently Marquis was always hard up for stuff to fill his space. Adams was a great editor, an insatiable proofreader, a good makeup man. Marquis was none of these. Adams, operating his Conning Tower in the *World,* moved in the commodious margins of column-and-a-half width and built up a reliable stable of contributors. Marquis, cramped by single-column width, produced his column largely without outside assistance. He never assembled a hard-hitting bunch of contributors and never tried to. He was impatient of hard work and humdrum restrictions, yet expression was the need of his soul. (It is significant that the first words Archy left in his machine were "expression is the need of my soul.")

The creation of Archy, whose communications were in free verse, was part inspiration, part desperation. It enabled Marquis to use short (sometimes very, very short) lines, which fill space rapidly, and at the same time it allowed his spirit to soar while viewing things from the under side, insect fashion. Even Archy's physical limitations (his inability to operate the shift key) relieved Marquis of the toilsome business of capital letters, apostrophes, and quotation marks, those small irritations that slow up all men who are hoping their spirit will soar in time to catch the edition. Typographically, the *vers libre* did away with the turned or runover line that every single-column practitioner suffers from.

Archy has endeared himself in a special way to thousands of poets and creators and newspaper slaves, and there are reasons for this beyond the sheer merit of his literary output. The details of his creative life make him blood brother to writing men. He cast himself with all his force upon a key, head downward. So do we all. And when he was through his labors, he fell to the floor, spent. He was vain (so are we all), hungry, saw things from the under side, and was continually bringing up the matter of whether he should be paid for his work. He was bold, disrespectful, possessed of the revolutionary spirit (he organized the Worms Turnverein), was never subservient to the boss yet always trying to wheedle food out of him, always getting right to the heart of the matter. And he was contemptuous of those persons who were absorbed in the mere technical details of his writing. "The question is whether the stuff is literature or not."

That question dogged his boss, it dogs us all. This book—and the fact that it sells steadily and keeps going into new editions—supplies the answer.

In one sense Archy and his racy pal Mehitabel are timeless. In another sense, they belong rather intimately to an era—an era in American letters when this century was in its teens and its early twenties, an era before the newspaper column had degenerated. In 1916 to hold a job on a daily paper, a columnist was expected to be something of a scholar and a poet—or if not a poet at least to harbor the transmigrated soul of a dead poet. Nowadays, to get a columning job a man need only have the soul of a Peep Tom or a third-rate prophet. There are plenty of loud clowns and bad poets at work on papers today, but there are not many columnists adding to belles lettres, and certainly there is no Don Marquis at work on any big daily, or if there is, I haven't encountered his stuff. This seems to me a serious falling off of the press. Mr. Marquis's cockroach was more than the natural issue of a creative and humorous mind. Archy was the child of compulsion, the stern compulsion of journalism. The compulsion is as great today as it ever was, but it is met in a different spirit. Archy used to come back from the golden companionship of the tavern with a poet's report of life as seen from the under side. Today's columnist returns from the platinum companionship of the night club with a dozen pieces of watered gossip and a few bottomless anecdotes. Archy returned carrying a heavy load of wine and dreams. These later cockroaches come sober from their taverns, carrying a basket of fluff. I think newspaper publishers in this decade ought to ask themselves why. What accounts for so great a falling off?

To interpret humor is as futile as explaining a spider's web in terms of geometry. Marquis was, and is, to me a very funny man, his product rich and satisfying, full of sad beauty, bawdy adventure, political wisdom, and wild surmise; full of pain and jollity, full of exact and inspired writing. The little dedication to this book

>   . . . to babs
>   with babs knows what
>   and babs knows why

is a characteristic bit of Marquis madness. It has hasty despair, the quick anguish, of an author who has just tossed another book to a publisher. It has the unmistakable whiff of
the tavern, and is free of the pretense and the studied affection
that so often pollute a dedicatory message.

The days of the Sun Dial were, as one gazes back on
them, pleasantly preposterous times and Marquis was made for
them, or they for him. *Vers libre* was in vogue, and tons of
souped-up prose and other dribble poured from young free-verse
artists who were suddenly experiencing a gorgeous release in the
disorderly high-sounding tangle of nonmetrical lines. Spiritualism
had captured people's fancy also. Sir Arthur Conan Doyle was in
close touch with the hereafter, and received frequent communications from the other side. Ectoplasm swirled around all our
heads in those days. (It was great stuff, Archy pointed out, to
mend broken furniture with.) Souls, at this period, were being
transmigrated in Pythagorean fashion. It was the time of "swat
the fly," dancing the shimmy, and speakeasies. Marquis imbibed
freely of this carnival air, and it all turned up, somehow, in
Archy's report. Thanks to Archy, Marquis was able to write
rapidly and almost (but not quite) carelessly. In the very act of
spoofing free verse, he was enjoying some of its obvious advantages. And he could always let the chips fall where they might,
since the burden of responsibility for his sentiments, prejudices,
and opinions was neatly shifted to the roach and the cat. It was
quite in character for them to write either beautifully or sourly,
and Marquis turned it on and off the way an orchestra plays first
hot, then sweet.

Archy and Mehitabel, between the two of them, performed the inestimable service of enabling their boss to be
profound without sounding self-important, or even self-con-

scious. Between them, they were capable of taking any theme the boss threw them, and handling it. The piece called "the old trouper" is a good example of how smoothly the combination worked. Marquis, a devoted member of The Players, had undoubtedly had a bellyful of the lamentations of aging actors who mourned the passing of the great days of the theatre. It is not hard to imagine him hastening from his club on Gramercy Park to his desk in the *Sun* office and finding, on examining Archy's report, that Mehitabel was inhabiting an old theatre trunk with a tom who had given his life to the theatre and who felt that actors today don't have it any more—"they don't have it here." (Paw on breast.) The conversation in the trunk is Marquis in full cry, ribbing his nostalgic old actors all in the most wildly fantastic terms, with the tomcat's grandfather (who trooped with Forrest) dropping from the fly gallery to play the beard. This is double-barreled writing, for the scene is funny in itself, with the disreputable cat and her platonic relationship with an old ham, and the implications are funny, with the author successfully winging a familiar type of bore. Double-barreled writing and, on George Herriman's part, double-barreled illustration. It seems to me Herriman deserves much credit for giving the right form and mien to these willful animals. They possess (as he drew them) the great soul. It would be hard to take Mehitabel if she were either more catlike or less. She is cat, yet not cat; and Archy's lineaments are unmistakably those of poet and pest.

Marquis was by temperament a city dweller, and both his little friends were of the city: the cockroach, most common of city bugs; the cat, most indigenous of city mammals. Both, too, were tavern habitués, as was their boss. Here were perfect transmigrations of an American soul, this dissolute feline who was a dancer and always the lady, *toujours gai*, and this troubled insect who was a poet—both seeking expression, both vainly trying to reconcile art and life, both finding always that one gets in the way of the other.

Marquis moved easily from one literary form to another.

He was parodist, historian, poet, clown, fable writer, satirist, reporter, and teller of tales. He had everything it takes and more. In this book you will find prose in the guise of bad *vers libre,* you will find poetry that is truly free verse, and you will find rhymed verse. Whatever fiddle he plucked, he always produced a song. I think he was at his best in a piece like "warty bliggens," which has the jewel-like perfection of poetry and contains cosmic reverberations along with high comedy. Beautiful to read, beautiful to think about.

At bottom Don Marquis was a poet, and his life followed the precarious pattern of a poet's existence. He danced on bitter nights with Boreas, he ground out copy on drowsy afternoons when he felt no urge to write and in newspaper offices where he didn't want to be. After he had exhausted himself columning, he tried playwriting and made a pot of money (on "The Old Soak") and then lost it all on another play (about the Crucifixion). He tried Hollywood and was utterly miserable and angry, and came away with a violent, unprintable poem in his pocket describing the place. In his domestic life he suffered one tragedy after another—the death of a young son, the death of his first wife, the death of his daughter, finally the death of his second wife. Then sickness and poverty. All these things happened in the space of a few years. He was never a robust man— usually had a puffy, overweight look and a gray complexion. He loved to drink, and was told by doctors that he mustn't. Some of the old tomcats at The Players remember the day when he came downstairs after a month on the wagon, ambled over to the bar, and announced: "I've conquered that god-damn will power of mine. Gimme a double scotch."

I think the new generation of newspaper readers is missing a lot that we used to have, and I am deeply sensible of what it meant to be a young man when Archy was at the top of his form and when Marquis was discussing the Almost Perfect State in the daily paper. Buying a paper then was quietly exciting, in a way that it has ceased to be.

BOOK COUNTRY

In writing about literature White does not presume to qualify as an expert. He approaches his task without the credentials of the scholar or the professional reviewer. The motley of the jester fits him more comfortably than the sober robes of the academic critic. His tone even implies that he is only an obscure member of the great fraternity of the common reader, a bewildered layman who knows little more about the arts than what he reads in the papers. Actually he is a most uncommon reader, a man who sees with a critic's perception but writes with a layman's freedom. Unburdened by the duty of close critical analysis, he can look at the whole tree without concentrating on the twigs. Making no pretense of critical disinterestedness and vowing no allegiance to the current fashions in art and language, he can express his personal prejudices in a clear human voice. His affection for his favorites (Don Marquis, Thoreau) is undisguised. He is not afraid to voice the universal longing for poets to be clearer (see p. 105), even though the attitude may look like the weary frown of the middlebrow. Like a good umpire, he calls them as he sees them.

Of the following selections, the first two illustrate White's gift for mimicry, a talent that combines close reading with attentive listening. The free verse imitation of Walt Whitman reflects an attitude that permeates the prose essays: suspicion of the institutionalism that inhibits the free thought and choice of the individual—in this instance, the mass seduction of the mail order book clubs. In "Across the Street and into the Grill" the parody has no other motive than respectful ridicule of the novel, *Across the River and into the Trees,* in which Hemingway's manner often degenerated into mannerism. Like all good parodies it catches both the spirit and the shortcomings of the original and comes across not only as amusing mockery but as provocative criticism. "Some Remarks on Humor" is an informal attempt to taste the flavor of a literary mode; White is faced with a problem familiar to all critics and anthologists—defining the indefinable. Finally, the reader is introduced to the two worlds of today and yesterday, White's Walden and Thoreau's. In both the essayist is too much at home to write with pure critical detachment. The two essays, each with its own method, reveal how a great book can be more than a passing diversion for the reader. When revisited again and again, it can be absorbed into his way of life.

FEBRUARY 19, 1944

A CLASSIC WAITS FOR ME

(With apologies to Walt Whitman, plus a trial membership in the Classics Club)

A classic waits for me, it contains all, nothing is lacking,
Yet all were lacking if taste were lacking, or if the en-
    dorsement of the right man were lacking.
O clublife, and the pleasures of membership,
O volumes for sheer fascination unrivalled.
Into an armchair endlessly rocking,
Walter J. Black my president,
I, freely invited, cordially welcomed to membership,
My arm around John Kieran, Pearl S. Buck,
My taste in books guarded by the spirits of William Lyon
    Phelps, Hendrik Willem van Loon,
(From your memories, sad brothers, from the fitful risings
    and callings I heard),
I to the classics devoted, brother of rough mechanics,
    beauty-parlor technicians, spot welders, radio-program
    directors
(It is not necessary to have a higher education to appreci-
    ate these books),
I, connoisseur of good reading, friend of connoisseurs of
    good reading everywhere,
I, not obligated to take any specific number of books, free

From *The Second Tree from the Corner*.

to reject any volume, perfectly free to reject Mon-
taigne, Erasmus, Milton,
I, in perfect health except for a slight cold, pressed for
time, having only a few more years to live,
Now celebrate this opportunity.
Come, I will make the club indissoluble,
I will read the most splendid books the sun ever shone
upon,
I will start divine magnetic groups,
 With the love of comrades,
 With the life-long love of distinguished
  committees.

I strike up for an Old Book.
Long the best-read figure in America, my dues paid, sitter
in armchairs everywhere, wanderer in populous cities,
weeping with Hecuba and with the late William
Lyon Phelps,
Free to cancel my membership whenever I wish,
Turbulent, fleshy, sensible,
Never tiring of clublife,
Always ready to read another masterpiece provided it has
the approval of my president, Walter J. Black,
Me imperturbe, standing at ease among writers,
Rais'd by a perfect mother and now belonging to a perfect
book club,
Bearded, sunburnt, gray-neck'd, astigmatic,
Loving the masters and the masters only
(I am mad for them to be in contact with me),
My arm around Pearl S. Buck, only American woman to
receive the Nobel Prize for Literature,
I celebrate this opportunity.
And I will not read a book nor the least part of a book but
has the approval of the Committee,
For all is useless without that which you may guess at
many times and not hit, that which they hinted at,

All is useless without readability.

By God! I will accept nothing which all cannot have their
  counterpart of on the same terms (89¢ for the Regular
  Edition or $1.39 for the De Luxe Edition, plus a few
  cents postage).

I will make inseparable readers with their arms around
  each other's necks,
  By the love of classics,
  By the manly love of classics.

OCTOBER 14, 1950

ACROSS THE STREET AND INTO
THE GRILL

(With my respects to Ernest Hemingway)

This is my last and best and true and only meal, thought Mr.
Perley as he descended at noon and swung east on the beat-up
sidewalk of Forty-fifth Street. Just ahead of him was the girl
from the reception desk. I am a little fleshed up around the crook
of the elbow, thought Perley, but I commute good.

He quickened his step to overtake her and felt the pain
again. What a stinking trade it is, he thought. But after what
I've done to other assistant treasurers, I can't hate anybody. Sixteen deads, and I don't know how many possibles.

The girl was near enough now so he could smell her fresh
receptiveness, and the lint in her hair. Her skin was light blue,
like the sides of horses.

"I love you," he said, "and we are going to lunch together
for the first and only time, and I love you very much."

"Hello, Mr. Perley," she said, overtaken. "Let's not think
of anything."

A pair of fantails flew over from the sad old Guaranty

From *The Second Tree from the Corner.*

Trust Company, their wings set for a landing. A lovely double, thought Perley, as he pulled. "Shall we go to the Hotel Biltmore, on Vanderbilt Avenue, which is merely a feeder lane for the great streets, or shall we go to Schrafft's, where my old friend Botticelli is captain of girls and where they have the mayonnaise in fiascos?"

"Let's go to Schrafft's," said the girl, low. "But first I must phone Mummy." She stepped into a public booth and dialled true and well, using her finger. Then she telephoned.

As they walked on, she smelled good. She smells good, thought Perley. But that's all right, I add good. And when we get to Schrafft's, I'll order from the menu, which I like very much indeed.

They entered the restaurant. The wind was still west, ruffling the edges of the cookies. In the elevator, Perley took the controls. "I'll run it," he said to the operator. "I checked out long ago." He stopped true at the third floor, and they stepped off into the men's grill.

"Good morning, my Assistant Treasurer," said Botticelli, coming forward with a fiasco in each hand. He nodded at the girl, who he knew was from the West Seventies and whom he desired.

"Can you drink the water here?" asked Perley. He had the fur trapper's eye and took in the room at a glance, noting that there was one empty table and three pretty waitresses.

Botticelli led the way to the table in the corner, where Perley's flanks would be covered.

"Alexanders," said Perley. "Eighty-six to one. The way Chris mixes them. Is this table all right, Daughter?"

Botticelli disappeared and returned soon, carrying the old Indian blanket.

"That's the same blanket, isn't it?" asked Perley.

"Yes. To keep the wind off," said the Captain, smiling from the backs of his eyes. "It's still west. It should bring the ducks in tomorrow, the chef thinks."

Mr. Perley and the girl from the reception desk crawled

down under the table and pulled the Indian blanket over them so it was solid and good and covered them right. The girl put her hand on his wallet. It was cracked and old and held his commutation book. "We are having fun, aren't we?" she asked.

"Yes, Sister," he said.

"I have here the soft-shelled crabs, my Assistant Treasurer," said Botticelli. "And another fiasco of the 1926. This one is cold."

"Dee the soft-shelled crabs," said Perley from under the blanket. He put his arm around the receptionist good.

"Do you think we should have a green pokeweed salad?" she asked. "Or shall we not think of anything for a while?"

"We shall not think of anything for a while, and Botticelli would bring the pokeweed if there was any," said Perley. "It isn't the season." Then he spoke to the Captain. "Botticelli, do you remember when we took all the mailing envelopes from the stockroom, spit on the flaps, and then drank rubber cement till the foot soldiers arrived?"

"I remember, my Assistant Treasurer," said the Captain. It was a little joke they had.

"He used to mimeograph pretty good," said Perley to the girl. "But that was another war. Do I bore you, Mother?"

"Please keep telling me about your business experiences, but not the rough parts." She touched his hand where the knuckles were scarred and stained by so many old mimeographings. "Are both your flanks covered, my dearest?" she asked, plucking at the blanket. They felt the Alexanders in their eyeballs. Eighty-six to one.

"Schrafft's is a good place and we're having fun and I love you," Perley said. He took another swallow of the 1926, and it was a good and careful swallow. "The stockroom men were very brave," he said, "but it is a position where it is extremely difficult to stay alive. Just outside that room there is a little bare-assed highboy and it is in the way of the stuff that is being brought up. The hell with it. When you make a breakthrough, Daughter, first you clean out the baskets and the half-wits, and all the time they have the fire escapes taped. They also shell you with old production orders, many of them approved by the general manager in charge of sales. I am boring you and I will not at this time discuss the general manager in charge of sales as we are unquestionably being listened to by that waitress over there who is setting out the decoys."

"I am going to give you my piano," the girl said, "so that when you look at it you can think of me. It will be something between us."

"Call up and have them bring the piano to the restaurant," said Perley. "Another fiasco, Botticelli!"

They drank the sauce. When the piano came, it wouldn't play. The keys were stuck good. "Never mind, we'll leave it here, Cousin," said Perley.

They came out from under the blanket and Perley tipped their waitress exactly fifteen per cent minus withholding. They left the piano in the restaurant, and when they went down the elevator and out and turned in to the old, hard, beat-up pavement of Fifth Avenue and headed south toward Forty-fifth Street, where the pigeons were, the air was as clean as your grandfather's howitzer. The wind was still west.

I commute good, thought Perley, looking at his watch. And he felt the old pain of going back to Scarsdale again.

1941

SOME REMARKS ON HUMOR

Analysts have had their go at humor, and I have read some of this interpretative literature, but without being greatly instructed. Humor can be dissected, as a frog can, but the thing dies in the process and the innards are discouraging to any but the pure scientific mind.

In a newsreel theatre the other day I saw a picture of a

From *The Second Tree from the Corner.*

man who had developed the soap bubble to a higher point than it had ever before reached. He had become the ace soap bubble blower of America, had perfected the business of blowing bubbles, refined it, doubled it, squared it, and had even worked himself up into a convenient lather. The effect was not pretty. Some of the bubbles were too big to be beautiful, and the blower was always jumping into them or out of them, or playing some sort of unattractive trick with them. It was, if anything, a rather repulsive sight. Humor is a little like that: it won't stand much blowing up, and it won't stand much poking. It has a certain fragility, an evasiveness, which one had best respect. Essentially, it is a complete mystery. A human frame convulsed with laughter, and the laughter becoming hysterical and uncontrollable, is as far out of balance as one shaken with the hiccoughs or in the throes of a sneezing fit.

One of the things commonly said about humorists is that they are really very sad people—clowns with a breaking heart. There is some truth in it, but it is badly stated. It would be more accurate, I think, to say that there is a deep vein of melancholy running through everyone's life and that the humorist, perhaps more sensible of it than some others, compensates for it actively and positively. Humorists fatten on trouble. They have always made trouble pay. They struggle along with a good will and endure pain cheerfully, knowing how well it will serve them in the sweet by and by. You find them wrestling with foreign languages, fighting folding ironing boards and swollen drainpipes, suffering the terrible discomfort of tight boots (or as Josh Billings wittily called them, "tite" boots). They pour out their sorrows profitably, in a form that is not quite fiction nor quite fact either. Beneath the sparkling surface of these dilemmas flows the strong tide of human woe.

Practically everyone is a manic depressive of sorts, with his up moments and his down moments, and you certainly don't have to be a humorist to taste the sadness of situation and mood. But there is often a rather fine line between laughing and crying, and if a humorous piece of writing brings a person to the point where his emotional responses are untrustworthy and seem likely to break over into the opposite realm, it is because humor, like poetry, has an extra content. It plays close to the big hot fire that is Truth, and sometimes the reader feels the heat.

The world likes humor, but it treats it patronizingly. It decorates its serious artists with laurel, and its wags with Brussels sprouts. It feels that if a thing is funny it can be presumed to be something less than great, because if it were truly great it would be wholly serious. Writers know this, and those who take their literary selves with great seriousness are at considerable pains never to associate their name with anything funny or flippant or nonsensical or "light." They suspect it would hurt their reputation, and they are right. Many a poet writing today signs his real name to his serious verse and a pseudonym to his comical verse, being unwilling to have the public discover him in any but a pensive and heavy moment. It is a wise precaution. (It is often a bad poet, too.)

When I was reading over some of the parody diaries of Franklin P. Adams, I came across this entry for April 28, 1926:

> Read H. Canby's book, *Better Writing*, very excellent. But when he says, "A sense of humour is worth gold to any writer," I disagree with him vehemently. For the writers who amass the greatest gold have, it seems to me, no sense of humour; and I think also that if they had, it would be a terrible thing for them, for it would paralyze them so that they would not write at all. For in writing, emotion is more to be treasured than a sense of humour, and the two are often in conflict.

That is a sound observation. The conflict is fundamental. There constantly exists, for a certain sort of person of high emotional content, at work creatively, the danger of coming to a point where something cracks within himself or within the paragraph under construction—cracks and turns into a snicker. Here, then, is the very nub of the conflict: the careful form of art, and the careless shape of life itself. What a man does with this uninvited snicker (that may closely resemble a sob, at that) decides his destiny. If he resists it, conceals it, destroys it, he may keep his architectural scheme intact and save his building, and the world will never know. If he gives in to it, he becomes a humorist, and the sharp brim of the fool's cap leaves a mark forever on his brow.

I think the stature of humor must vary some with the times. The court fool in Shakespeare's day had no social standing and was no better than a lackey, but he did have some artistic standing and was listened to with considerable attention, there being a well-founded belief that he had the truth hidden somewhere about his person. Artistically he stood probably higher than the humorist of today, who has gained social position but not the ear of the mighty. (Think of the trouble the world would save itself if it would pay some attention to nonsense!) A narrative poet at court, singing of great deeds, enjoyed a higher standing than the fool and was allowed to wear fine clothes; yet I suspect that the ballad singer was more often than not a second-rate stooge, flattering his monarch lyrically, while the fool must often have been a first-rate character, giving his monarch good advice in bad puns.

In the British Empire of our time, satirical humor of the Gilbert and Sullivan sort enjoys a solid position in the realm, and *Punch*, which is as British as vegetable marrow, is socially acceptable everywhere an Englishman is to be found. The *Punch* editors not only write the jokes but they help make the laws of England. Here in America we have an immensely humorous people in a land of milk and honey and wit, who cherish the ideal of the "sense" of humor and at the same time are highly suspicious of anything that is nonserious. Whatever else an American believes or disbelieves about himself, he is absolutely sure he has a sense of humor.

Frank Moore Colby, one of the most intelligent humorists operating in this country in the early years of the century, in an essay called "The Pursuit of Humor" described how the American loves and guards his most precious treasure:

> . . . Now it is the commonest thing in the world to hear people call the absence of a sense of humor the one fatal defect. No matter how owlish a man is, he will tell you that. It is a miserable falsehood, and it does incalculable harm. A life without humor is like a life without legs. You are haunted by a sense of incompleteness, and you cannot go where your friends go. You are also somewhat of a burden. But the only really fatal thing is the shamming of humor when you have it not. There are people whom nature meant to be solemn from their cradle to their grave. They are under bonds to remain so. In so far as they are true to themselves they are safe company for any one; but outside their proper field they are terrible. Solemnity is relatively a blessing, and the man who was born with it should never be encouraged to wrench himself away.

> We have praised humor so much that we have started an insincere cult, and there are many who think they must glorify it when they hate it from the bottom of their hearts. False humor-worship is the deadliest of social sins, and one of the commonest. People without a grain of humor in their composition will eulogize it by the hour. Men will confess to treason, murder, arson, false teeth, or a wig. How many of them will own up to a lack of humor? The courage that could draw this confession from a man would atone for everything.

Relatively few American humorists have become really famous, so that their name is known to everyone in the land in the way that many novelists and other solemn literary characters have become famous. Mark Twain made it. He had, of course, an auspicious start, since he was essentially a story teller and his humor was an added attraction. (It was also very, very good.) In the 1920's and 30's, Ring Lardner was the idol of professional humorists and of plenty of other people, too; but I think I am correct in saying that at the height of his career he was not one of the most widely known literary figures in this country, and the name Lardner was not known to the millions but only to the thousands. He never reached Mr. and Mrs. America and all the ships at sea, to the extent that Mark Twain reached them, and I doubt if he ever will. On the whole, humorists who give pleasure to a wide audience are the ones who create characters and tell tales, the ones who are story tellers at heart. Lardner told stories and gave birth to some characters, but I think he was a realist and a parodist and a satirist first of all, not essentially a writer of fiction. The general public needs something to get a grip on—a Penrod, a Huck Finn, a Br'er Rabbit, or a Father Day. The subtleties of satire and burlesque and nonsense and parody and criticism are not to the general taste; they are for the top (or, if you want, for the bottom) layer of intellect. Clarence Day, for example, was relatively inconspicuous when he was oozing his incomparable "Thoughts without Words," which are his best creations; he became generally known and generally loved only after he had brought Father to life. (Advice to young writers who want to get ahead without any annoying delays: don't write about Man, write about *a* man.)

I was interested, in reading DeVoto's "Mark Twain in Eruption," to come across some caustic remarks of Mr. Clemens's about an anthology of humor that his copyright lawyer had sent him and that Mark described as "a great fat, coarse, offensive volume." He was not amused. "This book is a cemetery," he wrote.

> In this mortuary volume [he went on] I find Nasby, Artemus Ward, Yawcob Strauss, Derby, Burdette, Eli Perkins, the Danbury News Man, Orpheus C. Kerr, Smith O'Brien, Josh Billings, and a score of others, maybe two score, whose writings and sayings were once in everybody's mouth but are now heard of no more and are no longer mentioned. Seventy-eight seems an incredible crop of well-known humorists for one forty-year period to have produced, and yet this book has not harvested the entire crop—far from it. It has no mention of Ike Partington, once so wel-

come and so well known; it has no mention of Doesticks, nor of the Pfaff crowd, nor of Artemus Ward's numerous and perishable imitators, nor of three very popular Southern humorists whose names I am not able to recall, nor of a dozen other sparkling transients whose light shone for a time but has now, years ago, gone out.

Why have they perished? Because they were merely humorists. Humorists of the "mere" sort cannot survive. Humor is only a fragrance, a decoration. Often it is merely an odd trick of speech and of spelling, as in the case of Ward and Billings and Nasby and the "Disbanded Volunteer," and presently the fashion passes and the fame along with it.

Not long ago I plunged back fifty to a hundred years into this school of dialect humor that Mark Twain found perishable. Then was the heyday of the crackerbarrel philosopher, sometimes wise, always wise-seeming, and when read today rather dreary. It seemed to me, in reading the dialect boys, that a certain basic confusion often exists in the use of tricky or quaint or illiterate spelling to achieve a humorous effect. I mean, it is not always clear whether the author intends his character to be writing or speaking—and I, for one, feel that unless I know at least this much about what I am reading, I am off to a bad start. For instance, here are some spellings from the works of Petroleum V. Nasby: he spells "would" *wood*, "of" *uv*, "you" *yoo*, "hence" *hentz*, "office" *offis*.

Now, it happens that I pronounce "office" *offis*. And I pronounce "hence" *hentz*, and I even pronounce "of" *uv*. Therefore, I infer that Nasby's character is supposed not to be speaking but to be writing. Yet in either event, justification for this perversion of the language is lacking; for if the character is speaking, the queer spelling is unnecessary, since the pronunciation is almost indistinguishable from the natural or ordinary pronunciation, and if the character is writing, the spelling is most unlikely. Who ever wrote "uv" for "of"? Nobody. Anyone who knows how to write at all knows how to spell a simple word like "of." If you can't spell "of" you wouldn't be able to spell anything and wouldn't be attempting to set words to paper—much less words like "solissitood." A person who can't spell "of" is an illiterate, and the only time such a person attempts to write anything down is in a great crisis. He doesn't write political essays or diaries or letters or satirical paragraphs.

In the case of Dooley, the Irish dialect is difficult but worth the effort, and it smooths out after the first hundred miles. Finley Peter Dunne was a sharp and gifted humorist, who wrote no second-rate stuff, and he had the sympathetic feeling for his character that is indispensable. This same sympathy is discernible in contemporary Jewish humor—in the work of Milt Gross, Arthur Kober, Leonard Q. Ross. It is sympathy, not contempt or derision, that makes their characters live. Lardner's ballplayer was born because the author had a warm feeling for ballplayers, however boyish or goofy. The spelling in all these cases is not a device for gaining a humorous effect but a necessary tool for working the material, that is inherently humorous.

I suspect that the popularity of all dialect stuff derives in part from flattery of the reader—giving him a pleasant sensation of superiority which he gets from working out the intricacies of misspelling, and the satisfaction of detecting boorishness or illiteracy in someone else. This is not the whole story but it has some bearing in the matter. Incidentally, I am told by an authority on juvenile literature that dialect is tops with children. They like to puzzle out the words. When they catch on to the thing, they must feel that first fine glow of maturity—the ability to exercise higher intellectual powers than those of the character they are looking at.

But to get back to Mark Twain and the "great fat, coarse volume" that offended him so:

> There are those [he continued], who say that a novel should be a work of art solely, and you must not preach in it, you must not teach in it. That may be true as regards novels but it is not true as regards humor. Humor must not professedly teach, and it must not professedly preach, but it must do both

if it would live forever. By forever I mean thirty years. With all its preaching it is not likely to outlive so long a term as that. The very things it preaches about, and which are novelties when it preaches about them, can cease to be novelties and become commonplaces in thirty years. Then that sermon can thenceforth interest no one.

I have always preached. That is the reason that I have lasted thirty years. If the humor came of its own accord and uninvited, I have allowed it a place in my sermon, but I was not writing the sermon for the sake of humor. I should have written the sermon just the same, whether any humor applied for admission or not. I am saying these vain things in this frank way because I am a dead person speaking from the grave. Even I would be too modest to say them in life. I think we never become really and genuinely our entire and honest selves until we are dead—and not then until we have been dead years and years. People ought to start dead, and then they would be honest so much earlier.

I don't think I agree that humor must preach in order to live; it need only speak the truth—and I notice it usually does. But there is no question at all that people ought to start dead.

JUNE   1939

WALDEN

Miss Nims, take a letter to Henry David Thoreau. Dear Henry: I thought of you the other afternoon as I was approaching Concord doing fifty on Route 62. That is a high speed at which to hold a philosopher in one's mind, but in this century we are a nimble bunch.

On one of the lawns in the outskirts of the village a woman was cutting the grass with a motorized lawn mower. What made me think of you was that the machine had rather got away from her, although she was game enough, and in the

From *One Man's Meat*.

brief glimpse I had of the scene it appeared to me that the lawn was mowing the lady. She kept a tight grip on the handles, which throbbed violently with every explosion of the one-cylinder motor, and as she sheered around bushes and lurched along at a reluctant trot behind her impetuous servant, she looked like a puppy who had grabbed something that was too much for him. Concord hasn't changed much, Henry; the farm implements and the animals still have the upper hand.

I may as well admit that I was journeying to Concord with the deliberate intention of visiting your woods; for although I have never knelt at the grave of a philosopher nor placed wreaths on moldy poets, and have often gone a mile out of my way to avoid some place of historical interest, I have always wanted to see Walden Pond. The account that you left of your sojourn there is, you will be amused to learn, a document of increasing pertinence; each year it seems to gain a little headway, as the world loses ground. We may all be transcendental yet, whether we like it or not. As our common complexities increase, any tale of individual simplicity (and yours is the best written and the cockiest) acquires a new fascination; as our goods accumulate, but not our well-being, your report of an existence without material adornment takes on a certain awkward credibility.

My purpose in going to Walden Pond, like yours, was not to live cheaply or to live dearly there, but to transact some private business with the fewest obstacles. Approaching Concord, doing forty, doing forty-five, doing fifty, the steering wheel held snug in my palms, the highway held grimly in my vision, the crown of the road now serving me (on the righthand curves), now defeating me (on the lefthand curves), I began to rouse myself from the stupefaction that a day's motor journey induces. It was a delicious evening, Henry, when the whole body is one sense, and imbibes delight through every pore, if I may coin a phrase. Fields were richly brown where the harrow, drawn by the stripped Ford, had lately sunk its teeth; pastures were green; and overhead the sky had that same everlasting great look which you will find on Page 144 of the Oxford pocket edition. I could feel the road entering me, through tire, wheel, spring, and cushion; shall I not have intelligence with earth too? Am I not partly leaves and vegetable mold myself?—a man of infinite horsepower, yet partly leaves.

Stay with me on 62 and it will take you into Concord. As I say, it was a delicious evening. The snake had come forth to die in a bloody S on the highway, the wheel upon its head, its bowels flat now and exposed. The turtle had come up too to cross the road and die in the attempt, its hard shell smashed under the rubber blow, its intestinal yearning (for the other side of the road) forever squashed. There was a sign by the wayside which announced that the road had a "cotton surface." You wouldn't know what that is, but neither, for that matter, did I. There is a cryptic ingredient in many of our modern improvements—we are awed and pleased without knowing quite what we are enjoying. It is something to be traveling on a road with a cotton surface.

The civilization round Concord today is an odd distillation of city, village, farm, and manor. The houses, yards, fields look not quite suburban, not quite rural. Under the bronze beech and the blue spruce of the departed baron grazes the milch goat of the heirs. Under the porte-cochère stands the reconditioned station wagon; under the grape arbor sit the puppies for sale. (But why do men degenerate ever? What makes families run out?)

It was June and everywhere June was publishing her immemorial stanza; in the lilacs, in the syringa, in the freshly edged paths and the sweetness of moist beloved gardens, and the little wire wickets that preserve the tulips' front. Farmers were already moving the fruits of their toil into their yards, arranging the rhubarb, the asparagus, the strictly fresh eggs on the painted stands under the little shed roofs with the patent shingles. And though it was almost a hundred years since you had taken your ax and started cutting out your home on Walden Pond, I was interested to observe that the philosophical spirit was still alive in Massachusetts: in the center of a vacant lot some boys were assembling the framework of the rude shelter, their whole mind and skill concentrated in the rather inauspicious helter-skeleton of studs and rafters. They too were escaping from town, to live naturally, in a rich blend of savagery and philosophy.

That evening, after supper at the inn, I strolled out into the twilight to dream my shapeless transcendental dreams and see that the car was locked up for the night (first open the right front door, then reach over, straining, and pull up the handles of the left rear and the left front till you hear the click, then the handle of the right rear, then shut the right front but open it again, remembering that the key is still in the ignition switch, remove the key, shut the right front again with a bang, push the tiny keyhole cover to one side, insert key, turn, and withdraw). It is what we all do, Henry. It is called locking the car. It is said to confuse thieves and keep them from making off with the laprobe. Four doors to lock behind one robe. The driver himself never uses a laprobe, the free movement of his legs being vital to the operation of the vehicle; so that when he locks the car it is a pure and unselfish act. I have in my life gained very little essential heat from laprobes, yet I have ever been at pains to lock them up.

The evening was full of sounds, some of which would have stirred your memory. The robins still love the elms of New England villages at sundown. There is enough of the thrush in them to make song inevitable at the end of day, and enough of the tramp to make them hang round the dwellings of men. A robin, like many another American, dearly loves a white house with green blinds. Concord is still full of them.

Your fellow-townsmen were stirring abroad—not many afoot, most of them in their cars; and the sound that they made in Concord at evening was a rustling and a whispering. The sound lacks steadfastness and is wholly unlike that of a train. A train, as you know who lived so near the Fitchburg line, whistles once or twice sadly and is gone, trailing a memory in smoke, soothing to ear and mind. Automobiles, skirting a village green, are like flies that have gained the inner ear—they buzz, cease, pause, start, shift, stop, halt, brake, and the whole effect is a nervous polytone curiously disturbing.

As I wandered along, the toc toc of ping pong balls drifted from an attic window. In front of the Reuben Brown house a Buick was drawn up. At the wheel, motionless, his hat upon his head, a man sat, listening to Amos and Andy on the radio (it is a drama of many scenes and without an end). The deep voice of Andrew Brown, emerging from the car, although it originated more than two hundred miles away, was unstrained by distance. When you used to sit on the shore of your pond on Sunday morning, listening to the church bells of Acton and Concord, you were aware of the excellent filter of the intervening atmosphere. Science has attended to that, and sound now maintains its intensity without regard for distance. Properly sponsored, it goes on forever.

A fire engine, out for a trial spin, roared past Emerson's house, hot with readiness for public duty. Over the barn roofs the martins dipped and chittered. A swarthy daughter of an asparagus grower, in culottes, shirt, and bandanna, pedalled past on her bicycle. It was indeed a delicious evening, and I returned to the inn (I believe it was your house once) to rock with the old ladies on the concrete veranda.

Next morning early I started afoot for Walden, out Main Street and down Thoreau, past the depot and the Minuteman Chevrolet Company. The morning was fresh, and in a bean field along the way I flushed an agriculturalist, quietly studying his beans. Thoreau Street soon joined Number 126, an artery of the State. We number our highways nowadays, our speed being so great we can remember little of their quality or character and are lucky to remember their number. (Men have an indistinct notion that if they keep up this activity long enough all will at length ride somewhere, in next to no time.) Your pond is on 126.

I knew I must be nearing your woodland retreat when the Golden Pheasant lunchroom came into view—Sealtest ice cream, toasted sandwiches, hot frankfurters, waffles, tonics, and lunches. Were I the proprietor, I should add rice, Indian meal, and molasses—just for old time's sake. The Pheasant, incidentally, is for sale: a chance for some nature lover who wishes to set himself up beside a pond in the Concord atmosphere and live deliberately, fronting only the essential facts of life on Number 126. Beyond the Pheasant was a place called Walden Breezes, an oasis whose porch pillars were made of old green shutters sawed into lengths. On the porch was a distorting mirror, to give the traveler a comical image of himself, who had miraculously learned to gaze in an ordinary glass without smiling. Behind the Breezes, in a sun-parched clearing, dwelt your philosophical descendants in their trailers, each trailer the size of your hut, but all grouped together for the sake of congeniality. Trailer people leave the city, as you did, to discover solitude and in any weather, at any hour of the day or night, to improve the nick of time; but they soon collect in villages and get bogged deeper in the mud than ever. The camp behind Walden Breezes was just rousing itself to the morning. The ground was packed hard under the heel, and the sun came through the clearing to bake the soil and enlarge the wry smell of cramped housekeeping. Cushman's bakery truck had stopped to deliver an early basket of rolls. A camp dog, seeing me in the road, barked petulantly. A man emerged from one of the trailers and set forth with a bucket to draw water from some forest tap.

Leaving the highway I turned off into the woods toward the pond, which was apparent through the foliage. The floor of the forest was strewn with dried old oak leaves and *Transcripts*. From beneath the flattened popcorn wrapper (*granum explosum*) peeped the frail violet. I followed a footpath and descended to the water's edge. The pond lay clear and blue in the morning light, as you have seen it so many times. In the shallows a man's waterlogged shirt undulated gently. A few flies came out to greet me and convoy me to your cove, past the No Bathing signs on which the fellows and the girls had scrawled their names. I felt strangely excited suddenly to be snooping around your premises, tiptoeing along watchfully, as though not to tread by mistake upon the intervening century. Before I got to the cove I heard something that seemed to me quite wonderful: I heard your frog, a full, clear *troonk,* guiding me, still hoarse and solemn, bridging the years as the robins had bridged them in the sweetness of the village evening. But he soon quit, and I came on a couple of young boys throwing stones at him.

Your front yard is marked by a bronze tablet set in a stone. Four small granite posts, a few feet away, show where the house was. On top of the tablet was a pair of faded blue bathing trunks with a white stripe. Back of it is a pile of stones, a sort of cairn, left by your visitors as a tribute I suppose. It is a rather ugly little heap of stones, Henry. In fact the hillside itself seems faded, browbeaten; a few tall skinny pines, bare of lower limbs, a smattering of young maples in suitable green, some birches and oaks, and a number of trees felled by the last big wind. It was from the bole of one of these fallen pines, torn up by the roots, that I extracted the stone that I added to the cairn—a sentimental act in which I was interrupted by a small terrier from a nearby picnic group, who confronted me and wanted to know about the stone.

I sat down for a while on one of the posts of your house to listen to the bluebottles and the dragonflies. The invaded glade sprawled shabby and mean at my feet, but the flies were tuned to the old vibration. There were the remains of a fire in your ruins, but I doubt that it was yours; also two beer bottles trodden into the soil and become part of earth. A young oak had taken root in your house, and two or three ferns, unrolling like the ticklers at a banquet. The only other furnishings were a DuBarry pattern sheet, a page torn from a picture magazine, and some crusts in wax paper.

Before I quit I walked clear round the pond and found the place where you used to sit on the northeast side to get the sun in the fall, and the beach where you got sand for scrubbing your floor. On the eastern side of the pond, where the highway borders it, the State has built dressing rooms for swimmers, a float with diving towers, drinking fountains of porcelain, and rowboats for hire. The pond is in fact a State Preserve, and carries a twenty-dollar fine for picking wild flowers, a decree signed in all solemnity by your fellow-citizens Walter C. Wardwell, Erson B. Barlow, and Nathaniel I. Bowditch. There was a smell of creosote where they had been building a wide wooden stairway to the road and the parking area. Swimmers and boaters were arriving; bodies plunged vigorously into the water and emerged wet and beautiful in the bright air. As I left, a boatload of town boys were splashing about in mid-pond, kidding and fooling, the young fellows singing at the tops of their lungs in a wild chorus:

> *Amer-ica, Amer-ica, God shed his grace on thee,*
> *And crown thy good with brotherhood—*
> *From sea to shi-ning sea!*

I walked back to town along the railroad, following your custom. The rails were expanding noisily in the hot sun, and on the slope of the roadbed the wild grape and the blackberry sent up their creepers to the track.

The expense of my brief sojourn in Concord was:

Canvas shoes	$1.95	
Baseball bat	.25 ⎫	gifts to take back
Left-handed fielder's glove	1.25 ⎭	to a boy
Hotel and meals	4.25	
In all	$7.70	

As you see, this amount was almost what you spent for food for eight months. I cannot defend the shoes or the expenditure for shelter and food: they reveal a meanness and grossness in my nature which you would find contemptible. The baseball equipment, however, is the kind of impediment with which you were never on even terms. You must remember that the house where you practiced the sort of economy that I respect was haunted only by mice and squirrels. You never had to cope with a shortstop.

SEPTEMBER   1954

A SLIGHT SOUND AT EVENING

Allen Cove, Summer, 1954

In his journal for July 10–12, 1841, Thoreau wrote: "A slight sound at evening lifts me up by the ears, and makes life seem inexpressibly serene and grand. It may be in Uranus, or it may be in the shutter." The book into which he later managed to pack both Uranus and the shutter was published in 1854, and now, a hundred years having gone by, *Walden,* its serenity and grandeur unimpaired, still lifts us up by the ears, still translates for us that language we are in danger of forgetting, "which all things and events speak without metaphor, which alone is copious and standard."

Walden is an oddity in American letters. It may very well be the oddest of our distinguished oddities. For many it is a great deal too odd, and for many it is a particular bore. I have not found it to be a well-liked book among my acquaintances, although usually spoken of with respect, and one literary critic for whom I have the highest regard can find no reason for anyone's giving *Walden* a second thought. To admire the book is, in fact, something of an embarrassment, for the mass of men have an indistinct notion that its author was a sort of Nature Boy.

I think it is of some advantage to encounter the book at a period in one's life when the normal anxieties and enthusiasms and rebellions of youth closely resemble those of Thoreau in that spring of 1845 when he borrowed an ax, went out to the woods, and began to whack down some trees for timber. Received at such a juncture, the book is like an invitation to life's dance, assuring the troubled recipient that no matter what befalls him in the way of success or failure he will always be welcome at the

A "Letter from the East" in *The Points of My Compass.*

party—that the music is played for him too, if he will but listen and move his feet. In effect, that is what the book is—an invitation, unengraved; and it stirs one as a young girl is stirred by her first big party bid. Many think it a sermon; many set it down as an attempt to rearrange society; some think it an exercise in nature-loving; some find it a rather irritating collection of inspirational puffballs by an eccentric show-off. I think it none of these. It still seems to me the best youth's companion yet written by an American, for it carries a solemn warning against the loss of one's valuables, it advances a good argument for travelling light and trying new adventures, it rings with the power of positive adoration, it contains religious feeling without religious images, and it steadfastly refuses to record bad news. Even its pantheistic note is so pure as to be noncorrupting—pure as the flute-note blown across the pond on those faraway summer nights. If our colleges and universities were alert, they would present a cheap pocket edition of the book to every senior upon graduating, along with his sheepskin, or instead of it. Even if some senior were to take it literally and start felling trees, there could be worse mishaps: the ax is older than the Dictaphone and it is just as well for a young man to see what kind of chips he leaves before listening to the sound of his own voice. And even if some were to get no farther than the table of contents, they would learn how to name eighteen chapters by the use of only thirty-nine words and would see how sweet are the uses of brevity.

If Thoreau had merely left us an account of a man's life in the woods or if he had simply retreated to the woods and there recorded his complaints about society, or even if he had contrived to include both records in one essay, *Walden* would probably not have lived a hundred years. As things turned out, Thoreau, very likely without knowing quite what he was up to, took man's relation to Nature and man's dilemma in society and man's capacity for elevating his spirit and he beat all these matters together, in a wild free interval of self-justification and delight, and produced an original omelette from which people can draw nourishment in a hungry day. *Walden* is one of the first of the vitamin-enriched American dishes. If it were a little less good than it is, or even a little less queer, it would be an abominable book. Even as it is, it will continue to baffle and annoy the literal mind and all those who are unable to stomach its caprices and imbibe its theme. Certainly the plodding economist will continue to have rough going if he hopes to emerge from the book with a clear system of economic thought. Thoreau's assault on the Concord society of the mid-nineteenth century has the quality of a modern Western: he rides into the subject at top speed, shooting in all directions. Many of his shots ricochet and nick him on the rebound, and throughout the melee there is a horrendous cloud of inconsistencies and contradictions, and when the shooting dies down and the air clears, one is impressed chiefly by the courage of the rider and by how splendid it was that somebody should have ridden in there and raised all that ruckus.

When he went to the pond, Thoreau struck an attitude and did so deliberately, but his posturing was not to draw the attention of others to him but rather to draw his own attention more closely to himself. "I learned this at least by my experiment: that if one advances confidently in the direction of his dreams, and endeavors to live the life which he has imagined, he will meet with a success unexpected in common hours." The sentence has the power to resuscitate the youth drowning in his sea of doubt. I recall my exhilaration upon reading it, many years ago, in a time of hesitation and despair. It restored me to health. And now in 1954 when I salute Henry Thoreau on the hundredth birthday of his book, I am merely paying off an old score—or an installment on it.

In his journal for May 3–4, 1838—Boston to Portland—he wrote: "Midnight—head over the boat's side—between sleeping and waking—with glimpses of one or more lights in the vicinity of Cape Ann. Bright moonlight—the effect heightened by seasickness." The entry illuminates the man, as the moon the sea on that night in May. In Thoreau the natural scene was heightened, not depressed, by a disturbance of the stomach, and nausea met its match at last. There was a steadiness in at least one passenger if there was none in the boat. Such steadiness (that in some would be called intoxication) is at the heart of *Walden*—confidence, faith, the discipline of looking always at what is to be seen, undeviating gratitude for the life-everlasting that he found growing in his front yard. "There is nowhere recorded a simple and irrepressible satisfaction with the gift of life, any memorable praise of God." He worked to correct that deficiency. *Walden* is his acknowledgment of the gift of life. It is the testament of a man in a high state of indignation because (it seemed to him) so few ears heard the uninterrupted poem of creation, the morning wind that forever blows. If the man sometimes wrote as though all his readers were male, unmarried, and well-connected, it is because he gave his testimony during the callow years, and, for that matter, never really grew up. To reject the book because of the immaturity of the author and the bugs in the logic is to throw away a bottle of good wine because it contains bits of the cork.

Thoreau said he required of every writer, first and last, a simple and sincere account of his own life. Having delivered himself of this chesty dictum, he proceeded to ignore it. In his books and even in his enormous journal, he withheld or disguised most of the facts from which an understanding of his life could be drawn. *Walden*, subtitled "Life in the Woods," is not a simple and sincere account of a man's life, either in or out of the woods; it is an account of a man's journey into the mind, a toot on the trumpet to alert the neighbors. Thoreau was well aware that no one can alert his neighbors who is not wide-awake himself, and he went to the woods (among other reasons) to make sure that he would stay awake during his broadcast. What actually took place during the years 1845–47 is largely unrecorded, and the reader is excluded from the private life of the author, who supplies almost no gossip about himself, a great deal about his neighbors and about the universe.

As for me, I cannot in this short ramble give a simple and sincere account of my own life, but I think Thoreau might find it instructive to know that this memorial essay is being written in a house that, through no intent on my part, is the same size and shape as his own domicile on the pond—about ten by fifteen, tight, plainly finished, and at a little distance from my Concord. The house in which I sit this morning was built to accommodate a boat, not a man, but by long experience I have learned that in most respects it shelters me better than the larger dwelling where my bed is, and which, by design, is a manhouse not a boathouse. Here in the boathouse I am a wilder and, it would appear, a healthier man, by a safe margin. I have a chair, a bench, a table, and I can walk into the water if I tire of the land. My house fronts a cove. Two fishermen have just arrived to spot fish from the air—an osprey and a man in a small yellow plane who works for the fish company. The man, I have noticed, is less well equipped than the hawk, who can dive directly on his fish and carry it away, without telephoning. A mouse and a squirrel share the house with me. The building is, in fact, a multiple dwelling, a semidetached affair. It is because I am semidetached while here that I find it possible to transact this private business with the fewest obstacles.

There is also a woodchuck here, living forty feet away under the wharf. When the wind is right, he can smell my house; and when the wind is contrary, I can smell his. We both use the wharf for sunning, taking turns, each adjusting his schedule to the other's convenience. Thoreau once ate a woodchuck. I think he felt he owed it to his readers, and that it was little enough, considering the indignities they were suffering at his hands and the dressing-down they were taking. (Parts of *Walden* are pure scold.) Or perhaps he ate the woodchuck because he believed every man should acquire strict business habits, and the woodchuck was destroying his market beans. I do not know. Thoreau had a strong experimental streak in him. It is probably no harder to eat a woodchuck than to construct a sentence that lasts a hundred years. At any rate, Thoreau is the only writer I know who prepared himself for his great ordeal by eating a woodchuck; also the only one who got a hangover from drinking too much water. (He was drunk the whole time, though he seldom touched wine or coffee or tea.)

Here in this compact house where I would spend one day as deliberately as Nature if I were not being pressed by the editor of a magazine, and with a woodchuck (as yet uneaten) for neighbor, I can feel the companionship of the occupant of the pondside cabin in Walden woods, a mile from the village, near the Fitchburg right of way. Even my immediate business is no barrier between us: Thoreau occasionally batted out a magazine piece, but was always suspicious of any sort of purposeful work that cut into his time. A man, he said, should take care not to be thrown off the track by every nutshell and mosquito's wing that falls on the rails.

There has been much guessing as to why he went to the pond. To set it down to escapism is, of course, to misconstrue what happened. Henry went forth to battle when he took to the woods, and *Walden* is the report of a man torn by two powerful and opposing drives—the desire to enjoy the world (and not be derailed by a mosquito wing) and the urge to set the world straight. One cannot join these two successfully, but sometimes, in rare cases, something good or even great results from the attempt of the tormented spirit to reconcile them. Henry went forth to battle, and if he set the stage himself, if he fought on his own terms and with his own weapons, it was because it was his nature to do things differently from most men, and to act in a cocky fashion. If the pond and the woods seemed a more plausible site for a house than an in-town location, it was because a cowbell made for him a sweeter sound than a churchbell. *Walden,* the book, makes the sound of a cowbell, more than a churchbell, and proves the point, although both sounds are in it, and both remarkably clear and sweet. He simply preferred his churchbell at a little distance.

I think one reason he went to the woods was a perfectly simple and commonplace one—and apparently he thought so, too. "At a certain season of our life," he wrote, "we are accustomed to consider every spot as the possible site of a house." There spoke the young man, a few years out of college, who had not yet broken away from home. He hadn't married, and he had found no job that measured up to his rigid standards of employment, and like any young man, or young animal, he felt uneasy and on the defensive until he had fixed himself a den. Most young men, of course, casting about for a site, are content merely to draw apart from their kinfolks. Thoreau, convinced that the greater part of what his neighbors called good was bad, withdrew from a great deal more than family: he pulled out of everything for a while, to serve everybody right for being so stuffy, and to try his own prejudices on the dog.

The house-hunting sentence above, that starts the chapter called "Where I Lived, and What I Lived For," is followed by another passage that is worth quoting here because it so beautifully illustrates the offbeat prose that Thoreau was master of, a prose at once strictly disciplined and wildly abandoned. "I have surveyed the country on every side within a dozen miles of where I live," continued this delirious young man. "In imagination I have bought all the farms in succession, for all were to be bought, and I knew their price. I walked over each farmer's premises, tasted his wild apples, discoursed on husbandry with him, took his farm at his price, at any price, mortgaging it to him in my mind; even put a higher price on it—took everything but a deed of it—took his word for his deed, for I dearly love to talk—cultivated it, and him too to some extent, I trust, and withdrew when I had enjoyed it long enough, leaving him to carry it on." A copy-desk man would get a double hernia trying to clean up that sentence for the management, but the sentence needs no fixing, for it perfectly captures the meaning of the writer and the quality of the ramble.

"Wherever I sat, there I might live, and the landscape radiated from me accordingly." Thoreau, the home-seeker, sitting on his hummock with the entire State of Massachusetts radiating from him, is to me the most humorous of the New England figures, and *Walden* the most humorous of the books, though its humor is almost continuously subsurface and there is nothing deliberately funny anywhere, except a few weak jokes and bad puns that rise to the surface like the perch in the pond that rose to the sound of the maestro's flute. Thoreau tended to write in sentences, a feat not every writer is capable of, and *Walden* is, rhetorically speaking, a collection of certified sentences, some of them, it would now appear, as indestructible as they are errant. The book is distilled from the vast journals, and this accounts for its intensity: he picked out bright particles that pleased his eye, whirled them in the kaleidoscope of his content, and produced the pattern that has endured—the color, the form, the light.

On this its hundredth birthday, Thoreau's *Walden* is pertinent and timely. In our uneasy season, when all men unconsciously seek a retreat from a world that has got almost completely out of hand, his house in the Concord woods is a haven. In our culture of gadgetry and the multiplicity of convenience, his cry "Simplicity, simplicity, simplicity!" has the insistence of a fire alarm. In the brooding atmosphere of war and the gathering radioactive storm, the innocence and serenity of his summer afternoons are enough to burst the remembering heart, and one gazes back upon that pleasing interlude—its confidence, its purity, its deliberateness—with awe and wonder, as one would look upon the face of a child asleep.

"This small lake was of most value as a neighbor in the intervals of a gentle rain-storm in August, when, both air and water being perfectly still, but the sky overcast, midafternoon had all the serenity of evening, and the wood-thrush sang around, and was heard from shore to shore." Now, in the perpetual overcast in which our days are spent, we hear with extra perception and deep gratitude that song, tying century to century.

I sometimes amuse myself by bringing Henry Thoreau back to life and showing him the sights. I escort him into a phone booth and let him dial Weather. "This is a delicious evening," the girl's voice says, "when the whole body is one sense, and imbibes delight through every pore." I show him the spot in the Pacific where an island used to be, before some magician made it vanish. "We know not where we are," I murmur. "The light which puts out our eyes is darkness to us. Only that day dawns to which we are awake." I thumb through the latest copy of *Vogue* with him. "Of two patterns which differ only by a few threads more or less of a particular color," I read, "the one will be sold readily, the other lie on the shelf, though it frequently happens that, after the lapse of a season, the latter becomes the most fashionable." Together we go outboarding on the Assabet, looking for what we've lost—a hound, a bay horse, a turtledove. I show him a distracted farmer who is trying to repair a hay baler before the thundershower breaks. "This farmer," I remark, "is endeavoring to solve the problem of a livelihood by a formula more complicated than the problem itself. To get his shoestrings he speculates in herds of cattle."

I take the celebrated author to Twenty-One for lunch, so the waiters may study his shoes. The proprietor welcomes us. "The gross feeder," remarks the proprietor, sweeping the room with his arm, "is a man in the larva stage." After lunch we visit a classroom in one of those schools conducted by big corporations to teach their superannuated executives how to retire from business without serious injury to their health. (The shock to men's systems these days when relieved of the exacting routine of amassing wealth is very great and must be cushioned.) "It is not necessary, says the teacher to his pupils, "that a man should earn his living by the sweat of his brow, unless he sweats easier than I do. We are determined to be starved before we are hungry."

I turn on the radio and let Thoreau hear Winchell beat the red hand around the clock. "Time is but the stream I go a-fishing in," shouts Mr. Winchell, rattling his telegraph key. "Hardly a man takes a half hour's nap after dinner, but when he wakes he holds up his head and asks, 'What's the news?' If we read of one man robbed, or murdered, or killed by accident, or one house burned, or one vessel wrecked, or one steamboat blown up, or one cow run over on the Western Railroad, or one mad dog killed, or one lot of grasshoppers in the winter—we need never read of another. One is enough."

I doubt that Thoreau would be thrown off balance by the

fantastic sights and sounds of the twentieth century. "The Concord nights," he once wrote, "are stranger than the Arabian nights." A four-engined airliner would merely serve to confirm his early views on travel. Everywhere he would observe, in new shapes and sizes, the old predicaments and follies of men—the desperation, the impedimenta, the meanness—along with the visible capacity for elevation of the mind and soul. "This curious world which we inhabit is more wonderful than it is convenient; more beautiful than it is useful; it is more to be admired and enjoyed than used." He would see that today ten thousand engineers are busy making sure that the world shall be convenient even if it is destroyed in the process, and others are determined to increase its usefulness even though its beauty is lost somewhere along the way.

At any rate, I'd like to stroll about the countryside in Thoreau's company for a day, observing the modern scene, inspecting today's snowstorm, pointing out the sights, and offering belated apologies for my sins. Thoreau is unique among writers in that those who admire him find him uncomfortable to live with—a regular hairshirt of a man. A little band of dedicated Thoreauvians would be a sorry sight indeed: fellows who hate compromise and have compromised, fellows who love wildness and have lived tamely, and at their side, censuring them and chiding them, the ghostly figure of this upright man, who long ago gave corroboration to impulses they perceived were right and issued warnings against the things they instinctively knew to be their enemies. I should hate to be called a Thoreauvian, yet I wince every time I walk into the barn I'm pushing before me, seventy-five feet by forty, and the author of *Walden* has served as my conscience through the long stretches of my trivial days.

Hairshirt or no, he is a better companion than most, and I would not swap him for a soberer or more reasonable friend even if I could. I can reread his famous invitation with undiminished excitement. The sad thing is that not more acceptances have been received, that so many decline for one reason or another, pleading some previous engagement or ill health. But the invitation stands. It will beckon as long as this remarkable book stays in print—which will be as long as there are August afternoons in the intervals of a gentle rainstorm, as long as there are ears to catch the faint sounds of the orchestra. I find it agreeable to sit here this morning, in a house of correct proportions, and hear across a century of time his flute, his frogs, and his seductive summons to the wildest revels of them all.

HABITATS

The essays in this section are all marked, like "Walden," by White's unusual talent for distilling the essence of a place. One piece has its setting on a beach in Florida, three are centered in the city (two specifically in Manhattan), and another in Maine. White's chief concern is less with establishing the specific facts of setting than with conjuring up the mysterious spirit that is inadequately called atmosphere. He knows that the best way to realize the atmosphere of any place is to feel the pulses of the inhabitants.

In spite of his preference for labeling his essays with both date and place, White's perspective is not limited by a calendar or a compass. "Time," he could say with Thoreau, "is but the stream I go a-fishing in." As for place, he makes it clear in the foreword to *The Points of My Compass* that no orthodox prejudices about geography could restrain his own vagrant mood:

Not wanting to rule out any portion of the globe as my territory, or any subject matter as my concern, I invented a new compass and a more accommodating wind vane. . . . I selected my office in midtown Manhattan as a locus —a spot in air between Forty-third and Forty-fourth streets, between Fifth and Sixth. In my new design anything east of this point was "the East," anything west of it was "the West," and so on. Thus, by merely walking half a block over to Sixth Avenue, I was in a position to write a "Letter from the West." You can readily see what a convenience this was to a foreign correspondent—no passport fuss, no plane reservations, no packing of suitcases, no trouble with customs, no dysentery from eating raw food. All I had to do was sit down anywhere and I was somewhere.

A writer's home is where he stables his typewriter. To travel anywhere else he needs no passport other than his imagination. Though White has made his home in both Manhattan and Maine, his point of view has not been limited by metropolitan sophistication or down-east rusticity. He has written from Maine about "keeping green the memory of the cities," and he has been neighbor to the birds—not merely to the pigeons—frequenting a midtown apartment. He has never assumed the romantic provincial view that God made the country and man made the town, though he may have firm convictions about who made the suburbs and the exurbs. Just as Thoreau could see the universe reflected in a pond near Concord, White can find global significance in the synthetic coloring of a Florida orange.

FEBRUARY   1941

ON A FLORIDA KEY

I am writing this in a beach cottage on a Florida key. It is raining to beat the cars. The rollers from a westerly storm are creaming along the shore, making a steady boiling noise instead of the usual intermittent slap. The Chamber of Commerce has drawn the friendly blind against this ugliness and is busy getting out some advance notices of the style parade that is to be held next Wednesday at the pavilion. The paper says cooler tomorrow.

The walls of my room are of matched boarding, applied horizontally and painted green. On the floor is a straw mat. Under the mat is a layer of sand that has been tracked into the cottage and has sifted through the straw. I have thought some of taking the mat up and sweeping the sand into a pile and removing it, but have decided against it. This is the way keys form, apparently, and I have no particular reason to interfere. On a

From *One Man's Meat.*

small wooden base in one corner of the room is a gas heater, supplied from a tank on the premises. This device can raise the temperature of the room with great rapidity by converting the oxygen of the air into heat. In deciding whether to light the heater or leave it alone, one has only to choose whether he wants to congeal in a well-ventilated room or suffocate in comfort. After a little practice, a nice balance can be established—enough oxygen left to sustain life, yet enough heat generated to prevent death from exposure.

On the west wall hangs an Indian rug, and to one edge of the rug is pinned a button that carries the legend: Junior Programs Joop Club. Built into the north wall is a cabinet made of pecky cypress. On the top shelf are three large pine cones, two of them painted emerald-green, the third painted brick-red. Also a gilded candlestick in the shape of a Roman chariot. Another shelf holds some shells that, at the expenditure of considerable effort on somebody's part, have been made to look like birds. On the bottom shelf is a tiny toy collie, made of rabbit fur, with a tongue of red flannel.

In the kitchenette just beyond where I sit is a gas stove and a small electric refrigerator of an ancient vintage. The ice trays show deep claw marks, where people have tried to pry them free, using can openers and knives and screwdrivers and petulance. When the refrigerator snaps on it makes a noise that can be heard all through the cottage and the lights everywhere go dim for a second and then return to their normal brilliancy. This refrigerator contains the milk, the butter, and the eggs for tomorrow's breakfast. More milk will arrive in the morning, but I will save it for use on the morrow, so that every day I shall use the milk of the previous day, never taking advantage of the opportunity to enjoy perfectly fresh milk. This is a situation that could be avoided if I had the guts to throw away a whole bottle of milk, but nobody has that much courage in the world today. It is a sin to throw away milk and we know it.

The water that flows from the faucets in the kitchen sink and in the bathroom contains sulphur and is not good to drink. It leaves deep-brown stains around the drains. Applied to the face with a shaving brush, it feels as though fine sandpaper were being drawn across your jowls. It is so hard and sulphurous that ordinary soap will not yield to it, and the breakfast dishes have to be washed with a washing powder known as Dreft.

On the porch of the cottage, each in a special stand, are two carboys of spring water—for drinking, making coffee, and brushing teeth. There is a deposit of two dollars on bottle and stand, and the water itself costs fifty cents. Two rival companies furnish water to the community, and I happened to get mixed up with both of them. Every couple of days a man from one or the other of the companies shows up and hangs around for a while, whining about the presence on my porch of the rival's carboy. I have made an attempt to dismiss one company and retain the other, but to accomplish it would require a dominant personality and I haven't one. I have been surprised to see how long it takes a man to drink up ten gallons of water. I should have thought I could have done it in half the time it has taken me.

This morning I read in the paper of an old Negro, one hundred and one years old, and he was boasting of the quantity of whisky he had drunk in his life. He said he had once worked in a distillery and they used to give him half a gallon of whisky a day to take home, which kept him going all right during the week, but on weekends, he said, he would have to buy a gallon extry, to tide him over till Monday.

In the kitchen cabinet is a bag of oranges for morning juice. Each orange is stamped "Color Added." The dyeing of an orange, to make it orange, is Man's most impudent gesture to date. It is really an appalling piece of effrontery, carrying the clear implication that Nature doesn't know what she is up to. I think an orange, dyed orange, is as repulsive as a pine cone painted green. I think it is about as ugly a thing as I have ever seen, and it seems hard to believe that here, within ten miles, probably, of the trees that bore the fruit, I can't buy an orange that somebody hasn't smeared with paint. But I doubt that there are many who feel that way about it, because fraudulence has become a national virtue and is well thought of in many circles. In the past twenty-four hours, I see by this morning's paper, one hundred and thirty-six cars of oranges have been shipped. There are probably millions of children today who have never seen a natural orange—only an artificially colored one. If they should see a natural orange they might think something had gone wrong with it.

There are two moving picture theaters in the town to which my key is attached by a bridge. In one of them colored people are allowed in the balcony. In the other, colored people are not allowed at all. I saw a patriotic newsreel there the other day that ended with a picture of the American flag blowing in the breeze, and the words: one nation indivisible, with liberty and justice for all. Everyone clapped, but I decided I could not clap for liberty and justice (for all) while I was in a theater from which Negroes had been barred. And I felt there were too many people in the world who think liberty and justice for all means liberty and justice for themselves and their friends. I sat there wondering what would happen to me if I were to jump up and say in a loud voice: "If you folks like liberty and justice so much, why do you keep Negroes from this theater?" I am sure it would have surprised everybody very much and it is the kind of thing I dream about doing but never do. If I had done it I suppose the management would have taken me by the arm and marched me out of the theater, on the grounds that it is disturbing the peace to speak up for liberty just as the feature is coming on. When a man is in the South he must do as the Southerners do; but although I am willing to call my wife "Sugar" I am not willing to call a colored person a nigger.

Northerners are quite likely to feel that Southerners are bigoted on the race question, and Southerners almost invariably figure that Northerners are without any practical experience and therefore their opinions aren't worth much. The Jim Crow philosophy of color is unsatisfying to a Northerner, but is regarded as sensible and expedient to residents of towns where the

Negro population is as large as or larger than the white. Whether one makes a practical answer or an idealistic answer to a question depends partly on whether one is talking in terms of one year, or ten years, or a hundred years. It is, in other words, conceivable that the Negroes of a hundred years from now will enjoy a greater degree of liberty if the present restrictions on today's Negroes are not relaxed too fast. But that doesn't get today's Negroes in to see Hedy Lamarr.

I have to laugh when I think about the sheer inconsistency of the Southern attitude about color: the Negro barred from the movie house because of color, the orange with "color added" for its ultimate triumph. Some of the cities in this part of the State have fête days to commemorate the past and advertise the future, and in my mind I have been designing a float which I would like to enter in the parades. It would contain a beautiful Negro woman riding with the other bathing beauties and stamped with the magical words, Color Added.

In the cottage next door is a lady who is an ardent isolationist and who keeps running in and out with pamphlets, books, and marked-up newspapers, hoping to convince me that America should mind its own business. She tracks sand in, as well as ideas, and I have to sweep up after her two or three times a day.

Floridians are complaining this year that business is below par. They tell you that the boom in industry causes this unwholesome situation. When tycoons are busy in the North they have no time for sunning themselves, or even for sitting in a semitropical cottage in the rain. Miami is appropriating a few extra thousand dollars for its advertising campaign, hoping to lure executives away from the defense program for a few golden moments.

Although I am no archaeologist, I love Florida as much for the remains of her unfinished cities as for the bright cabanas on her beaches. I love to prowl the dead sidewalks that run off into the live jungle, under the broiling sun of noon, where the cabbage palms throw their spiny shade across the stillborn streets and the creepers bind old curbstones in a fierce sensual embrace and the mocking birds dwell in song upon the remembered grandeur of real estate's purple hour. A boulevard that has been reclaimed by Nature is an exciting avenue; it breathes a strange prophetic perfume, as of some century still to come, when the birds will remember, and the spiders, and the little quick lizards that toast themselves on the smooth hard surfaces that once held the impossible dreams of men. Here along these bristling walks is a decayed symmetry in a living forest—straight lines softened by a kindly and haphazard Nature, pavements nourishing life with the beginnings of topsoil, the cracks in the walks possessed by root structures, the brilliant blossoms of the domesticated vine run wild, and overhead the turkey buzzard in the clear sky, on quiet wings, awaiting new mammalian death among the hibiscus, the yucca, the Spanish bayonet, and the palm. I remember the wonderful days and the tall dream of rainbow's end; the offices with the wall charts, the pins in the charts, the orchestras playing gently to prepare the soul of the wanderer for the mysteries of subdivision, the free bus service to the rainbow's beginning, the luncheon served on the little tables under the trees, the warm sweet air so full of the deadly contagion, the dotted line, the signature, and the premonitory qualms and the shadow of the buzzard in the wild wide Florida sky.

I love these rudimentary cities that were conceived in haste and greed and never rose to suffer the scarifying effects of human habitation, cities of not quite forgotten hopes, untouched by neon and by filth. And I love the beaches too, out beyond the cottage colony, where they are wild and free still, visited by the sandpipers that retreat before each wave, like children, and by an occasional hip-sprung farmwife hunting shells, or sometimes by a veteran digging for *Donax variabilis* to take back to his hungry mate in the trailer camp.

The sound of the sea is the most time-effacing sound there is. The centuries reroll in a cloud and the earth becomes young again when you listen, with eyes shut, to the sea—a young green time when the water and the land were just getting acquainted and had known each other for only a few billion years and the mollusks were just beginning to dip and creep in the shallows; and now man the invertebrate, under his ribbed umbrella, anoints himself with oil and pulls on his Polaroid glasses to stop the glare and stretches out his long brown body at ease upon a towel on the warm sand and listens.

The sea answers all questions, and always in the same way; for when you read in the papers the interminable discussions and the bickering and the prognostications and the turmoil, the disagreements and the fateful decisions and agreements and the plans and the programs and the threats and the counter threats, then you close your eyes and the sea dispatches one more big roller in the unbroken line since the beginning of the world and it combs and breaks and returns foaming and saying: "So soon?"

NOVEMBER   1939

THE CITIES

In the cities (but the cities are to be destroyed) lights continue to burn on into the morning, in the hotel bedrooms that open into the dark court, in the little sitting rooms off the bedrooms, where the breakfast things linger, with the light gleaming on the half grapefruit and the bright serving covers and the coffee thermos, the ice melting around the grapefruit-rind all through the morning and shades going up across the areaway where the other people in dressing gowns and bathrobes and pajamas are lifting the receiver from the hook and calling room service and ordering the half grapefruit and the toast and marmalade and running the water behind the shower curtain. The city wakens, but to its own internal suns, each lamp with its parchment shade and the cord, dusty twisted, that connects it to the center of light and of power, the umbilicals of the solar system.

From "Poetry" in *One Man's Meat.*

(But they tell me the cities are all to be destroyed and that people will no longer live in the impractical cities, but the time has not yet come.) Nevertheless I must begin keeping green the memory of the cities, the ferns and tiger plants in the boxes under the lights in the dining rooms and the restaurants and the grills, the opening and closing of the doors of the elevators, and the finger always on the button summoning the elevator, waiting silently with the others (there are always others in the city) and the ascent and descent always with the others, but never speaking. In the bookshops the clerks, wanting to know if they can help, but you say no you are just looking around, and the terrible excitement of so great a concentration of books in one place under one roof, each book wanting the completion of being read. Under the marquee, after the show, huddling out of the rain with the rain on the roofs of the cabs and the look on the faces of the city people desperate in the rain, and the men in their black coats and hats darting out into the withering fire of raindrops to seek the turbulent headwaters of the stream of taxis, and the petulance and impatience and desperation of the women in their dresses waiting for the return of the men who are gone so long into the fierce bewildering night, and the mass urgency, there under the marquee, as though unless they all escaped safely into a cab within five minutes they would die. (You must leave the key at the desk when you go out. Even though the cities are to be destroyed, don't forget to leave the key at the desk when you go out.)

JULY 10, 1943

TRANCE

That delicious Sabbath trance induced by the study of the Sunday *Times* reaches its glassiest phase when we get into the changeless ads on the garden page of the Drama-

From *The Second Tree from the Corner*.

Screen-Radio-Music-Dance-Art-Stamps-Resorts-Travel-Gardens-Women's News-Bridge Section. It is here, among the strange accoutrements of the horticultural life, that we forget, losing ourself completely. The senses float in pale regions of total intellectual stupor. A flexible blade to increase the efficiency of the lawn mower that we know we will never push over lawns measureless to man; a citronella candle to banish the imaginary mosquito from the imaginary porch on the fancied terrible summer night; twenty pachysandras for one dollar—how calm we feel, reading about them, how sweetly safe and indolent behind the walls of this stifling room in town! Here is a device for dehydrating vegetables, here a treatise on the breeding of earthworms for the feeding of hens in confinement, here a lovely silver gazing ball for the informal coppice. As our lids slowly droop, the scene expands and lightens, and we stand in the center of this unearthly pleasure spot, this garden close, this green maze, with the cutworms and the laying pullets creeping around our feet, the liquid repellent for dogs and beetles gurgling over the mossy stones of the artificial brook, and an incredibly beautiful woman staring steadily into the gazing ball. No matter that this is the century of trouble: it is Sunday in the living room and there is a panacea for every ill.

APRIL   1949

HERE IS NEW YORK

There are roughly three New Yorks. There is, first, the New York of the man or woman who was born here, who takes the city for granted and accepts its size and its turbulence as natural and inevitable. Second, there is the New York of the commuter—the city that is devoured by locusts each day and spat out each night. Third, there is the New York of the person who was born somewhere else and came to New York in quest of

From *Here Is New York*.

something. Of these three trembling cities the greatest is the last—the city of final destination, the city that is a goal. It is this third city that accounts for New York's high-strung disposition, its poetical deportment, its dedication to the arts, and its incomparable achievements. Commuters give the city its tidal restlessness; natives give it solidity and continuity; but the settlers give it passion. And whether it is a farmer arriving from Italy to set up a small grocery store in a slum, or a young girl arriving from a small town in Mississippi to escape the indignity of being observed by her neighbors, or a boy arriving from the Corn Belt with a manuscript in his suitcase and a pain in his heart, it makes no difference: each embraces New York with the intense excitement of first love, each absorbs New York with the fresh eyes of an adventurer, each generates heat and light to dwarf the Consolidated Edison Company.

The commuter is the queerest bird of all. The suburb he inhabits has no essential vitality of its own and is a mere roost where he comes at day's end to go to sleep. Except in rare cases, the man who lives in Mamaroneck or Little Neck or Teaneck, and works in New York, discovers nothing much about the city except the time of arrival and departure of trains and buses, and the path to a quick lunch. He is desk-bound, and has never, idly roaming in the gloaming, stumbled suddenly on Belvedere Tower in the Park, seen the ramparts rise sheer from the water of the pond, and the boys along the shore fishing for minnows, girls stretched out negligently on the shelves of the rocks; he has never come suddenly on anything at all in New York as a loiterer, because he has had no time between trains. He has fished in Manhattan's wallet and dug out coins, but has never listened to Manhattan's breathing, never awakened to its morning, never dropped off to sleep in its night. About 400,000 men and women come charging onto the Island each week-day morning, out of the mouths of tubes and tunnels. Not many among them have ever spent a drowsy afternoon in the great rustling oaken silence of the reading room of the Public Library, with the book elevator (like an old water wheel) spewing out books onto the trays. They tend their furnaces in Westchester and in Jersey, but have never seen the furnaces of the Bowery, the fires that burn in oil drums on zero winter nights. They may work in the financial district downtown and never see the extravagant plantings of Rockefeller Center—the daffodils and grape hyacinths and birches and the flags trimmed to the wind on a fine morning in spring. Or they may work in a midtown office and may let a whole year swing round without sighting Governors Island from the sea wall. The commuter dies with tremendous mileage to his credit, but he is no rover. His entrances and exits are more devious than those in a prairie-dog village; and he calmly plays bridge while buried in the mud at the bottom of the East River. The Long Island Rail Road alone carried forty million commuters last year; but many of them were the same fellow retracing his steps.

The terrain of New York is such that a resident sometimes travels farther, in the end, than a commuter. Irving Berlin's journey from Cherry Street in the lower East Side to an apartment uptown was through an alley and was only three or four miles in length; but it was like going three times around the world.

JANUARY   1943

COLD WEATHER

There has been more talk about the weather around here this year than common, but there has been more weather to talk about. For about a month now we have had solid cold—firm, business-like cold that stalked in and took charge of the countryside as a brisk housewife might take charge of someone else's kitchen in an emergency. Clean, hard, purposeful cold, unyielding and unremitting. Some days have been clear and cold, others have been stormy and cold. We have had cold with snow and cold without snow, windy cold and quiet cold, rough cold and indulgent peace-loving cold. But always cold. The kitchen door-

From *One Man's Meat.*

yard is littered with the cylinders of ice from frozen water buckets that have been thawed out in the morning with hot water. Storm windows weren't enough this winter—we resorted to the simplest and best insulating material available, the daily newspaper applied to north windows with thumbtacks. Mornings the thermometer would register ten or twelve below. By noon it would have zoomed up to zero. As the night shut in, along about four-thirty, it would start dropping again. Even in the tight barn, insulated with tons of hay, the slobber from the cow's nose stiffened in small icicles, and the vapor rose from the warm milk into the milker's face. If you took hold of a latch with ungloved hands, the iron seized you by the skin and held on.

There is a fraternity of the cold, to which I am glad I belong. Nobody is kept from joining. Even old people sitting by the fire belong, as the floor draft closes in around their ankles. The members get along well together: extreme cold when it first arrives seems to generate cheerfulness and sociability. For a few hours all life's dubious problems are dropped in favor of the clear and congenial task of keeping alive. It is rather soothing when existence is reduced to the level of a woodbox that needs filling, a chink that needs plugging, a rug that needs pushing against a door.

I remember that first morning. It was twelve below just before daylight. Most of us had realized the previous afternoon that we were in for a cold night. There is something about the way things look that tells you of approaching cold—a tightening, a drawing in. Acting on this tip, I had laid a fire in the old drum stove in the garage, a few feet from the car's radiator. Before I went to bed I lit it and threw in another stick of wood. Then I went down to the sheep shed, whose door ordinarily stands open night and day, winter and summer, and kicked the snow away with my boot and closed the door. Then I handed the cow a forkful of straw instead of her usual teaspoonful of sawdust, and also threw some straw down through the hatch to the hog. We didn't open our windows much when we went to bed. (The windows in this house have to be propped up with a window stick, and on nights like this we don't use the window stick; we just take a piece of stove wood and lay it flat on the sill and let the window down on that.)

Morning comes and bed is a vise from which it is almost impossible to get free. Once up, things seem very fine and there are fires to be made all over the house, and the old dog has to be wrapped in a wool throw because of his rheumatism. (He and I have about the same amount of this trouble, but he makes more fuss about it than I do and is always thinking about wool throws.) Then everybody compares notes, each reads the thermometer for himself, and wonders whether the car will start. From the gray waters of the bay the vapor rises. In the old days when the vapor used to rise from the sea people would wink and say: "Farmer Jones is scalding his hog."

The phone jingles. It's the mailman. He can't start his car. I'm to pick him up if my car will start and carry him to the town line. The phone rings again (cold weather stirs up the telephone). It's Mrs. Dow. I am to pick her up on my way back from the store because it's most too cold to walk it this morning. Thanks to my all-night fire in the drum stove my car starts easily, third time over. The garage is still comfortably warm from the night before and there are embers in the stove.

The question of clothes becomes a topic for everybody. The small boy, who has relied thus far on a hunting cap with flaps down, digs up an old stocking cap as midwinter gear. I exhume my Army underdrawers, saved from the little war of 1918. The snow squeaks under the rubber tread of the boot, and the windows of the car frost up immediately. The geese, emerging from their hole in the barn, trample a yard for themselves in the deep drift. They complain loudly about a frozen water pan, and their cornmeal mash is golden-yellow against the blue snow.

The mailman is full of charitable explanations about his car—he thinks it was sediment in the carburetor. The general cheerfulness is in part surprise at discovering that it is entirely possible to exist in conditions that would appear, offhand, to be fatal. The cold hasn't a chance really against our club, against our walls, our wool, the blaze in the stove, the clever mitten, the harsh sock, the sound of kindling, the hot drink, the bright shirt that matches the bright cap. A truck driver, through the slit in his frosted windshield, grins at me and I grin back through the slit in mine. This interchange, translated means: "Some cold, Bud, but nothing but what your buggy and my buggy can handle." Word gets round that the school bus won't start. Children wait, chilly but busy, along the route, testing surfaces for skis and runners, some of them waiting indoors and peering out the windows. A truckman has to go down and tow the bus to get it started. Scholars will be tardy today. This makes *them* cheerful. It is a fine thing to be late for school all together in one vast company of mass delinquency, with plenty of support and a cold bus for alibi.

If a man were in any doubt as to whether it is a cold day or not there is one way he can always tell. On a really cold day the wooden handle of a pitchfork is as cold as a pinchbar. And when he picks up a scrubbing brush to clean out a water pail the brush has turned to stone. I don't know any object much colder than a frozen brush.

SHADOW OF THE FUTURE

To a random reader of this book it should be evident that E. B. White's world is not restricted by the boundaries traditionally assigned to the old-fashioned genre of the personal essay: his intimate pictures of himself, selected others, the books he has read, and the places he has inhabited. Beyond the circle of White's immediate concerns looms the whole world. For all his efforts to build himself a private Walden, he has never succeeded in escaping from the public utopia of man the architect. If the natural world, as White sees it, is sometimes frightening, the synthetic world of *Homo faber* can be infinitely frightful. The unexpected fall of an old tree is not so awesome as the calculated fallout from a new bomb. When White reflects on the passing of the railroads, the denaturing of good food, or the defeat of the old kitchen stove by an arsenal of electronic gadgets, he may heave a nostalgic sigh and raise impudent questions about the meaning of scientific progress. But when he considers how we quietly commit race suicide by slow poison as we noisily threaten to obliterate the planet in

a sudden flash, the cool urbanity of the personal essayist sometimes gives way to the mordant irony of the satirist.

White does not offer us the standard caricature of the
literary man standing on the high brow of his own culture taunting
the Philistines in the dismal swamps of Science and Technology.
He is unhappy about a world in which the prophets of many
secular faiths are equally indifferent to the menace of the bomb
and the miracle of the egg. He "would feel more optimistic about
a bright future for man if [man] spent less time proving that he
can outwit Nature and more time tasting her sweetness and re-
specting her seniority." White does not always prophesy disaster;
he has never forsaken the dream of one world, with its sovereign
walls demolished, in which supranationalism would be the only
natural political creed. ("Before you can be an internationalist
you have first to be a naturalist and feel the ground under you
making a whole circle.") He believes simply that better living is
more likely to come about through human brotherhood than
through chemistry.

Of the three selections in the following group, the first
two antedate the horror of the bomb. "The Supremacy of Uruguay"
is a parable predicting disaster in an old-fashioned world; a
world ignorant of atomic fission but already expert in the politics
of nationalism and the science of capturing man's eardrums and
destroying his sanity with noise. "The Door" is a fantasy that
portrays a civilization in which the genius of modern man, having
succeeded in driving rats crazy in the laboratory, is triumphantly
maddening his own kind in the maze of the metropolis. "Sootfall and Fallout" (written before the test ban of 1963) begins as
a pleasant idyll of city life and ends as an earnest discourse on
the menace of dusty death.

NOVEMBER 25, 1933

THE SUPREMACY OF URUGUAY

Fifteen years after the peace had been made at Versailles,
Uruguay came into possession of a very fine military secret. It
was an invention, in effect so simple, in construction so cheap,
that there was not the slightest doubt that it would enable

From *Quo Vadimus?*

Uruguay to subdue any or all of the other nations of the earth. Naturally the two or three statesmen who knew about it saw visions of aggrandizement; and although there was nothing in history to indicate that a large country was any happier than a small one, they were very anxious to get going.

The inventor of the device was a Montevideo hotel clerk named Martín Casablanca. He had got the idea for the thing during the 1933 mayoralty campaign in New York City, where he was attending a hotel men's convention. One November evening, shortly before election, he was wandering in the Broadway district and came upon a street rally. A platform had been erected on the marquee of one of the theatres, and in an interval between speeches a cold young man in an overcoat was singing into a microphone. "Thanks," he crooned, "for all the lovely dee-light I found in your embrace . . ." The inflection of the love words was that of a murmurous voice, but the volume of the amplified sound was enormous; it carried for blocks, deep into the ranks of the electorate. The Uruguayan paused. He was not unfamiliar with the delight of a lovely embrace, but in his experience it had been pitched lower—more intimate, concentrated. This sprawling, public sound had a curious effect on him. "And thanks for unforgettable nights I never can replace . . ." People swayed against him. In the so bright corner in the too crowded press of bodies, the dominant and searching booming of the love singer struck sharp into him and he became for a few seconds, as he later realized, a loony man. The faces, the mask-faces, the chill air, the advertising lights, the steam rising from the jumbo cup of A. & P. Coffee high over Forty-seventh Street, these added to his enchantment and his unbalance. At any rate, when he left and walked away from Times Square and the great slimy sounds of the love embrace, this was the thought that was in his head:

> If it unhinged me to hear such a soft crooning sound slightly amplified, what might it not do to me to hear a far greater sound greatlier amplified?

Mr. Casablanca stopped. "Good Christ!" he whispered to himself; and his own whisper frightened him, as though it, too, had been amplified.

Chucking his convention, he sailed for Uruguay the following afternoon. Ten months later he had perfected and turned over to his government a war machine unique in military history—a radio-controlled plane carrying an electric phonograph with a retractable streamlined horn. Casablanca had got hold of Uruguay's loudest tenor, and had recorded the bar of music he had heard in Times Square. "Thanks," screamed the tenor, "for unforgettable nights I never can replace . . ." Casablanca prepared to step it up a hundred and fifty thousand times, and grooved the record so it would repeat the phrase endlessly. His theory was that a squadron of pilotless planes scattering this unendurable sound over foreign territories would immediately reduce the populace to insanity. Then Uruguay, at her leisure, could send in her armies, subdue the idiots, and annex the land. It was a most engaging prospect.

The world at this time was drifting rapidly into a nationalistic phase. The incredible cancers of the World War had been forgotten, armaments were being rebuilt, hate and fear sat in every citadel. The Geneva gesture had been prolonged, but only by dint of removing the seat of disarmament to a walled city on a neutral island and quartering the delegates in the waiting destroyers of their respective countries. The Congress of the United States had appropriated another hundred million dollars for her naval program; Germany had expelled the Jews and recast the steel of her helmets in a firmer mold; and the world was re-living the 1914 prologue. Uruguay waited till she thought the moment was at hand, and then struck. Over the slumbrous hemispheres by night sped swift gleaming planes, and there fell upon all the world, except Uruguay, a sound the equal of which had never been heard before on land or sea.

The effect was as Casablanca had predicted. In forty-eight hours the peoples were hopelessly mad, ravaged by an ineradicable noise, ears shattered, minds unseated. No defence had been possible because the minute anyone came within range of the sound, he lost his sanity and, being daft, proved ineffectual in a military way. After the planes had passed over, life went on much as before, except that it was more secure, sanity being gone. No one could hear anything except the noise in his own head. At the actual moment when people had been smitten with the noise, there had been, of course, some rather amusing incidents. A lady in West Philadelphia happened to be talking to her butcher on the phone. "Thanks," she had just said, "for taking back that tough steak yesterday. And thanks," she added, as the plane passed over, "for unforgettable nights I never can replace." Linotype operators in composing-rooms chopped off in the middle of sentences, like the one who was setting a story about an admiral in San Pedro:

> I am tremendously grateful to all the ladies of San Pedro for the wonderful hospitality they have shown the men of the fleet during our recent maneuvers and thanks for unforgettable nights I never can replace and thanks for unforgettable nights I nev-

To all appearances Uruguay's conquest of the earth was complete. There remained, of course, the formal occupation by her armed forces. That her troops, being in possession of all their faculties, could establish her supremacy among idiots, she never for a moment doubted. She assumed that with nothing but lunacy to combat, the occupation would be mildly stimulating and enjoyable. She supposed her crazy foes would do a few rather funny, picturesque things with their battleships and their tanks, and then surrender. What she failed to anticipate was that her foes, being mad, had no intention of making war at all. The occupation proved bloodless and singularly unimpressive. A detachment of her troops landed in New York, for example, and took up quarters in the RKO Building, which was fairly empty at the time; and they were no more conspicuous around town than the Knights of Pythias. One of her battleships steamed for

England, and the commanding officer grew so enraged when no hostile ship came out to engage him that he sent a wireless (which of course nobody in England heard): "Come on out, you yellow-bellied rats!"

It was the same story everywhere. Uruguay's supremacy was never challenged by her silly subjects, and she was very little noticed. Territorially her conquest was magnificent; politically it was a fiasco. The peoples of the world paid slight attention to the Uruguayans, and the Uruguayans, for their part, were bored by many of their territorials—in particular by the Lithuanians, whom they couldn't stand. Everywhere crazy people lived happily as children, in their heads the old refrain: "And thanks for unforgettable nights . . ." Billions dwelt contentedly in a fool's paradise. The earth was bountiful and there was peace and plenty. Uruguay gazed at her vast domain and saw the whole incident lacked authenticity.

It wasn't till years later, when the descendants of some early American idiots grew up and regained their senses, that there was a wholesale return of sanity to the world, land and sea forces were restored to fighting strength, and the avenging struggle was begun that eventually involved all the races of the earth, crushed Uruguay, and destroyed mankind without a trace.

MARCH 25, 1939

THE DOOR

Everything (he kept saying) is something it isn't. And everybody is always somewhere else. Maybe it was the city, being in the city, that made him feel how queer everything was and that it was something else. Maybe (he kept thinking) it was the names of the things. The names were tex and frequently koid. Or they were flex and oid or they were duroid (sani) or flexsan (duro), but everything was glass (but not quite glass) and the

From *The Second Tree from the Corner.*

thing that you touched (the surface, washable, crease-resistant) was rubber, only it wasn't quite rubber and you didn't quite touch it but almost. The wall, which was glass but thrutex, turned out on being approached not to be a wall, it was something else, it was an opening or doorway—and the doorway (through which he saw himself approaching) turned out to be something else, it was a wall. And what he had eaten not having agreed with him.

He was in a washable house, but he wasn't sure. Now about those rats, he kept saying to himself. He meant the rats that the Professor had driven crazy by forcing them to deal with problems which were beyond the scope of rats, the insoluble problems. He meant the rats that had been trained to jump at the square card with the circle in the middle, and the card (because it was something it wasn't) would give way and let the rat into a place where the food was, but then one day it would be a trick played on the rat, and the card would be changed, and the rat would jump but the card wouldn't give way, and it was an impossible situation (for a rat) and the rat would go insane and into its eyes would come the unspeakably bright imploring look of the frustrated, and after the convulsions were over and the frantic racing around, then the passive stage would set in and the willingness to let anything be done to it, even if it was something else.

He didn't know which door (or wall) or opening in the house to jump at, to get through, because one was an opening that wasn't a door (it was a void, or koid) and the other was a wall that wasn't an opening, it was a sanitary cupboard of the same color. He caught a glimpse of his eyes staring into his eyes, in the thrutex, and in them was the expression he had seen in the picture of the rats—weary after convulsions and the frantic racing around, when they were willing and did not mind having anything done to them. More and more (he kept saying) I am confronted by a problem which is incapable of solution (for this time even if he chose the right door, there would be no food behind it) and that is what madness is, and things seeming different from what they are. He heard, in the house where he was, in the city to which he had gone (as toward a door which might, or might not, give way), a noise—not a loud noise but more of a low prefabricated humming. It came from a place in the base of the wall (or stat) where the flue carrying the filterable air was, and not far from the Minipiano, which was made of the same material nailbrushes are made of, and which was under the stairs. "This, too, has been tested," she said, pointing, but not at it, "and found viable." It wasn't a loud noise, he kept thinking, sorry that he had seen his eyes, even though it was through his own eyes that he had seen them.

First will come the convulsions (he said), then the exhaustion, then the willingness to let anything be done. "And you better believe it *will* be."

All his life he had been confronted by situations that were incapable of being solved, and there was a deliberateness behind all this, behind this changing of the card (or door), because they would always wait till you had learned to jump at the certain card (or door)—the one with the circle—and then they would change it on you. There have been so many doors changed on me, he said, in the last twenty years, but it is now becoming clear that it is an impossible situation, and the question is whether to jump again, even though they ruffle you in the rump with a blast of air—to make you jump. He wished he wasn't standing by the Minipiano. First they would teach you the prayers and the Psalms, and that would be the right door (the one with the circle), and the long sweet words with the holy sound, and that would be the one to jump at to get where the food was. Then one day you jumped and it didn't give way, so that all you got was the bump on the nose, and the first bewilderment, the first young bewilderment.

I don't know whether to tell her about the door they substituted or not, he said, the one with the equation on it and the picture of the amoeba reproducing itself by division. Or the one with the photostatic copy of the check for thirty-two dollars and fifty cents. But the jumping was so long ago, although the bump is . . . how those old wounds hurt! Being crazy this way wouldn't be so bad if only, if only. If only when you put your foot forward to take a step, the ground wouldn't come up to meet your foot the way it does. And the same way in the street (only I may never get back to the street unless I jump at the right door), the curb coming up to meet your foot, anticipating ever so delicately the weight of the body, which is somewhere else. "We could take your name," she said, "and send it to you." And it wouldn't be so bad if only you could read a sentence all the way through without jumping (your eye) to something else on the same page; and then (he kept thinking) there was that man out in Jersey, the one who started to chop his trees down, one by one, the man who began talking about how he would take his house to pieces, brick by brick, because he faced a problem incapable of solution, probably, so he began to hack at the trees in the yard, began to pluck with trembling fingers at the bricks in the house. Even if a house is not washable, it is worth taking down. It is not till later that the exhaustion sets in.

But it is inevitable that they will keep changing the doors on you, he said, because that is what they are for; and the thing is to get used to it and not let it unsettle the mind. But that would mean not jumping, and you can't. Nobody can not jump. There will be no not-jumping. Among rats, perhaps, but among people never. Everybody has to keep jumping at a door (the one with the circle on it) because that is the way everybody is, specially some people. You wouldn't want me, standing here, to tell you, would you, about my friend the poet (deceased) who said, "My heart has followed all my days something I cannot name"? (It had the circle on it.) And like many poets, although few so beloved, he is gone. It killed him, the jumping. First, of course, there were the preliminary bouts, the convulsions, and the calm and the willingness.

I remember the door with the picture of the girl on it (only it was spring), her arms outstretched in loveliness, her dress (it was the one with the circle on it) uncaught, beginning the slow, clear, blinding cascade—and I guess we would all like to try that door again, for it seemed like the way and for a while

it was the way, the door would open and you would go through
winged and exalted (like any rat) and the food would be there,
the way the Professor had it arranged, everything O.K., and you
had chosen the right door for the world was young. The time
they changed that door on me, my nose bled for a hundred
hours—how do you like that, Madam? Or would you prefer to
show me further through this so strange house, or you could take
my name and send it to me, for although my heart has followed
all my days something I cannot name, I am tired of the jumping
and I do not know which way to go, Madam, and I am not even
sure that I am not tried beyond the endurance of man (rat, if
you will) and have taken leave of sanity. What are you following these days, old friend, after your recovery from the last
bump? What is the name, or is it something you cannot name?
The rats have a name for it by this time, perhaps, but I don't
know what they call it. I call it plexikoid and it comes in sheets,
something like insulating board, unattainable and ugli-proof.

And there was the man out in Jersey, because I keep
thinking about his terrible necessity and the passion and trouble
he had gone to all those years in the indescribable abundance of
a householder's detail, building the estate and the planting of the
trees and in spring the lawn-dressing and in fall the bulbs for the
spring burgeoning, and the watering of the grass on the long
light evenings in summer and the gravel for the driveway (all
had to be thought out, planned) and the decorative borders,
probably, the perennials and the bug spray, and the building of
the house from plans of the architect, first the sills, then the
studs, then the full corn in the ear, the floors laid on the floor
timbers, smoothed, and then the carpets upon the smooth floors
and the curtains and the rods therefor. And then, almost without warning, he would be jumping at the same old door and it
wouldn't give: they had changed it on him, making life no
longer supportable under the elms in the elm shade, under the
maples in the maple shade.

"Here you have the maximum of openness in a small
room."

It was impossible to say (maybe it was the city) what

made him feel the way he did, and I am not the only one either, he kept thinking—ask any doctor if I am. The doctors, they know how many there are, they even know where the trouble is only they don't like to tell you about the prefrontal lobe because that means making a hole in your skull and removing the work of centuries. It took so long coming, this lobe, so many, many years. (Is it something you read in the paper, perhaps?) And now, the strain being so great, the door having been changed by the Professor once too often . . . but it only means a whiff of ether, a few deft strokes, and the higher animal becomes a little easier in his mind and more like the lower one. From now on, you see, that's the way it will be, the ones with the small prefrontal lobes will win because the other ones are hurt too much by this incessant bumping. They can stand just so much, eh, Doctor? (And what is that, pray, that you have in your hand?) Still, you never can tell, eh, Madam?

He crossed (carefully) the room, the thick carpet under him softly, and went toward the door carefully, which was glass and he could see himself in it, and which, at his approach, opened to allow him to pass through; and beyond he half expected to find one of the old doors that he had known, perhaps the one with the circle, the one with the girl her arms outstretched in loveliness and beauty before him. But he saw instead a moving stairway, and descended in light (he kept thinking) to the street below and to the other people. As he stepped off, the ground came up slightly, to meet his foot.

NOVEMBER 3, 1956

SOOTFALL AND FALLOUT

Turtle Bay, October 18, 1956

This is a dark morning in the apartment, but the block is gay with yellow moving vans disgorging Mary Martin's belongings in front of a house a couple of doors east of here, into which

A "Letter from the East" in *The Points of My Compass*.

(I should say from the looks of things) she is moving. People's lives are so exposed at moments like this, their possessions lying naked in the street, the light of day searching out every bruise and mark of indoor living. It is an unfair exposé—end tables with nothing to be at the end of, standing lamps with their cords tied up in curlers, bottles of vermouth craning their long necks from cartons of personal papers, and every wastebasket carrying its small cargo of miscellany. The vans cause a stir in the block. Heads appear in the windows of No. 230, across the way. Passers-by stop on the sidewalk and stare brazenly into the new home through the open door. I have a mezzanine seat for the performance; like a Peeping Tom, I lounge here in my bathrobe and look down, held in the embrace of a common cold, before which scientists stand in awe although they have managed to split the atom, infect the topsoil with strontium 90, break the barrier of sound, and build the Lincoln Tunnel.

What a tremendous lot of stuff makes up the cumulus called "the home"! The trivet, the tiny washboard, the fire tools, the big copper caldron large enough to scald a hog in, the metal filing cabinets, the cardboard filing cabinets, the record player, the glass and the china invisible in their barrels, the carpet sweeper. (I wonder whether Miss Martin knows that she owns an old-fashioned carpet sweeper in a modern shade of green.) And here comes a bright little hacksaw, probably the apple of Mr. Halliday's eye. When a writing desk appears, the movers take the drawers out, to lighten the load, and I am free to observe what a tangle Mary Martin's stationery and supplies are in—like my wife's, everything at sixes and sevens. And now the bed, under the open sky above Forty-eighth Street. And now the mattress. A wave of decency overtakes me. I avert my gaze.

The movers experience the worst trouble with two large house plants, six-footers, in their great jars. The jars, on being sounded, prove to be a third full of water and have to be emptied into the gutter. Living things are always harder to lift, somehow, than inanimate objects, and I think any mover would rather walk up three flights with a heavy bureau than go into a waltz with a rubber plant. There is really no way for a man to put his arms around a big house plant and still remain a gentleman.

Out in back, away from the street, the prospect is more pleasing. The yellow cat mounts the wisteria vine and tries to enter my bedroom, stirred by dreams of a bullfinch in a cage. The air is hazy, smoke and fumes being pressed downward in what the smog reporter of the *Times* calls "a wigwam effect." I don't know what new gadget the factories of Long Island are making today to produce such a foul vapor—probably a new jet applicator for the relief of nasal congestion. But whatever it is, I would swap it for a breath of fresh air. On every slight stirring of the breeze, the willow behind Mary Martin's wigwam lets drop two or three stylish yellow leaves, and they swim lazily down like golden fish to where Paul, the handyman, waits with his broom. In the ivy border along the wall, watchful of the cat, three thrushes hunt about among the dry leaves. I can't pronounce "three thrushes," but I can see three thrushes from this window, and this is the first autumn I have ever seen three at once. An October miracle. I think they are hermits, but the visibility is so poor I can't be sure.

This section of Manhattan boasts the heaviest sootfall in town, and the United States of America boasts the heaviest fallout in the world, and when you take the sootfall and the fallout and bring smog in on top of them, I feel I am in a perfect position to discuss the problem of universal pollution. The papers, of course, are full of the subject these days, as they follow the Presidential campaigners around the nation from one contaminated area to another.

I have no recent figures on sootfall in the vicinity of Third Avenue, but the *Times* last Saturday published some figures on fallout from Dr. Willard F. Libby, who said the reservoir of radioactive materials now floating in the stratosphere from the tests of all nations was roughly twenty-four billion tons. That was Saturday. Sunday's *Times* quoted Dr. Laurence H. Snyder as saying, "In assessing the potential harm [of weapons-testing], statements are always qualified by a phrase such as 'if the testing of weapons continues at the present rate . . .' This qualification is usually obsolete by the time the statement is printed." I have an idea the figure twenty-four billion tons may have been obsolete when it appeared in the paper. It may not have included, for instance, the radioactive stuff from the bomb the British set off in Australia a week or two ago. Maybe it did, maybe it didn't. The point of Dr. Snyder's remark is clear. A thermonuclear arms race is, as he puts it, self-accelerating. Bomb begets bomb. A begets H. Anything you can build, I can build bigger.

"Unhappily," said Governor Harriman the other night, "we are still thinking in small, conventional terms, and with unwarranted complacency."

The habit of thinking in small, conventional terms is, of course, not limited to us Americans. You could drop a leaflet or a Hubbard squash on the head of any person in any land and you would almost certainly hit a brain that was whirling in small, conventional circles. There is something about the human mind that keeps it well within the confines of the parish, and only one outlook in a million is nonparochial. The impression one gets from campaign oratory is that the sun revolves around the earth, the earth revolves around the United States, and the United States revolves around whichever city the speaker happens to be in at the moment. This is what a friend of mine used to call the Un-Copernican system. During a Presidential race, candidates sometimes manage to create the impression that their thoughts are ranging widely and that they have abandoned conventional thinking. I love to listen to them when they are in the throes of these quadrennial seizures. But I haven't heard much from either candidate that sounded unconventional—although I have heard some things that sounded sensible and sincere. A candidate could easily commit political suicide if he were to come up with an unconventional thought during a Presidential tour.

I think Man's gradual, creeping contamination of the planet, his sending up of dust into the air, his strontium additive in our bones, his discharge of industrial poisons into rivers that once flowed clear, his mixing of chemicals with fog on the east wind add up to a fantasy of such grotesque proportions as to make everything said on the subject seem pale and anemic by contrast. I hold one share in the corporate earth and am uneasy about the management. Dr. Libby said there is new evidence that the amount of strontium reaching the body from topsoil impregnated by fallout is "considerably less than the seventy per cent of the topsoil concentration originally estimated." Perhaps we should all feel elated at this, but I don't. The correct amount of strontium with which to impregnate the topsoil is *no* strontium. To rely on "tolerances" when you get into the matter of strontium 90, with three sovereign bomb testers already testing, independently of one another, and about fifty potential bomb testers ready to enter the stratosphere with their contraptions, is to talk with unwarranted complacency. I belong to a small, unconventional school that believes that *no* rat poison is the correct amount to spread in the kitchen where children and puppies can get at it. I believe that *no* chemical waste is the correct amount to discharge into the fresh rivers of the world, and I believe that if there is a way to trap the fumes from factory chimneys, it should be against the law to set these deadly fumes adrift where they can mingle with fog and, given the right conditions, suddenly turn an area into another Donora, Pa.

"I have seen the smoky fury of our factories—rising to the skies," said President Eisenhower pridefully as he addressed the people of Seattle last night. Well, I can see the smoky fury of our factories drifting right into this room this very minute; the fury sits in my throat like a bundle of needles, it explores my nose, chokes off my breath, and makes my eyes burn. The room smells like a slaughterhouse. And the phenomenon gets a brief mention in the morning press.

One simple, unrefuted fact about radioactive substances is that scientists do not agree about the "safe" amount. All radiation is harmful, all of it shortens life, all is cumulative, nobody keeps track of how much he gets in the form of X-rays and radiotherapy, and all of it affects not only the recipient but his heirs.

Both President Eisenhower and Governor Stevenson have discussed H-bomb testing and the thermonuclear scene, and their views differ. Neither of them, it seems to me, has quite told the changing facts of life on earth. Both tend to speak of national security as though it were still capable of being dissociated from universal well-being; in fact, sometimes in these political addresses it sounds as though this nation, or any nation, through force of character or force of arms, could damn well rise *above* planetary considerations, as though we were greater than our environment, as though the national verve somehow transcended the natural world.

"Strong we shall stay free," said President Eisenhower in Pittsburgh. And Governor Stevenson echoed the statement in Chicago: ". . . only the strong can be free."

This doctrine of freedom through strength deserves a second look. It would have served nicely in 1936, but nobody thought of it then. Today, with the H-bomb deterring war, we are free and we are militarily strong, but the doctrine is subject to a queer, embarrassing amendment. Today it reads, "Strong we shall stay free, *provided we do not have to use our strength.*" That's not quite the same thing. What was true in 1936, if not actually false today, is at best a mere partial, or half, truth. A nation wearing atomic armor is like a knight whose armor has grown so heavy he is immobilized; he can hardly walk, hardly sit his horse, hardly think, hardly breathe. The H-bomb is an extremely effective deterrent to war, but it has little virtue as a *weapon* of war, because it would leave the world uninhabitable.

For a short while following the release of atomic energy, a strong nation was a secure nation. Today, no nation, whatever its thermonuclear power, is a strong nation in the sense that it is a fully independent nation. All are weak, and all are weak from the same cause: each depends on the others for salvation, yet none likes to admit this dependence, and there is no machinery for interdependence. The big nations are weak because the strength has gone out of their arms—which are too terrifying to use, too poisonous to explode. The little nations are weak because they have always been relatively weak and now they have to breathe the same bad air as the big ones. Ours is a balance, as Mr. Stevenson put it, not of power but of terror. If anything, the H-bomb rather favors small nations that don't as yet possess it; they feel slightly more free to jostle other nations, having discovered that a country can stick its tongue out quite far these days without provoking war, so horrible are war's consequences.

The atom, then, is a proper oddity. It has qualified the meaning of national security, it has very likely saved us from a third world war, it has given a new twist to the meaning of power, and it has already entered our bones with a cancer-producing isotope. Furthermore, it has altered the concept of personal sacrifice for moral principle. Human beings have always been willing to shed their blood for what they believe in. Yesterday this was clear and simple; we would pay in blood because, after the price was exacted, there was still a chance to make good the gain. But the modern price tag is not blood. Today our leaders and the leaders of other nations are, in effect, saying, "We will defend our beliefs not alone with our blood—by God, we'll defend them, if we have to, with our genes." This is bold, resolute talk, and one can't help admiring the spirit of it. I admire the spirit of it, but the logic of it eludes me. I doubt whether any noble principle—or any ignoble principle, either, for that matter—can be preserved at the price of genetic disintegration.

The thing I watch for in the speeches of the candidates is some hint that the thermonuclear arms race may be bringing people nearer together, rather than forcing them farther apart. I suspect that because of fallout we may achieve a sort of universality sooner than we bargained for. Fallout may compel us to fall in. The magic-carpet ride on the mushroom cloud has left us dazed—we have come so far so fast. There is a passage in Anne Lindbergh's book *North to the Orient* that captures the curious lag between the mind and the body during a plane journey, between the slow unfolding of remembered images and the swift blur of modern flight. Mrs. Lindbergh started her flight to the

Orient by way of North Haven, her childhood summer home. "The trip to Maine," she wrote, "used to be a long and slow one. There was plenty of time in the night, spattered away in the sleeper, in the morning spent ferrying across the river at Bath, in the afternoon syncopated into a series of calls on one coast town after another—there was plenty of time to make the mental change coinciding with our physical change. . . . But on this swift flight to North Haven in the *Sirius* my mind was so far behind my body that when we flew over Rockland Harbor the familiar landmarks below me had no reality."

Like the girl in the plane, we have arrived, but the familiar scene lacks reality. We cling to old remembered forms, old definitions, old comfortable conceptions of national coziness, national self-sufficiency. The Security Council meets solemnly and takes up Suez, eleven sovereign fellows kicking a sovereign ditch around while England threatens war to defend her "life-lines," when modern war itself means universal contamination, universal deathlines, and the end of ditches. I would feel more hopeful, more *secure,* if the Councilmen suddenly changed their tune and began arguing the case for mud turtles and other ancient denizens of ponds and ditches. That is the thing at stake now, and it is what will finally open the Canal to the world's ships in perfect concord.

Candidates for political office steer clear of what Mrs. Luce used to call "globaloney," for fear they may lose the entire American Legion vote and pick up only Norman Cousins. Yet there are indications that supranational ideas are alive in the back of a few men's minds. Through the tangle of verbiage, the idea of "common cause" skitters like a shy bird. Mr. Dulles uses the word "interdependent" in one sentence, then returns promptly to the more customary, safer word "independent." We give aid to Yugoslavia to assure her "independence," and the very fact of the gift is proof that neither donor nor recipient enjoys absolute independence any more; the two are locked in mortal *inter*-dependence. Mr. Tito says he is for "new forms and new laws." I haven't the vaguest notion of what he means by that, and I doubt whether he has, either. Certainly there are no *old* laws, if by "laws" he means enforceable rules of conduct by which the world community is governed. But I'm for new forms, all right. Governor Stevenson, in one of his talks, said, "Nations have become so accustomed to living in the dark that they find it hard to learn to live in the light." What light? The light of government? If so, why not say so? President Eisenhower ended a speech the other day with the phrase "a peace of justice in a world of law." Everything else in his speech dealt with a peace of justice in a world of anarchy.

The riddle of disarmament, the riddle of peace, seems to me to hang on the interpretation of these conflicting and contradictory phrases—and on whether or not the men who use them really mean business. Are we independent or interdependent? We can't possibly be both. Do we indeed seek a peace of justice in a world of law, as the President intimates? If so, when do we start, and how? Are we for "new forms," or will the old ones do? In 1945, after the worst blood bath in history, the nations settled immediately back into old forms. In its structure, the United Nations reaffirms everything that caused World War II. At the end of a war fought to defeat dictators, the U.N. welcomed Stalin and Péron to full membership, and the Iron Curtain quickly descended to put the seal of authority on this inconsistent act. The drafters of the Charter assembled in San Francisco and defended their mild, inadequate format with the catchy phrase "Diplomacy is the art of the possible." Meanwhile, a little band of physicists met in a squash court and said, "The hell with the art of the possible. Watch this!"

The world organization debates disarmament in one room and, in the next room, moves the knights and pawns that make national arms imperative. This is not justice and law, and this is not light. It is not new forms. The U.N. is modern in intent, old-fashioned in shape. In San Francisco in 1945, the victor nations failed to create a constitution that placed a higher value on principle than on sovereignty, on common cause than on special cause. The world of 1945 was still a hundred percent parochial.

The world of 1956 is still almost a hundred percent parochial. But at last we have a problem that is clearly a community problem, devoid of nationality—the problem of the total pollution of the planet.

We have, in fact, a situation in which the deadliest of all weapons, the H-bomb, together with its little brother, the A-bomb, is the latent source of great agreement among peoples. The bomb is universally hated, and it is universally feared. We cannot escape it with collective security; we shall have to face it with united action. It has given us a few years of grace without war, and now it offers us a few millenniums of oblivion. In a paradox of unbelievable jocundity, the shield of national sovereignty suddenly becomes the challenge of national sovereignty. And, largely because of events beyond our control, we are able to sniff the faint stirring of a community ferment—something every man can enjoy.

The President speaks often of "the peaceful uses of atomic energy," and they are greatly on his mind. I believe the peaceful use of atomic energy that should take precedence over all other uses is this: stop it from contaminating the soil and the sea, the rain and the sky, and the bones of man. That is elementary. It comes ahead of "good-will" ships and it comes ahead of cheap power. What good is cheap power if your child already has an incurable cancer?

The hydrogen-garbage-disposal program unites the people of the earth in a common anti-litterbug drive for salvation. Radioactive dust has no nationality, is not deflected by boundaries; it falls on Turk and Texan impartially. The radio-strontium isotope finds its way into the milk of Soviet cow and English cow with equal ease. This simple fact profoundly alters the political scene and calls for political leaders to echo the physicists and say, "Never mind the art of the possible. Watch this!"

To me, living in the light means an honest attempt to discover the germ of common cause in a world of special cause, even against the almost insuperable odds of parochialism and national fervor, even in the face of the dangers that always attend political growth. Actually, nations are already enjoying little pockets of unity. The European coal-steel authority is apparently a success. The U.N., which is usually impotent in political disputes, has nevertheless managed to elevate the world's children and the world's health to a community level. The trick is to encourage and hasten this magical growth, this benign condition—encourage it and get it on paper, while children still have healthy bones and before we have all reached the point of no return. It will not mean the end of nations; it will mean the true beginning of nations.

Paul-Henri Spaak, addressing himself to the Egyptian government the other day, said, "We are no longer at the time of the absolute sovereignty of states." We are not, and we ought by this time to know we are not. I just hope we learn it in time. In the beautiful phrase of Mrs. Lindbergh's there used to be "plenty of time in the night." Now there is hardly any time at all.

Well, this started out as a letter and has turned into a discourse. But I don't mind. If a candidate were to appear on the scene and come out for the dignity of mud turtles, I suppose people would hesitate to support him, for fear he had lost his reason. But he would have my vote, on the theory that in losing his reason he had kept his head. It is time men allowed their imagination to infect their intellect, time we all rushed headlong into the wilder regions of thought where the earth again revolves around the sun instead of around the Suez, regions where no individual and no group can blithely assume the right to sow the sky with seeds of mischief, and where the sovereign nation at last begins to function as the true friend and guardian of sovereign man.

SONG TRIO

In an essay "How to Tell a Major Poet from a Minor Poet" (*Quo Vadimus?*), E. B. White made the distinction as clear as it often is in academic headnotes: "Serious verse is verse written by a major poet; light verse is verse written by a minor poet. . . ." According to this circular definition, White is unquestionably a minor poet. Much of his output can be identified by the standard hallmarks of light verse: the sparkling wordplay; the smooth precision (or calculated imprecision) of well-oiled (or creaky) meter; the profusion of rhyme—internal and external, mono- and polysyllabic, delightfully apt or intentionally inept; a gamut of tones ranging from airy nonsense to nipping (but seldom biting) irony.

The tide of light verse, which was at the full in the earnest Victorian England of W. S. Gilbert, Lewis Carroll, and Edward Lear, is now at a low ebb. The reason may be, as White suggests in "Some Remarks on Humor," that writers are reluctant to be light or flippant in a world that "decorates its serious artists with laurel, and its wags with Brussels sprouts." Though he has often signed his light verses with only initials, he does not, like some of his comtemporaries, conceal them surreptitiously under a pseudonym. A genre good enough for W. H. Auden, Robert Frost, or T. S. Eliot (or Browning, Byron, or Shakespeare) is good enough for him.

Major or minor, serious or light, whether in prose or in verse, White is a poet. He sees with a poet's eye for compact imagery, reflects with a poet's sensitivity to paradox, and listens with a poet's ear for the music and rhythm of life and language. Though he may not aspire to the fine frenzy that Shakespeare described, he obviously shares with Keats the intuition that the poetry of earth is never dead.

The following "occasional" poems (a more accurate word than "light") suggest both the variety of White's verse and the extent to which his poems are in tune with his prose. In "The Red Cow Is Dead" (no lighter perhaps than Thomas Gray's mock elegy on a favorite cat) the freedom of verse is subtly controlled by the natural use of rhyme (mostly internal) and consonance (udder-adder, snake-sneak). The poem reflects White's awareness of the humorous music of the folk idiom and his familiarity with the perils of the farmyard. "The Tennis" suspends the magic of an autumn afternoon in translucent free verse. With the words rearranged to carry a less persistent rhythm, the poem might become (like "The Day of Days" or "The Cities" or "Trance") a piece of "poetic" prose. The third poem is a free-wheeling tour de force in which the poet takes full advantage of the light versifier's license—reveling in short lines and long lines, on-rhymes and off-rhymes, doggerel and birderel. Far from hiding under a nom de plume, he identifies himself as a gay, though gaunt, bird named E. B. White. Yet behind this happy ornithological nonsense lurks uncommon sense. He incorporates here an indirect parody of more earnest poems on skylarks and nightingales and a sympathetic ridicule of a familiar joker in White's pack—the expert who strives in vain to simplify the mysterious processes of nature.

JUNE 1, 1946

THE RED COW IS DEAD

ISLE OF WIGHT (AP)—Sir Hanson Rowbotham's favorite Red Polled cow is dead. Grazing in the lush pastures of the Wellow Farm, she was bitten on the udder by an adder.— *The Herald Tribune.*

Toll the bell, fellow,
This is a sad day at Wellow:
Sir Hanson's cow is dead,
His red cow,
Bitten on the udder by an adder.

Spread the bad news! What is more sudden,
What sadder than udder stung by adder?
He's never been madder, Sir Hanson Rowbotham.

The Red Polled cow is dead.
The grass was lush at very last,
And the snake (a low sneak)
Passed, hissed,
Struck.

Now a shadow goes across the meadow,
Wellow lies fallow.

From *The Second Tree from the Corner.*

The red cow is dead, and the stories go round.
"Bit in the teat by a dog in a fit."
"A serpent took Sir Hanson's cow—
A terrible loss, a king's ransom."

A blight has hit Wight:
The lush grass, the forked lash, the quick gash
Of adder, torn bleeding udder,
The cow laid low,
The polled cow dead, the bell not yet tolled
(A sad day at Wellow),
Sir Hanson's cow,
Never again to freshen, never again
Bellow with passion—
A ruminant in death's covenant,
Smitten, bitten, gone.
Toll the bell, young fellow!

OCTOBER 6, 1956

THE TENNIS

Circled by trees, ringed with the faded folding chairs,
The court awaits the finalists on this September day,
A peaceful level patch, a small precise green pool
In a chrysanthemum wood, where the air smells of grapes.
Someone has brought a table for the silver cup.
Someone has swept the tapes. The net is low;
Racket is placed on racket for the stretch.
Dogs are the first arrivals, loving society,
To roll and wrestle on the sidelines through the match.
Children arrive on bicycles. Cars drift and die, murmuring.
Doors crunch. The languorous happy people stroll and wave,
Slowly arrange themselves and greet the players.

From *The New Yorker*.

Here, in this unpretentious glade, everyone knows everyone.
And now the play. The ball utters its pugging sound:
Pug pug, pug pug—commas in the long sentence
Of the summer's end, slowing the syntax of the dying year.
Love—thirty. Fifteen—thirty. Fault.
The umpire sits his highchair like a solemn babe.
Voices are low—the children have been briefed on etiquette;
They do not call and shout. Even the dogs know where to stop,
And all is mannerly and well behaved, a sweet, still day.
What is the power of this bland American scene
To claim, as it does, the heart? What is this sudden
Access of love for the rich overcast of fall?
Is it the remembered Saturdays of "no school"—
All those old Saturdays of freedom and reprieve?
It strikes as quickly at the heart as when the contemptuous jay
Slashes the silence with his jagged cry.

JULY 4, 1959

A LISTENER'S GUIDE TO THE BIRDS

(After a binge with Roger Tory Peterson in his famous guide
book)

Wouldst know the lark?
Then hark!
Each natural bird
Must be seen *and* heard.
The lark's "Tee-ee" is a tinkling entreaty,
But it's not always "Tee-ee"—
Sometimes it's "Tee-titi."
  So watch yourself.

Birds have their love-and-mating song,
Their warning cry, their hating song;

From *The New Yorker.*

Some have a night song, some a day song,
A lilt, a tilt, a come-what-may song;
Birds have their careless bough and teeter song
And, of course, their Roger Tory Peter song.

The studious oven-bird (pale pinkish legs)
Calls, "Teacher, teacher, teacher!"
The chestnut-sided warbler begs
To see Miss Beecher.
   "I wish to see Miss Beecher."
(Sometimes interpreted as "Please please please ta meetcha.")

The red-wing (frequents swamps and marshes)
Gurgles, "Konk-la-reeee,"
Eliciting from the wood duck
The exclamation "Jeeee!"
   (But that's the *male* wood duck, remember.
   If it's his wife you seek,
   Wait till you hear a distressed "Whoo-eek!")

Nothing is simpler than telling a barn owl from a veery:
One says, "Kschh!" in a voice that is eerie,
The other says, "Vee-ur," in a manner that is breezy.
   (I told you it was easy.)
On the other hand, distinguishing between the veery
And the olive-backed thrush
Is another matter. It couldn't be worse.
The thrush's song is similar to the veery's,
Only it's in reverse.

Let us suppose you hear a bird say, "Fitz-bew,"
The things you can be sure of are two:
First, the bird is an alder flycatcher (*Empidonax traillii traillii*);
Second, you are standing in Ohio—or, as some people call it,
      O-hee-o—
Because, although it may come as a surprise to you,

The alder flycatcher, in New York or New England, does not
    say, "Fitz-bew,"
It says, "Wee-bé-o."

"Chu-chu-chu" is the note of the harrier,
Copied, of course from our common carrier.
The osprey, thanks to a lucky fluke,
Avoids "Chu-chu" and cries, "Chewk, chewk!"
    So there's no difficulty there.

The chickadee likes to pronounce his name;
It's extremely helpful and adds to his fame.
But in spring you can get the heebie-jeebies
Untangling chickadees from phoebes.
The chickadee, when he's all afire,
Whistles, "Fee-bee," to express desire.
He should be arrested and thrown in jail
For impersonating another male.
    (There's a way you can tell which bird is which,
    But just the same, it's a nasty switch.)
Our gay deceiver may fancy-free be
But he never does fool a female phoebe.

Oh, sweet the random sounds of birds!
The old squaw, practicing his thirds;
The distant bittern, driving stakes,
The lonely loon on haunted lakes;
The white-throat's pure and tenuous thread—
They go to my heart, they go to my head.
How hard it is to find the words
With which to sing the praise of birds!
Yet birds, when *they* get singing praises,
Don't lack for words—they know some daisies:
    "Fitz-bew,"
    "Konk-la-reeee,"
    "Hip-three-cheers,"

"Onk-a-lik, ow-owdle-ow,"
"Cheedle cheedle chew,"
And dozens of other inspired phrases.

—E. B. WHITE (gray cheeks, inconspicuous eye-ring;
frequents bars and glades)

EPILOGUE

Each of the closing selections in this book is full of the spirit of a particular locale—a lake in Maine, the winter quarters of a circus in Florida. But each is distinguished from the other pictures of habitats by White's persistent emphasis on the mystery of time. At the lake of his childhood the time is always August. During the shining ten minutes of a circus girl's ride the time is the eternity of youth.

A writer may, like any ordinary pedestrian, view time as flowing in a straight line from yesterday to today to tomorrow, each tick of the clock signaling inexorable change. Or he may see it as a circle on which change cannot plot a point of no return. On such a map the writer can return to yesterday and find it still unchanged. He can suspend time in the amber of his imagination. He can treat both time and change as phantoms. In such a world, the practical man—with his neurotic concern for making time, or saving time, or losing time, or cutting down on time—becomes the foolish dreamer.

In these two essays White never completely loses himself in the magic circle. Something has changed at the lake—something more profound than the noise of the motor boats; the final sentence is eloquent proof of that. Even in Florida, the fountain of youth is a mirage. As White noted later in a postscript, "Time has not stood still for anybody but the dead, and even the dead must be able to hear the acceleration of little sports cars and know that things have changed." But his willing reader resists disenchantment. By performing sleight of hand tricks with the calendar and the clock, White wrote two of his most haunting essays—combining the accurate observation of the reporter with the rare insight of the poet.

AUGUST   1941

ONCE MORE TO THE LAKE

One summer, along about 1904, my father rented a camp on a lake in Maine and took us all there for the month of August. We all got ringworm from some kittens and had to rub Pond's Extract on our arms and legs night and morning, and my father rolled over in a canoe with all his clothes on; but outside of that the vacation was a success and from then on none of us ever thought there was any place in the world like that lake in Maine. We returned summer after summer—always on August 1st for one month. I have since become a salt-water man, but sometimes in summer there are days when the restlessness of the tides and the fearful cold of the sea water and the incessant wind that blows across the afternoon and into the evening make me wish for the placidity of a lake in the woods. A few weeks ago this feeling got so strong I bought myself a couple of bass hooks and a spinner and returned to the lake where we used to go, for a week's fishing and to revisit old haunts.

I took along my son, who had never had any fresh water up his nose and who had seen lily pads only from train windows. On the journey over to the lake I began to wonder what it would be like. I wondered how time would have marred this unique, this holy spot—the coves and streams, the hills that the sun set behind, the camps and the paths behind the camps. I was sure that the tarred road would have found it out and I wondered in what other ways it would be desolated. It is strange how much you can remember about places like that once you allow your mind to return into the grooves that lead back. You remember one thing, and that suddenly reminds you of another thing. I guess I remembered clearest of all the early mornings, when the lake was cool and motionless, remembered how the bedroom

From *One Man's Meat*.

smelled of the lumber it was made of and of the wet woods whose scent entered through the screen. The partitions in the camp were thin and did not extend clear to the top of the rooms, and as I was always the first up I would dress softly so as not to wake the others, and sneak out into the sweet outdoors and start out in the canoe, keeping close along the shore in the long shadows of the pines. I remembered being very careful never to rub my paddle against the gunwale for fear of disturbing the stillness of the cathedral.

The lake had never been what you would call a wild lake. There were cottages sprinkled around the shores, and it was in farming country although the shores of the lake were quite heavily wooded. Some of the cottages were owned by nearby farmers, and you would live at the shore and eat your meals at the farmhouse. That's what our family did. But although it wasn't wild, it was a fairly large and undisturbed lake and there were places in it which, to a child at least, seemed infinitely remote and primeval.

I was right about the tar: it led to within half a mile of the shore. But when I got back there, with my boy, and we settled into a camp near a farmhouse and into the kind of summertime I had known, I could tell that it was going to be pretty much the same as it had been before—I knew it, lying in bed the first morning, smelling the bedroom, and hearing the boy sneak quietly out and go off along the shore in a boat. I began to sustain the illusion that he was I, and therefore, by simple transposition, that I was my father. This sensation persisted, kept cropping up all the time we were there. It was not an entirely new feeling, but in this setting it grew much stronger. I seemed to be living a dual existence. I would be in the middle of some simple act, I would be picking up a bait box or laying down a table fork, or I would be saying something, and suddenly it would be not I but my father who was saying the words or making the gesture. It gave me a creepy sensation.

We went fishing the first morning. I felt the same damp moss covering the worms in the bait can, and saw the dragonfly

alight on the tip of my rod as it hovered a few inches from the
surface of the water. It was the arrival of this fly that convinced
me beyond any doubt that everything was as it always had been,
that the years were a mirage and there had been no years. The
small waves were the same, chucking the rowboat under the chin
as we fished at anchor, and the boat was the same boat, the same
color green and the ribs broken in the same places, and under the
floor-boards the same fresh-water leavings and débris—the dead
helgramite, the wisps of moss, the rusty discarded fishhook, the
dried blood from yesterday's catch. We stared silently at the tips
of our rods, at the dragonflies that came and went. I lowered the
tip of mine into the water, tentatively, pensively dislodging the
fly, which darted two feet away, poised, darted two feet back,
and came to rest again a little farther up the rod. There had been
no years between the ducking of this dragonfly and the other
one—the one that was part of memory. I looked at the boy, who
was silently watching his fly, and it was my hands that held his
rod, my eyes watching. I felt dizzy and didn't know which rod I
was at the end of.

   We caught two bass, hauling them in briskly as though
they were mackerel, pulling them over the side of the boat in a
businesslike manner without any landing net, and stunning them
with a blow on the back of the head. When we got back for a
swim before lunch, the lake was exactly where we had left it, the
same number of inches from the dock, and there was only the
merest suggestion of a breeze. This seemed an utterly enchanted
sea, this lake you could leave to its own devices for a few hours
and come back to, and find that it had not stirred, this constant
and trustworthy body of water. In the shallows, the dark, water-
soaked sticks and twigs, smooth and old, were undulating in
clusters on the bottom against the clean ribbed sand, and the
track of the mussel was plain. A school of minnows swam by,
each minnow with its small individual shadow, doubling the
attendance, so clear and sharp in the sunlight. Some of the other
campers were in swimming, along the shore, one of them with a
cake of soap, and the water felt thin and clear and unsubstantial.

Over the years there had been this person with the cake of soap, this cultist, and here he was. There had been no years.

Up to the farmhouse to dinner through the teeming, dusty field, the road under our sneakers was only a two-track road. The middle track was missing, the one with the marks of the hooves and splotches of dried, flaky manure. There had always been three tracks to choose from in choosing which track to walk in; now the choice was narrowed down to two. For a moment I missed terribly the middle alternative. But the way led past the tennis court, and something about the way it lay there in the sun reassured me; the tape had loosened along the backline, the alleys were green with plantains and other weeds, and the net (installed in June and removed in September) sagged in the dry noon, and the whole place steamed with midday heat and hunger and emptiness. There was a choice of pie for dessert, and one was blueberry and one was apple, and the waitresses were the same country girls, there having been no passage of time, only the illusion of it as in a dropped curtain—the waitresses were still fifteen; their hair had been washed, that was the only difference—they had been to the movies and seen the pretty girls with the clean hair.

Summertime, oh summertime, pattern of life indelible, the fadeproof lake, the woods unshatterable, the pasture with the sweetfern and the juniper forever and ever, summer without end; this was the background, and the life along the shore was the design, the cottagers with their innocent and tranquil design, their tiny docks with the flagpole and the American flag floating against the white clouds in the blue sky, the little paths over the roots of the trees leading from camp to camp and the paths leading back to the outhouses and the can of lime for sprinkling, and at the souvenir counters at the store the miniature birch-bark canoes and the post cards that showed things looking a little better than they looked. This was the American family at play, escaping the city heat, wondering whether the newcomers in the camp at the head of the cove were "common" or "nice," wondering whether it was true that the people who drove up for Sunday dinner at the farmhouse were turned away because there wasn't enough chicken.

It seemed to me, as I kept remembering all this, that those times and those summers had been infinitely precious and worth saving. There had been jollity and peace and goodness. The arriving (at the beginning of August) had been so big a business in itself, at the railway station the farm wagon drawn up, the first smell of the pine-laden air, the first glimpse of the smiling farmer, and the great importance of the trunks and your father's enormous authority in such matters, and the feel of the wagon under you for the long ten-mile haul, and at the top of the last long hill catching the first view of the lake after eleven months of not seeing this cherished body of water. The shouts and cries of the other campers when they saw you, and the trunks to be unpacked, to give up their rich burden. (Arriving was less exciting nowadays, when you sneaked up in your car and parked it under a tree near the camp and took out the bags and in five minutes it was all over, no fuss, no loud wonderful fuss about trunks.)

Peace and goodness and jollity. The only thing that was wrong now, really, was the sound of the place, an unfamiliar nervous sound of the outboard motors. This was the note that jarred, the one thing that would sometimes break the illusion and set the years moving. In those other summertimes all motors were inboard; and when they were at a little distance, the noise they made was a sedative, an ingredient of summer sleep. They were one-cylinder and two-cylinder engines, and some were make-and-break and some were jump-spark, but they all made a sleepy sound across the lake. The one-lungers throbbed and fluttered, and the twin-cylinder ones purred and purred, and that was a quiet sound too. But now the campers all had outboards. In the daytime, in the hot mornings, these motors made a petulant, irritable sound; at night, in the still evening when the afterglow lit the water, they whined about one's ears like mosquitoes. My boy loved our rented outboard, and his great desire was to achieve singlehanded mastery over it, and authority, and he soon learned the trick of choking it a little (but not too much), and the adjustment of the needle valve. Watching him I would remember the things you could do with the old one-cylinder engine with the heavy flywheel, how you could have it eating out of your hand if you got really close to it spiritually. Motor boats in those days didn't have clutches, and you would make a landing by shutting off the motor at the proper time and coasting in with a dead rudder. But there was a way of reversing them, if you learned the trick, by cutting the switch and putting it on again exactly on the final dying revolution of the flywheel, so that it would kick back against compression and begin reversing. Approaching a dock in a strong following breeze, it was difficult to slow up sufficiently by the ordinary coasting method, and if a boy felt he had complete mastery over his motor, he was tempted to keep it running beyond its time and then reverse it a few feet from the dock. It took a cool nerve, because if you threw the switch a twentieth of a second too soon you would catch the flywheel when it still had speed enough to go up past center, and the boat would leap ahead, charging bull-fashion at the dock.

We had a good week at the camp. The bass were biting well and the sun shone endlessly, day after day. We would be tired at night and lie down in the accumulated heat of the little bedrooms after the long hot day and the breeze would stir almost imperceptibly outside and the smell of the swamp drift in through the rusty screens. Sleep would come easily and in the morning the red squirrel would be on the roof, tapping out his gay routine. I kept remembering everything, lying in bed in the mornings—the small steamboat that had a long rounded stern like the lip of a Ubangi, and how quietly she ran on the moon-light sails, when the older boys played their mandolins and the girls sang and we ate doughnuts dipped in sugar, and how sweet the music was on the water in the shining night, and what it had felt like to think about girls then. After breakfast we would go up to the store and the things were in the same place—the minnows in a bottle, the plugs and spinners disarranged and pawed over by the youngsters from the boys' camp, the fig

newtons and the Beeman's gum. Outside, the road was tarred
and cars stood in front of the store. Inside, all was just as it had
always been, except there was more Coca Cola and not so much
Moxie and root beer and birch beer and sarsaparilla. We would
walk out with a bottle of pop apiece and sometimes the pop
would backfire up our noses and hurt. We explored the streams,
quietly, where the turtles slid off the sunny logs and dug their
way into the soft bottom; and we lay on the town wharf and fed
worms to the tame bass. Everywhere we went I had trouble
making out which was I, the one walking at my side, the one
walking in my pants.

One afternoon while we were there at that lake a thun-
derstorm came up. It was like the revival of an old melodrama
that I had seen long ago with childish awe. The second-act
climax of the drama of the electrical disturbance over a lake in
America had not changed in any important respect. This was the
big scene, still the big scene. The whole thing was so familiar,
the first feeling of oppression and heat and a general air around
camp of not wanting to go very far away. In midafternoon (it
was all the same) a curious darkening of the sky, and a lull in
everything that had made life tick; and then the way the boats
suddenly swung the other way at their moorings with the coming
of a breeze out of the new quarter, and the premonitory rumble.
Then the kettle drum, then the snare, then the bass drum and
cymbals, then crackling light against the dark, and the gods
grinning and licking their chops in the hills. Afterward the calm,
the rain steadily rustling in the calm lake, the return of light and
hope and spirits, and the campers running out in joy and relief
to go swimming in the rain, their bright cries perpetuating the
deathless joke about how they were getting simply drenched, and
the children screaming with delight at the new sensation of
bathing in the rain, and the joke about getting drenched linking
the generations in a strong indestructible chain. And the comedian who waded in carrying an umbrella.

When the others went swimming my son said he was
going in too. He pulled his dripping trunks from the line where

they had hung all through the shower, and wrung them out. Languidly, and with no thought of going in, I watched him, his hard little body, skinny and bare, saw him wince slightly as he pulled up around his vitals the small, soggy, icy garment. As he buckled the swollen belt suddenly my groin felt the chill of death.

APRIL 7, 1956

THE RING OF TIME

Fiddler's Bayou, March 22, 1956

After the lions had returned to their cages, creeping angrily through the chutes, a little bunch of us drifted away and into an open doorway nearby, where we stood for a while in semidarkness, watching a big brown circus horse go harumphing around the practice ring. His trainer was a woman of about forty, and the two of them, horse and woman, seemed caught up in one of those desultory treadmills of afternoon from which there is no apparent escape. The day was hot, and we kibitzers were grateful to be briefly out of the sun's glare. The long rein, or tape, by which the woman guided her charge counterclockwise in his dull career formed the radius of their private circle, of which she was the revolving center; and she, too, stepped a tiny circumference of her own, in order to accommodate the horse and allow him his maximum scope. She had on a short-skirted costume and a conical straw hat. Her legs were bare and she wore high heels, which probed deep into the loose tanbark and kept her ankles in a state of constant turmoil. The great size and meekness of the horse, the repetitious exercise, the heat of the afternoon, all exerted a hypnotic charm that invited boredom; we spectators were experiencing a languor—we neither expected relief nor felt entitled to any. We had paid a dollar to get into the grounds, to be sure, but we had got our dollar's worth a few

A "Letter from the South" in *The Points of My Compass*.

minutes before, when the lion trainer's whiplash had got caught around a toe of one of the lions. What more did we want for a dollar?

Behind me I heard someone say, "Excuse me, please," in a low voice. She was halfway into the building when I turned and saw her—a girl of sixteen or seventeen, politely threading her way through us onlookers who blocked the entrance. As she emerged in front of us, I saw that she was barefoot, her dirty little feet fighting the uneven ground. In most respects she was like any of two or three dozen showgirls you encounter if you wander about the winter quarters of Mr. John Ringling North's circus, in Sarasota—cleverly proportioned, deeply browned by the sun, dusty, eager, and almost naked. But her grave face and the naturalness of her manner gave her a sort of quick distinction and brought a new note into the gloomy octagonal building where we had all cast our lot for a few moments. As soon as she had squeezed through the crowd, she spoke a word or two to the older woman, whom I took to be her mother, stepped to the ring, and waited while the horse coasted to a stop in front of her. She gave the animal a couple of affectionate swipes on his enormous neck and then swung herself aboard. The horse immediately resumed his rocking canter, the woman goading him on, chanting something that sounded like "Hop! Hop!"

In attempting to recapture this mild spectacle, I am merely acting as recording secretary for one of the oldest of societies—the society of those who, at one time or another, have surrendered, without even a show of resistance, to the bedazzlement of a circus rider. As a writing man, or secretary, I have always felt charged with the safekeeping of all unexpected items of worldly or unworldly enchantment, as though I might be held personally responsible if even a small one were to be lost. But it is not easy to communicate anything of this nature. The circus comes as close to being the world in microcosm as anything I know; in a way, it puts all the rest of show business in the shade. Its magic is universal and complex. Out of its wild disorder comes order; from its rank smell rises the good aroma of courage and daring; out of its preliminary shabbiness comes the final splendor. And buried in the familiar boasts of its advance agents lies the modesty of most of its people. For me the circus is at its best before it has been put together. It is at its best at certain moments when it comes to a point, as through a burning glass, in the activity and destiny of a single performer out of so many. One ring is always bigger than three. One rider, one aerialist, is always greater than six. In short, a man has to catch the circus unawares to experience its full impact and share its gaudy dream.

The ten-minute ride the girl took achieved—as far as I was concerned, who wasn't looking for it, and quite unbeknownst to her, who wasn't even striving for it—the thing that is sought by performers everywhere, on whatever stage, whether struggling in the tidal currents of Shakespeare or bucking the difficult motion of a horse. I somehow got the idea she was just cadging a ride, improving a shining ten minutes in the diligent way all serious artists seize free moments to hone the blade of their talent and keep themselves in trim. Her brief tour included only elementary postures and tricks, perhaps because they were all she was capable of, perhaps because her warmup at this hour was unscheduled and the ring was not rigged for a real practice session. She swung herself off and on the horse several times, gripping his mane. She did a few knee-stands—or whatever they are called—dropping to her knees and quickly bouncing back up on her feet again. Most of the time she simply rode in a standing position, well aft on the beast, her hands hanging easily at her sides, her head erect, her straw-colored ponytail lightly brushing her shoulders, the blood of exertion showing faintly through the tan of her skin. Twice she managed a one-foot stance—a sort of ballet pose, with arms outstretched. At one point the neck strap of her bathing suit broke and she went twice around the ring in the classic attitude of a woman making minor repairs to a garment. The fact that she was standing on the back of a moving horse while doing this invested the matter with a clown-ish significance that perfectly fitted the spirit of the circus— jocund, yet charming. She just rolled the strap into a neat ball and stowed it inside her bodice while the horse rocked and rolled beneath her in dutiful innocence. The bathing suit proved as self-reliant as its owner and stood up well enough without benefit of strap.

The richness of the scene was in its plainness, its natural condition—of horse, of ring, of girl, even to the girl's bare feet that gripped the bare back of her proud and ridiculous mount. The enchantment grew not out of anything that happened or was performed but out of something that seemed to go round and around and around with the girl, attending her, a steady gleam in the shape of a circle—a ring of ambition, of happiness, of youth. (And the positive pleasures of equilibrium under difficulties.) In a week or two, all would be changed, all (or almost all) lost: the girl would wear makeup, the horse would wear gold, the ring would be painted, the bark would be clean for the feet of the horse, the girl's feet would be clean for the slippers that she'd wear. All, all would be lost.

As I watched with the others, our jaws adroop, our eyes alight, I became painfully conscious of the element of time. Everything in the hideous old building seemed to take the shape of a circle, conforming to the course of the horse. The rider's gaze, as she peered straight ahead, seemed to be circular, as though bent by force of circumstance; then time itself began running in circles, and so the beginning was where the end was, and the two were the same, and one thing ran into the next and time went round and around and got nowhere. The girl wasn't so young that she did not know the delicious satisfaction of having a perfectly behaved body and the fun of using it to do a trick most people can't do, but she was too young to know that time does not really move in a circle at all. I thought: "She will never be as beautiful as this again"—a thought that made me acutely unhappy—and in a flash my mind (which is too much of a busybody to suit me) had projected her twenty-five years ahead, and she was now in the center of the ring, on foot, wearing a conical hat and high-heeled shoes, the image of the older woman, holding the long rein, caught in the treadmill of an afternoon long in the future. "She is at that enviable moment in life [I thought] when she believes she can go once around the ring, make one complete circuit, and at the end be exactly the same age as at the start." Everything in her movements, her expression, told you that for her the ring of time was perfectly formed, changeless, predictable, without beginning or end, like the ring in which she was travelling at this moment with the horse that wallowed under her. And then I slipped back into my trance, and time was circular again—time, pausing quietly with the rest of us, so as not to disturb the balance of a performer.

Her ride ended as casually as it had begun. The older woman stopped the horse, and the girl slid to the ground. As she walked toward us to leave, there was a quick, small burst of applause. She smiled broadly, in surprise and pleasure; then her face suddenly regained its gravity and she disappeared through the door.

It has been ambitious and plucky of me to attempt to describe what is indescribable, and I have failed, as I knew I would. But I have discharged my duty to my society; and besides, a writer, like an acrobat, must occasionally try a stunt that is too much for him. At any rate, it is worth reporting that long before the circus comes to town, its most notable performances have already been given. Under the bright lights of the finished show, a performer need only reflect the electric candle power that is directed upon him; but in the dark and dirty old training rings and in the makeshift cages, whatever light is generated, whatever excitement, whatever beauty, must come from original sources— from internal fires of professional hunger and delight, from the exuberance and gravity of youth. It is the difference between planetary light and the combustion of stars.

The South is the land of the sustained sibilant. Everywhere, for the appreciative visitor, the letter "s" insinuates itself in the scene: in the sound of sea and sand, in the singing shell, in the heat of sun and sky, in the sultriness of the gentle hours, in the siesta, in the stir of birds and insects. In contrast to the softness of its music, the South is also cruel and hard and prickly. A little striped lizard, flattened along the sharp green bayonet of a yucca, wears in its tiny face and watchful eye the pure look of death and violence. And all over the place, hidden at the bottom of their small sandy craters, the ant lions lie in wait for the ant that will stumble into their trap. (There are three kinds of lions in this region: the lions of the circus, the ant lions, and the Lions of the Tampa Lions Club, who roared their approval of segregation at a meeting the other day—all except one, a Lion named Monty Gurwit, who declined to roar and thereby got his picture in the paper.)

The day starts on a note of despair: the sorrowing dove, alone on its telephone wire, mourns the loss of night, weeps at the bright perils of the unfolding day. But soon the mockingbird wakes and begins an early rehearsal, setting the dove down by force of character, running through a few slick imitations, and trying a couple of original numbers into the bargain. The redbird takes it from there. Despair gives way to good humor. The Southern dawn is a pale affair, usually, quite different from our northern daybreak. It is a triumph of gradualism; night turns to day imperceptibly, softly, with no theatrics. It is subtle and undisturbing. As the first light seeps in through the blinds I lie in bed half awake, despairing with the dove, sounding the A for the brothers Alsop. All seems lost, all seems sorrowful. Then a mullet jumps in the bayou outside the bedroom window. It falls back into the water with a smart smack. I have asked several people why the mullet incessantly jump and I have received a variety of answers. Some say the mullet jump to shake off a parasite that annoys them. Some say they jump for the love of jumping—as the girl on the horse seemed to ride for the love of riding (although she, too, like all artists, may have been shaking off some parasite that fastens itself to the creative spirit and can be got rid of only by fifty turns around a ring while standing on a horse).

In Florida at this time of year, the sun does not take command of the day until a couple of hours after it has appeared in the east. It seems to carry no authority at first. The sun and the lizard keep the same schedule; they bide their time until the morning has advanced a good long way before they come fully forth and strike. The cold lizard waits astride his warming leaf for the perfect moment; the cold sun waits in his nest of clouds for the crucial time.

On many days, the dampness of the air pervades all life, all living. Matches refuse to strike. The towel, hung to dry, grows wetter by the hour. The newspaper, with its headlines about integration, wilts in your hand and falls limply into the coffee and the egg. Envelopes seal themselves. Postage stamps mate with one another as shamelessly as grasshoppers. But most of the time the days are models of beauty and wonder and comfort, with the kind sea stroking the back of the warm sand. At evening there are great flights of birds over the sea, where the light lingers; the gulls, the pelicans, the terns, the herons stay aloft for half an hour after land birds have gone to roost. They hold their ancient formations, wheel and fish over the Pass, enjoying the last of day like children playing outdoors after suppertime.

To a beachcomber from the North, which is my present status, the race problem has no pertinence, no immediacy. Here in Florida I am a guest in two houses—the house of the sun, the house of the State of Florida. As a guest, I mind my manners and do not criticize the customs of my hosts. It gives me a queer feeling, though, to be at the center of the greatest social crisis of my time and see hardly a sign of it. Yet the very absence of signs seems to increase one's awareness. Colored people do not come to the public beach to bathe, because they would not be made welcome there; and they don't fritter away their time visiting the circus, because they have other things to do. A few of them turn up at the ballpark, where they occupy a separate but equal section of the left-field bleachers and watch Negro players on the visiting Braves team using the same bases as the white players, instead of separate (but equal) bases. I have had only two small encounters with "color." A colored woman named Viola, who had been a friend of my wife's sister years ago, showed up one day with some laundry of ours that she had consented to do for us, and with the bundle she brought a bunch of nasturtiums, as a sort of natural accompaniment to the delivery of clean clothes. The flowers seemed a very acceptable thing and I was touched by them. We asked Viola about her daughter, and she said she was at Kentucky State College, studying voice.

The other encounter was when I was explaining to our cook, who is from Finland, the mysteries of bus travel in the American Southland. I showed her the bus stop, armed her with a timetable, and then, as a matter of duty, mentioned the customs of the Romans. "When you get on the bus," I said, "I think you'd better sit in one of the front seats—the seats in back are for colored people." A look of great weariness came into her face, as it does when we use too many dishes, and she replied, "Oh, I know—isn't it silly!"

Her remark, coming as it did all the way from Finland and landing on this sandbar with a plunk, impressed me. The Supreme Court said nothing about silliness, but I suspect it may play more of a role than one might suppose. People are, if anything, more touchy about being thought silly than they are about being thought unjust. I note that one of the arguments in the recent manifesto of Southern Congressmen in support of the doctrine of "separate but equal" was that it had been founded on "common sense." The sense that is common to one generation is uncommon to the next. Probably the first slave ship, with Negroes lying in chains on its decks, seemed commonsensical to the owners who operated it and to the planters who patronized it. But such a vessel would not be in the realm of common sense today. The only sense that is common, in the long run, is the sense of change—and we all instinctively avoid it, and object to the passage of time, and would rather have none of it.

The Supreme Court decision is like the Southern sun, laggard in its early stages, biding its time. It has been the law in Florida for two years now, and the years have been like the hours of the morning before the sun has gathered its strength. I think the decision is as incontrovertible and warming as the sun, and, like the sun, will eventually take charge.

But there is certainly a great temptation in Florida to duck the passage of time. Lying in warm comfort by the sea, you receive gratefully the gift of the sun, the gift of the South. This is true seduction. The day is a circle—morning, afternoon, and night. After a few days I was clearly enjoying the same delusion as the girl on the horse—that I could ride clear around the ring of day, guarded by wind and sun and sea and sand, and be not a moment older.

QUESTIONS FOR DISCUSSION

I. SAYING THE WORDS

The Duty of Writers

(1) White speaks of "a person engaged in the flimsy business of expressing himself on paper." Does he mean by "flimsy" that writing is essentially an unimportant pastime, especially in a time of crisis? (2) The word "significant" occurs once in the opening paragraph and twice in the third. What is its significance in these contexts, and why does "insignificant" in paragraph 4 occur in quotation marks? (3) According to paragraph 3, what kind of club should a writer not join? The Rotary Club? A country club? A fraternity? A literary club? A political party? (4) White asserts that a writer should "write in a way that comes easy." The playwright Sheridan once wrote: "Easy writing's curst hard reading." Can you resolve the apparent contradiction? Should White have written "comes easily"? (5) The last two sentences contain at least seven phrases (one included in another) that are metaphorical, i.e., not strictly literal. Can you identify them?

English Usage

(1) White uses "horribles" as a noun. *The American College Dictionary* classifies "horrible" only as an adjective. *Webster's Seventh Collegiate* lists "horrible" as a noun but not "terrible." How do you account for these differences? (2) What does your dictionary say about the use of "contact" as a verb? Is it bad grammar? If not, why do you think it made White wince? (3) Name some other "noun-verbs" in common use. If a plane can be grounded, why can't an automobile be garaged? If a house can sleep twelve, why can't it eat twenty? (4) What does your dictionary say about "ain't"? Can you cite other examples of its appropriate use? If White is to be taken literally, why should an old popular song have the refrain "Say

it isn't so"? (5) Explain the traditional grammatical objection to "My God, it's her!" (6) How would you express the sentence that trapped Dr. Canby?

The Word-handler's Aim

(1) Do you find the word "newspicture" in your dictionary? Why is it appropriate in White's first sentence? What is a neologism? (2) Is the word "cameraderie" in your dictionary? If not, why not? Why did White use it instead of "comradeship," "companionship," "fellowship," or "chumminess"? What is the difference between "denotation" and "connotation"? Explain the etymology of camera and comrade. (3) What is your reaction to the use of puns in speech or writing? (4) If White tossed off "a particularly neat ablative absolute," would he be writing English? What is a hanging participle and when should one be killed?

A Study of the Clinical "We"

(1) What is the purpose of the editorial "we"? Does White's comment on it seriously define its use? (2) Why might a writer use the second person (you) or the third person (he) in depicting his own experience? Can anything be said in defense of "the present writer," "the undersigned," or "your correspondent"? (3) Give some other examples of "a spoken form . . . rarely written." Is the quoted phrase an accurate definition of "colloquialism"? Does your dictionary label colloquialisms as such? (4) Is the dialogue beginning "Morning, Nurse . . ." an accurate attempt to reproduce natural conversation? If not, why not?

An Approach to Style

(1) What could White mean by admitting that he is offering "subtly dangerous hints"? (2) Can you characterize the differences between Faulkner and Hemingway and Frost and Whitman by analyzing the passages in greater detail than White? Do you agree that there is "nothing eccentric about the construction" of Faulkner's? (3) Why should White hit on the word "soulwise" for a

paraphrase of Paine, or characterize style as "non-detachable, un-filterable"? (4) What is the difference between a manner and a mannerism? (5) White's final passage is developed through analogy. Whether a writer uses an analogy to explain, describe, or persuade, the resemblance must be close enough to be convincing; the comparison must not be stretched too far or continued too long. Can you indicate what might have happened to White's analogy if he had pushed it much further? Can you think of another appropriate analogy to clarify the writer's occupation?

Prefer the Standard to the Offbeat

(1) A linguist reading this piece might point out that "deliberate infractions of grammatical rules," "crossbreeding of the parts of speech," and coining new words (coinages, neologisms) are normal processes that have contributed to the growth of English. Would this argument invalidate White's objections to the languages of advertising and business? (2) How many words can you name that function regularly as three or more different parts of speech? (3) What does your dictionary say about the use of "like" as a conjunction? Is White's objection to the notorious cigarette ad based strictly on grammar? (4) Are his objections to "accessorize" and "finalize" identical? Would he have similar objections to "mobilize," "realize," "humanize," or "feminize"? Would it be accurate to say that he is trying to standardize the language? How does your dictionary define "standard English"? (5) A recent ad in *Fortune* reads in part: "LIFE IS JUST ONE CADILLAC AFTER ANOTHER! No one knows better than a doorman that whenever people of consequence gather, the Cadillac car is a predominate part of the scene." How does this passage illustrate White's remarks about the special languages of advertising and business?

Calculating Machine

(1) Considering his attitude toward "accessorize" and "finalize" (pp. 17–18), why should White object to the word "personalize"? (2) According to your dictionary is White's use of "lief" in para-

graph 3 archaic? What is the difference between an archaic and an obsolete word? Can you defend the use of either? (3) Though White is discussing an abstract subject, he uses concrete words and metaphors throughout. Sometimes the metaphor is confined to a single phrase or sentence ("the person at the other end of the line"; "Already they have one foot caught in the brier patch of English usage"). Sometimes an entire paragraph is brought into focus with a sustained metaphor. Discuss the sustained metaphors in paragraphs 4 and 6. (4) What do you infer from the opening sentence in paragraph 6 about White's attitude toward the study of grammar? How do this statement and the piece as a whole compare with the view expressed in "English Usage"?

The Future of Reading

(1) In referring to "these audio-visual days" is White speaking only of "teaching aids"? (2) Do you agree that one audio-visual device in particular is "already giving the room the languor of an opium parlor"? (3) Of all your acquaintances, how many are readers and writers in White's sense of the words? If you do not belong to this minority, why not? (4) From what you know—or can learn from your dictionary—about the habits of bees (queen, drones, workers, busyness), discuss the effectiveness of the sustained metaphor in paragraph 1. What does White mean by "our modern hive of bees, substituting coaxial cable for spinal fluid"? (5) Where does White place "the scene of the accident" and why? What does this imply about the responsibilities of reporters?

Western Unity

(1) Is White's argument any less convincing as an editorial because he uses the singular personal pronoun instead of the editorial "we" or the impersonal point of view common to most writing by experts? (2) In paragraph 2 White twice uses the word "summit" in a metaphorical way. How has he prepared for this metaphor earlier? How does his use of "summit" differ from its common use

in contemporary diplomacy? (3) Explain the ironic paradox in the second sentence of paragraph 2. (4) From your knowledge of the two worlds of East and West, do you share White's confidence in the statement from the *Times* magazine?

The Wild Flag

(1) In a literal sense all language is symbolic, every word is a symbol. The combination of vowels and consonants that form the word "watermelon" symbolizes—stands for—the long green fruit with the pink, seedy insides. But in speaking of a short story or a poem as having symbolic language, the literary critic has in mind a more restricted kind of symbol. Thus the word "flag" can be doubly symbolic because it stands not only for a piece of cloth but also for the infinite gamut of facts and fancies that make a nation. There is a further distinction: though no two readers will react identically to any word ("bunting" may suggest an American flag to some and a squeeze play to others), there is general agreement about many conventional symbols—flag, cross, eight-ball, thirteen, black cat, true blue; but the writer, especially the poet, not only borrows conventional symbols from the general context of life, he devises original symbols in the context of a particular work of art—Blake's tiger, Eliot's hollow men, the giant cobweb of *Bleak House,* the green light in *The Great Gatsby,* the wild flag here. What does the wild flag symbolize, and what is the symbolic significance of the date of the piece? Name five symbols that are common in literature, citing, if possible, specific contexts. (2) Characterize each participant in the debate, distinguishing between what White tells the reader directly and what he implies by their speech and actions. (3) How does your dictionary account etymologically for the fact that modern English has the same word for a symbolic piece of cloth, a monocotyledonous flower, and a slab of stone? Etymologically speaking, how does "unpopular" lose most of its meaning in a world with only two hundred people? (4) According to one arbitrary division, any sentence of prose can be classified as statement, overstatement, or

understatement. Classify the language of the Chinese delegate and characterize White's intended effect. Is the final sentence a literal statement? (5) Why should White cast a Chinese in the role depicted here? Would the choice make any difference today, symbolically speaking?

Two Letters, Both Open

(1) What are the traditional differences in form and content between a business letter and a friendly letter? To what extent does White conform to these conventions? What does he mean by complaining that the note from the tax collector "didn't seem friendly"? Is either of his answers friendly? Should a business letter end with an invitation to eat Mrs. Freethy's cookies? (2) The expression "seizure and sale" appears at the beginning of the second letter and recurs—sometimes in a slightly different form—five times. Why does White repeat it so often? (3) To what extent does the signer of the two letters resemble the author of "The Duty of Writers" (p. 4)? (4) A familiar classification of levels or varieties of language has three overlapping divisions: vulgate, informal, and formal. Generally speaking, how would you classify the language in these letters? What other adjectives would you apply to their language? Considering White's intention, why does he use such language? What is his intention? (5) Analyze the logic of the following sentence: "Night chill is the most prevalent dachshund disorder, if you have never had one." What is an idiom?

The Day of Days

(1) The stanza to which White refers is as follows:

The sun was warm but the wind was chill.
You know how it is with an April day.
When the sun is out and the wind is still,
You're one month on in the middle of May.
But if you so much as dare to speak,
A cloud comes over the sunlit arch,

A wind comes off a frozen peak,
And you're two months back in the middle of March.*

Without reference to White's paraphrase, how would you characterize the tone of Frost's stanza? Considering both point of view and
tone, what do the stanza and the paraphrase have in common? How
do they differ? Why might "The Day of Days" be called a poem?
(2) The reference to Frost's poem is both an introduction and a
literary allusion. In some introductions the writer is merely warming
up on paper before he really begins. Some allusions are only academic exhibitionism. Would either of these complaints apply here?
If not, why not? (3) White calls the experience a "magical
moment." What details elsewhere in the piece are in key with this
description? Is the reference to "the twenty-eight-day grind" inconsistent with the dominant tone of the piece? (4) Poems (and prose
poems) about Spring are among the oldest and most familiar works
in English. What details or devices does White use to make this
piece ring true, not trite?

The Burning Question

(1) The dominant tone of this piece could be called "genial
ribbing." Against whom is the ribbing directed, and what makes it
genial? (2) While portraying himself directly as an inept neophyte
with a gun, White presents a less detailed sketch of his neighbors.
Using only the hints that he supplies, how would you characterize a
typical Maine deer-hunter? (3) Though he is writing about hunters
and hunting, White uses only one of these words, and that only
once. What phrases does he use instead, and how does the connotation of each contribute to the tone of the piece? (4) "The truth is I
have never given serious thought to the question of gunning." Do
you believe this is literally true? Is he giving serious thought to the

* From "Two Tramps in Mud Time" from *Complete Poems
of Robert Frost.* Copyright 1923 by Holt, Rinehart and Winston, Inc.
Copyright 1936, 1951 by Robert Frost. Copyright © 1964 by Lesley
Frost Ballantine. Reprinted by permission of Holt, Rinehart and Winston, Inc.

question in this piece? Would you picture the writer of "The Day of Days" (p. 37) as a man who would not give serious thought to hunting? (5) The effect of much humorous writing (or cartooning) could be described as "the incongruity of the unexpected." (A *New Yorker* cartoon pictures a proudly antlered deer sitting erect behind the wheel of a car, to whose left fender is lashed the crumpled corpse of a dead deerslayer.) How does this general definition fit White's essay?

Farewell, My Lovely!

(1) How does this title differ in tone from that of the essay as it appeared in book form: *Farewell to Model T*? (2) Considering White's own estimate of the tone ("the tribute of a sigh that is not a sob"), would you call the essay sentimental? How do you distinguish between sentimentality and sentiment? (3) How is White's attitude revealed in his treatment of the word "planetary"? In what other ways does the essay differ from a technical treatise by an earnest engineer or a promotion brochure from Detroit? (4) What does White mean by characterizing the vehicle and its driver as "heroic"? How is this note sustained throughout? (5) What does White mean by "the great days of lily-painting"? How does he contrive to keep his development of this point from degenerating into a monotonous inventory of spare parts? (6) The rhetorical device of *personification* is as familiar in everyday speech as in written poetry. The Model T, for example, was a "Tin Lizzy" or—even less elegantly on at least one occasion—"the son of a bitch." To what extent does White use this device, and what is its effect on the tone of the essay?

II.   THE CAREFUL FORM

Salt Water Farm

(1) The English language has a number of familiar clichés by which terms normally applied to the land are transferred to the sea: ploughing the ocean; the furrows of the waves. What fresh use

does White make of this device, and what is his purpose? (2) A writer, usually a bad one, may condescend to a reader who is presumably a stupid oaf beneath him; he may embrace the reader as a willing ally in a common enterprise (Now we can see, can't we?), or as a beloved friend (Dear reader); or he may write as if no human reader is expected to tune in on his isolated frequency. How does White approach the reader here, and how does this affect the tone of the piece? (3) White speaks of the cunners and the flounders as "hanging round" the dock piles. What does this suggest about the level of his language? Can you find other illustrations of the same sort of idiom? Is there any relation between the language and tone of the piece and the native attitude toward farming? How might both change if White were writing as an expert with a degree in agriculture?

Business Show

(1) Why should White begin a description of an indoor business show with an exterior setting? What is the relation between the beginning and the ending? What is the effect of the organization by which a writer returns finally to the point where he began? (2) Can you notice and account for any other instances of effective repetition? (3) How do the length and rhythm of the sentences relate to the dominant impression of the scene? (4) What is the writer's attitude toward the machines?

Coon Hunt

(1) This story is less concerned with the facts of the hunt than with developing a number of contrasting attitudes held by both two- and four-legged animals. How many different attitudes can you distinguish? How might the story differ in tone if it were written from the point of view of one of the veteran coon hunters? (2) What is White's attitude toward his fellow hunters, and how is it revealed? (3) How does White develop the setting and atmosphere in the story, including both sights and sounds? In what way is the setting related to the behavior of the puppy? (4) A hunting story—

Faulkner's "The Bear," for example—may have one or more themes with implications that transcend the immediate physical events. To what extent is this true of "Coon Hunt"?

The Second Tree from the Corner

(1) What is White's purpose in putting so many words between the psychiatrist's opening question and Trexler's answer? Why does Trexler give the answer he does? (2) What is Trexler's first attitude toward the psychiatrist, and how does it change once he is familiar with the routine? Is this change prepared for early in the story? (3) How would you define the essential differences between the two men? (4) If, as Trexler supposed, all men in general want the same thing, why does he want a tree and the doctor want a new wing on his house in Westport? (5) How does White vary the setting to suit the mood of his protagonist? (6) Would it be accurate to say that the point of this story is that some psychiatrists need psychiatry more than some of their patients?

Withholding

(1) Do you believe, as White apparently does, that the government should concern itself with the moral effect of its taxing methods rather than with their financial effectiveness? (2) Do you agree that the "whole setup of our democratic government assumes that the citizen is bright, honest, and at least as fundamentally sound as common stock"? (3) Is this a serious sermonette on self-reliance, or do you detect a different tone? (4) Analogy is a familiar device of persuasion. Are you persuaded of the soundness of the analogy in the final sentence?

Sound

(1) Although White is discussing an audible phenomenon in relation to an abstract principle of democracy, he makes his point with visible illustrations couched in concrete, figurative language. Identify the metaphors in the first paragraph and explain their

effectiveness. (2) This piece might have been called "The Paradox of Freedom." Explain. (3) White's "note to political candidates" is presumably not meant to be taken literally. Is it meant to be taken seriously? If not, why should he include it in an evidently serious piece of persuasion? (4) What does White mean by saying that modern man has "acquiesced in jumboism"? Illustrate from your own experience. (5) As a device of persuasion, how does the final sentence compare with the final sentence of "Withholding" (p. 74)?

The Age of Dust

(1) Horror stories often begin on a night of storms and blackness. What is the point of beginning a piece about atomic horror on a sunny morning under an apple tree? (2) Could the scientist effectively parry White's thrusts by pointing out that he had not, in "that queer sentence," exactly expressed his own meaning— that he was only guilty of "careless English"? (3) How does White's use of the word "purity" (three times) reflect the tone of the piece? (4) Why should a man who wants to write persuasive prose in a practical age present himself as a dreamer who pushes little girls in swings? (5) In what ways does this piece resemble and differ from "The Wild Flag" (p. 28)?

Motor Cars

(1) The opening sentence suggests that White is not strictly concerned with the design of automobiles. What other designs does he have on the reader? How does he carry them out? (2) A more technical explanation would be limited to a more precise statement of the facts. Where does White use overstatement? Does this departure from literal exactness distort the truth of his picture? How does it affect the tone of the essay? (3) How would you respond to the argument that White's piece is dated because the design of cars has changed since 1940? (4) A *double entendre* is not always a risqué remark or an obvious pun. Explain the double meanings in White's use of the following phrases: "symphonic styling"; "getting

into more scrapes"; "the bitter end"; "total immersion"; "blind flying." (5) What evidence in this essay suggests that it might have been written by the author of "Farewell, My Lovely!" (p. 40)?

Freedom

(1) What do the opening paragraphs of "Freedom" and "Motor Cars" (p. 79) have in common? (2) What fallacy do you find in each of the "strange remarks" that White has overheard in New York? (3) How does White's view of duty here compare with that in "The Duty of Writers" (p. 4)? (4) How is White's phrase "the anatomy of decadence" echoed by other anatomical metaphors? (5) How does his use of the words "innocent" and "innocence" reflect his tone? How does he sustain the image of being "in love with freedom"? (6) Why do you think he chose to call the explanation of his credo a "declaration"? (7) Informal as this essay may be, it is carefully organized to present three contrasts: between two attitudes toward tyranny, two kinds of freedom, and two views of the writer's value. Explain them. Instead of his final paragraph White might have settled for a simple proverbial statement: "The pen is mightier than the sword." Why didn't he?

Town Meeting

(1) The first paragraph presents two names for a New England town meeting, one abstract but dignified, the other recalling a commercial radio program. What evidence does White present to suggest that the two views may share the truth between them? (2) How do the remarks on masonry and Masons anticipate White's report of the actual meeting? (3) How many sentences can you find in which White is simply reporting the facts with complete detachment? Where and how does he reveal his personal bias? Does the existence of this bias add to or detract from the essential truth of the picture? (4) How does White use the devices of sustained metaphor, climax, and anticlimax to distil the essence of the meeting? (5) Do you think the delegation from the high school could have learned the lesson it had come to learn?

Twins

(1) In a piece about the birth of fawns in a zoo, why should White bother to mention the hearts and initials on a tree trunk or the feel of his new shoes? Why does he report the reactions of the other sightseers, including the child? (2) All good reporting presents particularizing details—to suggest that every experience, however typical, has a unique excitement all its own. How many such details can you single out here? (3) In what ways does this piece illustrate the essential virtues of good description and good narrative as discussed on pages 53–56 and 59–60? (4) Although White resorts to the editorial "we," his personal point of view is expressed with particular care. Explain. (5) Would you call the tone of this story sentimental? If not, why not?

About Myself

(1) White uses the word "declaration" to characterize both this piece and "Freedom" (p. 82). Does the word have the same meaning in both contexts? (2) Why does White repeat that he is a man of medium height? (3) What is the significance of what he tells about his father and mother? (4) What manner of man peeks through this tour de force, and what is the implied attitude here toward modern existence? Does he bear any resemblance to the author of "Two Letters, Both Open" (p. 32)? What is a tour de force?

Dudes and Flapsails

(1) What is White's attitude toward the "old sea dog" and how is it revealed? How does this miniature portrait anticipate the epigram at the end? (2) Would the piece have been more effective if White had begun with the last sentence and expanded his definition from there? If not, why not? What is the difference between induction and deduction? (3) What is White's reaction to dudes in general? Does he consider them good guys or bad guys? (4) This

piece is more than a definition of a human type; it is a comment on human nature. How does it resemble "The Second Tree from the Corner" (p. 66)?

Law and Justice

(1) According to White, what is the first requisite of law? (2) Do you agree with his implication that there is no such thing as international law? If this is true, why should anybody bother to study it? (3) Do you infer from White's argument that every word has only one meaning, and that we could solve international problems if only we could agree on definitions of words? Does he object to careless use of words because it is bad English? (4) Does he argue that the Japanese should not be punished because it would be unlawful and unjust?

Democracy

(1) Considering his attitude in "The Duty of Writers" (p. 4), why should White use the word "presumably" in the second sentence? (2) What does he mean by the opening sentence of the second paragraph? What is the relation between the tone of this sentence and that of the final sentence? If the Board knows what democracy is, why should they write for a definition? (3) How does White achieve variety in the second paragraph, and keep it from turning into a monotonous inventory? (4) Can you find any examples of literary allusion or intentional repetition?

Fascism

(1) According to your dictionary, how is "fascism" pronounced? Is the word as common today as it was in 1943? If not, how do you account for the decline in use? Can you name one or more "smear words" that are more commonly used in political controversy today? (2) What is White's special objection to indiscriminate use of the word? (3) In what ways, if any, does "fascist," as White defines it, differ from "communist," as you under-

stand it? (4) How do you distinguish between nationalism, patriotism, chauvinism, and jingoism?

Poetry

(1) To reduce high-level abstractions (poetry, the creative process) to concrete terms, White uses analogies, metaphors, and similes throughout. Identify each one, and show how some of them are sustained to help unify the piece. (2) How do you explain White's contention that poetry is "religious in tone, scientific in attitude"? (3) Do you agree with White that the majority should not rule in literature? (4) How many kinds of obscurity does White distinguish? From your reading of poetry, can you illustrate any of them or add any others? Do any of White's categories fit prose-writing? (5) Do you find any relation between White's attitude toward Gertrude Stein and the comment on style beginning on page 17?

Security

(1) Most dichotomies explaining human nature are loose generalizations at best. How closely does White's fit? Can you think of any others? (2) How can a wheel that creaks eternally on the same axle serve as a symbol of freedom? Why does Mr. G. W. G. Ferris belong with the immortals? How can a stroller swinging a prize cane on a country fair midway possibly have the world by the tail? In answering these questions, comment on the tone of the piece and the nature of the symbolism. (3) How does White illustrate his contention that the wheel was "only just holding its own"? What is the relation between the tattoo artist and the title? (4) Explain the significance of "jumbo tenderness" and "indelible ignominy." Why might the first phrase remind you of "Sound" (p. 75), and the second of "About Myself" (p. 95)?

Mrs. Wienckus

(1) What does White's use of quotation marks around the word "disorderliness" suggest about his attitude toward order, Mrs.

Wienckus, and the language of the law? How does this opening hint anticipate the paradox of the third paragraph? (2) Explain the structure of the second paragraph, accounting in particular for both the structure and the punctuation of the passages within parentheses. (3) Show how White's tidy illustration conveys a comment on the slovenliness of both national and world affairs. (4) How is White's comment on the seeking of hallways anticipated in the middle paragraph? How do you explain his choice of the phrase "all compact"?

Lime

(1) White is fond of short titles ("Sound," "Twins," "Security," "Lime") which do not pretend to convey the full meaning of the piece that follows. Can you suggest any reasons, other than the one already given, for not making these titles more complete? (2) A traditional grammarian might identify the opening statement as a "sentence fragment." Considering the style and tone of the whole piece, how do you account for White's decision to begin with a sentence without a subject? How do you explain the spelling and the verb-ending in the last sentence? (3) Although White twice states his belief in the Roosevelt Administration, he contends that he has no intention of taking sides over the question of three tons of lime. Considering the normal human tendency in political arguments, what are the advantages of this sort of fence-sitting? (4) How does White's use of lime as an illustration resemble his use of the Ferris wheel in "Security" (p. 108)? (5) White's large illustration is supported by smaller ones. How are the following related to the dominant theme: a cracked pot, a chocolate sundae, a permanent wave, a letter from a county agent?

Education

(1) How does White convey both the mundane and the heroic aspects of the country school teacher's job by calling it an "Augean task"? How does his adjective anticipate his later remarks about plumbing? What do you notice about the selection and

arrangement of the details of her task? (2) How does White's frank admission of his educational bias help to explain the tone of his description of the city school? What details in his description of the country school indicate that he still has the city school in mind? (3) To what extent is your own bias about education an attempt to justify your past? How rational is the normal process of rationalization? (4) According to White, what should really matter in elementary schools? Do you agree?

Beside the Shalimar

(1) Would it affect this piece in any way if White had known and explained exactly where the Shalimar is? (2) White might have organized his comparison by devoting his first paragraph to the music of the radio and his second to the tinkering of the mechanic (or vice versa). Why is the pattern he chose more effective? (3) Considering his attitude in "Sound" (p. 75), why should White be a captivated member of this captive audience? (4) Contrast his attitude toward the mechanic with his view of the designers in "Motor Cars" (p. 79).

Camp Meeting

(1) Is there method in White's stress of the fact that the audience is composed of Methodists? Would you characterize his attitude as intolerant? How does he sustain the religious tone of the meeting? (2) How is the description of the setting in paragraph 2 related to the rest of the piece? Point out details to show that White does not abandon the setting after he has established it. (3) According to White's view, is Dr. Townsend a typical demagogue, a hypocrite, a faker, or what? Considering both Townsend's message and his method, how do you account for the size of his national following in the 1930s? What could he teach a class in public speaking? (4) Though the dominant contrast of the piece is between Townsend weak and Townsend strong, White introduces other contrasts— between the promiser and the threatener, between the calmness of his manner and the audaciousness of his proposals, or between milk

and honey and everyday cookery. Discuss these contrasts and any others you may notice. (5) How does White depict his own role as a reporter? If this is no time for cynicism, what is his dominant tone?

Beloved Barriers

(1) Does White's metaphor of surrendering "ribs" have any special connotation, or does he use it merely to expand his alliteration (with "rights")? (2) How typical is White's picture of college fraternities? How accurate is his analogy between clubs and nations? Do you agree with him? Is he proposing the abolition of either fraternities or nations? (3) Why does he say that the prophecy is written on the wall when it is obviously being typed on paper? Who was Belshazzar?

The Shape of the U.N.

(1) How does White sustain his analogy between the shape of the U.N. and an old-fashioned flying machine? (2) Should a serious writer joke about such a serious subject? Is White being funny because he is a humorist or to provide comic relief? (3) What does White mean by calling the name "United Nations" a *euphemism?* Is such a euphemism defensible? Name some other euphemisms, political or otherwise, defensible or indefensible. (4) Does White mean that the fuzziness of the Charter can be cleared up by merely defining or using familiar words more accurately? If not, what does he mean? Would you conclude from his analysis that all problems are verbal? What do you know about semantics? (5) With particular reference to White's analysis of the job of the "dawn men," how does this piece resemble "Law and Justice" (p. 101)? To what extent does it reveal the same man who wrote "Western Unity" (p. 26), "The Wild Flag" (p. 28), and "Beloved Barriers" (p. 127)?

A Shepherd's Life

(1) What is the purpose of the opening paragraph in a piece that is primarily concerned with analyzing the process of birth? Why does White repeat the notion that "things work out if you leave

them alone"? (2) Why does he devote a paragraph in a modern essay to a consideration of ancient Celtic sheep-counting numerals? Is this merely an irrelevant touch of whimsy? What is whimsy? (3) How does his analysis differ in both technique and tone from the directions that might appear in a manual for professional veterinarians? Which analysis might be a more useful guide for the novice shepherd? (4) Compare and contrast "A Shepherd's Life" with "Twins" (p. 93). (5) Would you call White an escapist even though he worked long hours in the lambing season? What is your definition of an escapist?

Bedfellows

(1) Considering the adjective that often precedes the noun, what is the particular significance of White's title? (2) In spite of its title, this essay is an extended definition of democracy; it obviously differs from the piece earlier in this book (p. 102) in scope, purpose, organization, and tone. Explain the essential differences. (3) The connection between democracy and the memory of a departed dachshund is explained briefly in the headnote. Expand that explanation by illustrating the point in more detail. (4) "All writing slants the way a writer leans, and no man is born perpendicular, although many men are born upright." What does this statement reveal about White's attitude toward the press? Admitting that editorials are slanted, is there no such thing as unbiased factual reporting on the news pages? If not, why not? (5) What does the word "criticism" mean to you? Are you in favor of it as long as it is constructive, and not destructive? If so, would White and Adlai Stevenson agree with you? What is the difference between the two kinds of criticism? (6) With particular reference to White's attitudes on criticism and prayer, compare his opinions in "Bedfellows" and "Freedom" (p. 82).

Death of a Pig

(1) Considering both the pictures and White's technique in portraiture, compare the portraits of Fred in "Death of a Pig" and "Bedfellows" (p. 147). A standard view of dog-loving is revealed in

the cliché that "a man's best friend is his dog." Does this illustrate White's attitude toward Fred? (2) White depicts the experience as a departure from the standard script of a tragedy. How does he carry out this metaphor? Considering both the tone and the development of the plot, which of the two scripts comes closer to tragedy as you understand the term? Do you find any elements here of tragic irony, comic relief, or farce? (3) With particular reference to the uses of setting and point of view, how does this piece compare with "A Shepherd's Life" (p. 139)? If White is not primarily concerned with an exposition or analysis of the care of an ailing pig, how do you account for his extensive use of clinical details? (4) This story differs from "The Second Tree from the Corner" (p. 66) in arrangement of events and treatment of the time element. Explain the differences. (5) "Never send to know for whom the grave is dug, I said to myself, it's dug for thee." What is the literary allusion in this sentence, and how does the sentence summarize the point of view of the entire story? (6) The story is notably lacking in the conventional euphemisms attending human burial ("passed away," "lowered to rest," "no longer with us," "gone to his reward"). What does this indicate about the depth of the grief or the originality of the writing?

III. ONE MAN'S WORLD

First World War

(1) In what way does White's introduction of the two love songs set the tone of the entire essay? How is the beginning of the story related to the end? (2) White observes that the entries in his journal "are disappointingly lacking in solid facts." How many solid facts can you find in the comments that are not quoted directly from the journal? Can you defend the relevance of each of these facts to the piece as a whole? (3) To what extent is White's estimate of his own journal corroborated by the selections? If he were correcting the journal in 1939, what parts would he be most likely to attack with a red pencil? Does anything in the journal suggest that the author might some day grow up to be a distinguished writer? (4) The

entries quoted extend from mid-March in 1917 to late December in the year of the Armistice. Is there any evidence of change in the young man and his attitudes?

Removal

(1) Why does White choose to write about a mirror as "a sort of symbol of what [he] was trying to escape from?" Do you know of any other literary contexts in which a mirror is used as a symbol? (2) Can you suggest White's reasons for selecting the following details: a catcher's mitt and an old biology notebook; going out of the door hatless and in his shirtsleeves; the proprietor standing in the doorway; the El train; the two kibitzers. (3) The miserable miscellany in the junk shop is bruised, the El train chuckles, and the mirror is a bastard child. What do these details have in common, and what do they contribute to the story? (4) What does White mean by "catharsis" in paragraph 2? How is the word used in criticism of serious literature? (5) White might have ended with an explicit moral: "Nothing is more complicated than simplifying your life." Why didn't he? Why is his final sentence more effective?

Incoming Basket

(1) How could White's description of the incoming basket be considered a sequel to his story of the outgoing mirror (p. 180)? (2) Why does he repeat the word "desk" three times in the first three sentences when using pronouns (one, one, it) would make his essential meaning clear? What is a refrain? (3) A literal-minded reader might ask why White did not solve his problem efficiently by having two baskets in the country. Is the question relevant here? If so, why didn't he? (4) Why shouldn't a psychiatrist have an IN basket? In the context of this essay, what is White's apparent attitude toward physicists, psychiatrists, himself, and people in general?

Figures

(1) "Removal" (p. 180), "Incoming Basket" (p. 182), and "Figures" have a common theme; here White distinguishes the

simple aspects of his life from the complicated. Explain the distinction. Considering the conventional attitude toward figures and sheep farming, do you find the distinction paradoxical? What is paradoxical about White's way of seeing numbers, and what explanation does he suggest? (2) What words or phrases in paragraph 2 indicate that White is not stating the bare facts in strictly literal language? (3) Why is this essay organized into three paragraphs? Which paragraphs, if any, contain an explicit topic sentence? If a paragraph does not contain one, can you supply it?

Questionnaire

(1) What evidence from White's other essays supports his own estimate of his occupation? (2) How many names can you add to White's list of "pure" writers? Can you name works by all of White's "pure" writers? From your knowledge of Shakespeare's life, do you agree with White? (3) In the light of your experience with vocational guidance in school and elsewhere, is his attitude orthodox or unorthodox? (4) Do you notice anything unusual about his use of "as" in paragraph 2? What does he mean by "flibbertigibbet," "Jekyll and Hyde stuff," "inveterate loftsman"? Why did he choose a "single-hearted multipurpose machine operator" as an example of a clean-cut man?

The Sea and the Wind that Blows

(1) It is a common oversimplification to separate men into sea-lovers and landlubbers. What do you find in this essay and elsewhere in his writing to explain White's affection for the sea and the land? (2) In what other essays among the "Self-Portraits" does White fit the description of "men who ache all over for tidiness and compactness in their lives"? (3) In this piece White combines dream with reality, past with present. After carefully examining the organization, do you think he blends these elements successfully? (4) The lure of boats and of the sea is conveyed throughout by the use of analogy. Identify each analogy and explain its effectiveness.

Old Dameron

(1) How would you explain White's use of point of view here? (2) The most successful portraits in fact or fiction are a blend of the traits that particularize the individual and of the more general characteristics that he shares with others. To what extent is this true of the picture of Dameron? (3) Which of the five senses does White call on in describing Dameron and his environment? (4) At the beginning of World War Two, "freedom" was a household word, and "the common man" a household phrase. In the context of this piece do these expressions have the same connotation as in the standard political essay or editorial? How would Dameron's approach to freedom differ from White's attitude in "Freedom" (p. 82)? (5) "He cared for nobody, no not he, and nobody cared for him." Considering the evidence in "Death of a Pig" (p. 157), is this literally true of Dameron? How do you account for the rhythm of this sentence?

The Flocks We Watch by Night

(1) What do you infer about Charles from what he says and his way of saying it? What does White also reveal about himself, the boy, the dachshund, and Sarah? (2) How does White use the details of setting—place, season, time of day—to add extra dimensions to the picture? (3) The story is developed by a series of contrasts such as experience and innocence, cold and warmth, farce and pathos. What other contrasts can you identify? (4) Considering both character and characterization, to what extent do the two portraits of Charles Dameron (p. 191) resemble each other? (5) What is the full significance of the title?

Will Strunk

(1) Just as Charles Lamb can preface a tender discussion of the virtues of poverty by hymning the praise of old china, E. B. White can begin a tribute to a respected professor with a report of the battle against the mosquito in a midtown apartment. Though

such a beginning is not prescribed for most undergraduate assign-
ments, it usually has a more subtle organization and effect than may
be apparent to the casual reader. How, for example, does White
make the transition from paragraph 3 to paragraph 4? (2) "It is
encouraging to see how perfectly a book, even a dusty rulebook,
perpetuates and extends the spirit of a man." How much evidence
can you cite in support of this key sentence? (3) Of Will Strunk's
prescriptions and preferences, which ones, if any, do you find open
to challenge? If "student body" is to be proscribed as gruesome, why
shouldn't we outlaw all expressions ("body politic," "body of a
letter," "body of a book," "body of water") in which a body is not a
corpse? (4) If the ultimate test of usage is appropriateness, can it be
logically argued that any phrase should be "revised out of every
sentence in which it occurs"? (5) What is the point of White's
comparison of modern rhetoric and an automobile? (6) How does
the Strunkian elaboration on the theme of brevity reveal that repetition and wordiness are not synonymous? How do you distinguish
between needless and needful repetition? (7) Cite a passage from
this essay to indicate that White has practiced what Strunk
preached.

Don Marquis

(1) Why should Don Marquis have chosen to express
himself by using a cockroach and a cat? Why are they perfect
transmigrations of an American soul? (2) In what ways do Don
Marquis and his book reflect the peculiar spirit of an age? (3) What
is the significance of Archy's attitude toward capitalization, including the comment that "he was no e. e. cummings"? (4) In what
ways does the portrait of Don Marquis reflect White's own attitude
toward writing? Toward poetry? (5) How would you characterize
the tone of this essay? Cite specific instances to support your
opinion.

A Classic Waits for Me

(1) To what extent does White's choice of a literary form in
this "verse essay" compare with that of Don Marquis in *Archy and*

Mehitabel? Why should Whitman have occurred to White as a subject (or middleman) for this parody? (2) What is White's attitude toward the classics? (3) In this parody White dovetails echoes of Whitman with direct references to the advertisement he is ridiculing. Which lines clearly belong in which category? (4) How do you account for White's choice of the proper names, including Hecuba? (5) What does the parody reveal about the state of American culture? Do you think the situation has improved or deteriorated since 1944?

Across the Street and Into the Grill

(1) How many characteristic traits of Hemingway's manner and matter can you discern (whether or not you have read *Across the River and Into the Trees*)? (2) Although a sophisticated understanding of a parody depends on familiarity with the original, a good parody should be able to stand on its own. What aspects of this piece would appeal to you if you knew nothing about Hemingway? (3) Much of the humor here consists of implied contrasts—farcical or at least incongruous—based on the assumption that Hemingway's idioms, situations, and characters cannot all be transported from Italy (or Spain or Africa) to Manhattan (or Scarsdale) without suffering a sea change; mayonnaise in a *fiasco,* for example, or a captain of girls named Botticelli in, of all places, Schrafft's. How many similar contrasts can you identify?

Some Remarks on Humor

(1) What aspects of White's attitude toward humor are reflected in his portrait of Don Marquis (p. 205) or his own humorous parody of Hemingway (p. 215)? (2) "Practically everyone is a manic depressive of sorts. . . ." Assuming the truth of White's statement, to what extent would this account for or excuse the so-called "sick" comedian? (3) Can you add further evidence from your own experience (in or out of books) to support or refute White's assertion that the stature of humor has varied with time and clime? (4) What, according to White, is "the very nub of the conflict"? According to the editorial apparatus given here, is this

conflict restricted to humorous writing? (5) Name three humorists not listed by White, including at least two who "start dead," and discuss the extent to which his principles apply to them.

Walden

(1) Considering the style and tone of this piece, what is the advantage of White's opening device? (2) What evidence do you find in the "Self-Portraits" to suggest that White would be an unusually sympathetic reader of Thoreau? How does his sympathy for Thoreau affect the tone of the essay? (3) Why should White bother to explain to this nineteenth-century writer the exact process of locking a car? (4) What is the significance of the quotations from "America, the Beautiful" and from White's account book? (5) Explain the shape of this essay as a piece of description, showing how White shifts his point of view without diluting the dominant impression. (6) White might have written from the point of view of Thoreau returning to Concord a century later. Is his choice preferable? Why or why not?

A Slight Sound at Evening

(1) White clearly implies that the author of *Walden* was not "a sort of Nature Boy." Why not? (2) Explain the differences in point of view between this essay and the previous piece, and comment on the advantages of the point of view in each. (3) Does any experience in your own reading, either with *Walden* or any other book, support White's contention that the reaction to a book depends, to a great extent, on the age and mood of the reader? (4) White compares *Walden* to a vitamin-enriched American dish, a modern Western, and a toot on the trumpet. What is the pertinence of these analogies? (5) Why does he choose to illustrate the character of Thoreau by quoting the single journal entry for May 3–4, 1838? (6) In an anniversary essay on Thoreau why does White devote so much time to a description of his own boathouse? (7) How do you reconcile White's admiration of Thoreau's "offbeat prose" with his advice to writers in the selection beginning on

p. 17? (8) Can you explain the aptness of all the quotations that White uses on the guided tour of the modern scene?

On a Florida Key

(1) The first six paragraphs of this piece are essentially descriptive. What order does White follow in developing the picture of the cottage? (2) How are the themes of the sand and the sea woven into the total texture of the essay? (3) How is White's attitude toward the Chamber of Commerce expressed or implied throughout? (4) How does he squeeze a single illustration to make it yield contrasting attitudes toward nature and human nature? (5) Half way through the essay White gives a contemporary twist to an old Roman proverb. Does he accept his version of the proverb at its face value? (6) The tone of this essay might be defined as a blend of nostalgia and irony. Why?

The Cities

(1) How does the structure of the sentences and of the paragraph as a whole differ from the standards usually prescribed in the rhetoric books? How do you account for these differences? (2) Has White arranged the details of his description in an orderly way? Explain. (3) Can you account for White's use of repetition? Does he use any devices more commonly associated with poetry than with prose? (4) Can the final sentence be considered the key to the meaning of the whole piece?

Trance

(1) Although this paragraph has a different point of view (or focus) from "The Cities" (p. 251), the two pieces have obvious similarities. Compare and contrast them. (2) How does this piece differ from the standard ridicule of advertising in the affluent society? Do you notice any change in the writer's point of view or tone as the piece approaches its climax? (3) How does "Trance" illustrate the truth (see p. 90) that facts are such stuff as poems

and dreams are made on? Do you find any evidence in the piece that White may have a particular poem in mind?

Here is New York

(1) This passage from a much longer essay exemplifies three of the ways of development discussed in Part Two. Identify them and comment on the extent to which White's development of the material illustrates any points made in the editorial discussion of the three sections. (2) At the beginning of the essay (not here included) White characterizes New Yorkers as "to a large extent strangers who have pulled up stakes somewhere and come to town, seeking sanctuary or fullfillment or some greater or lesser grail." How does the selection sustain the note struck in this quotation? (3) Explain the paradox of the concluding paragraph. (4) In what specific ways does this passage remind you of "The Second Tree from the Corner" (p. 66) and "Don Marquis" (p. 205)?

Cold Weather

(1) How and why does White use repetition in the opening paragraph? (2) This piece consists almost entirely of "talk about the weather"—a tired subject that gives free rein to assorted bores. How does White's treatment differ from the typical idiom of the cliché expert testifying about the cold (or heat)? Would you regard part of this piece merely as an extension of the cliché that "misery loves company"? (3) Of St. Agnes Eve (the "coldest night of the year") Keats writes:

> The hare limped trembling through the frozen grass,
> And silent was the flock in wooly fold;

How does White's technique of description resemble the poet's? (4) How does the fraternity of the cold differ from other fraternities in your experience?

The Supremacy of Uruguay

(1) Why do you suppose White chose Uruguay instead of a mythological country? Why did he decide to have Casablanca get

the idea for his invention in New York City? (2) What devices or details does White use to make the reader suspend his disbelief? How incredible is the story? Is it dated? (3) A popular play in the 1930s referred to war as "Idiot's Delight." Does this phrase fit White's ironic conception here? (4) Does White's irony remind you of any other writer you have read—of Swift, for example, or George Orwell? Compare White's technique here with that in "The Wild Flag" (p. 28). (5) How does the theme of the story compare with the main point of "Sound" (p. 75)?

The Door

(1) In this piece White uses a technique common in modern fiction—known as *stream of consciousness* or *interior monologue*. How would you define these terms? Contrast them with other ways of telling a story or portraying a character? How does White's use of the method differ from any other instance with which you may be familiar? (2) It is an old cliché that modern life is a "rat-race." What new dimensions does White add to this familiar metaphor? (3) The opening sentence anticipates two interdependent themes: the central analogy between man and rat and the related comment on the wonderful world of Ersatz. How does White sustain each of these themes throughout? (4) What is meant by the sentence "Nobody can not jump."? (5) How is each of the following related to the story as a whole: "my friend the poet"; the picture of the girl; the man out in Jersey; "the curb coming up to meet your foot"; "the one with a circle"; the prefrontal lobe?

Sootfall and Fallout

(1) How does the opening sentence of the final paragraph serve as a comment on the development of the entire piece? (2) What, if any, is the relation between Mary Martin's moving and the central theme announced in the title? (3) Where does White first suggest his attitude toward modern scientists, and how would you define that attitude? Can you make any safe generalizations about his attitude toward politicians? (4) What does he mean by: "the Un-Copernican system"; "another Donora, Pa."; "a little band of physi-

cists . . . in a squash court"; "globaloney"; "the dignity of mud turtles"? (5) As Hemingway (and many others) have pointed out, "a serious writer is not to be confounded with a solemn writer"; like Shakespeare punning in mid-murder, he may play with words while handling the most awesome of subjects. How does White illustrate this here? (6) Considering both manner and matter, compare this essay with: "The Age of Dust" (p. 76), "Freedom" (p. 82), "The Shape of the U.N." (p. 130), "Mrs. Wienckus" (p. 110), "Bedfellows" (p. 147), and "Removal" (p. 180).

The Red Cow Is Dead

(1) How many examples of internal rhyme and consonance (see p. 279) can you find in the poem? How does White use repetition to achieve his effect? (2) What use has he made of the facts of the AP report? Is the report prosaic? (3) Why might this poem be called a *mock elegy*? What elements of parody does it contain? (4) Is the total effect funny or sad?

The Tennis

(1) How would you characterize the verse form of this poem? (2) How many plain facts do you find in the poem? How many similes, metaphors, or examples of alliteration or onomatopoeia are there? (3) Considering this poem a piece of description, do you find an orderly arrangement creating a dominant impression? Do you find a consistency of tone? (4) Compare and contrast the poem with "The Day of Days" (p. 37). (5) What is the relation between the verse form and White's apparent intention? (6) Does the poem bear out Marianne Moore's assertion that poets should be "literalists of the imagination" or Archibald MacLeish's statement that "A poem should not mean/But be"?

A Listener's Guide to the Birds

(1) Discuss White's use of rhyme for comic effect. (2) After reading the poem aloud, discuss the virtuosity of his versification. Where, if anywhere, does he use a standard meter? Why do

you think he did not choose to pour the whole poem into a standard verse mould? (3) The poem is a blend of birdsong (or an unreasonable facsimile) and man-speech. Where does White use prosaic colloquialisms for the sake of anticlimax. (4) What is his attitude toward birds, Roger Tory Peterson, and himself?

Once More to the Lake

(1) How do the first three paragraphs prepare the reader to accept the illusion explained in the fourth? How does White illustrate his statement that the illusion "grew much stronger" as he lingered at the lake? How does he use repetition in paragraphs 5 and 6 to emphasize his point? (2) Why does he refer to the lake as "an utterly enchanted sea"? (3) What is the significance, both literal and symbolic, of the missing middle track in the road? What other details are evidence of change or disenchantment? Would it be accurate to say that White's point is that you can change human nature but you can't change nature? (4) Discuss the paragraph on motorboats as an example of development by comparison and contrast. Considering other pieces by White, how do you account for his choice of "the only thing that was wrong"? (5) Explain the method by which he organized the paragraph on the storm. (6) What is the significance of the final paragraph?

The Ring of Time

(1) How is the metaphor of the title suggested in the opening paragraph and sustained throughout the piece? (2) The art of preparing the audience for the entrance of a member of the cast is not a monopoly of playwrights. How does White prepare the reader for the girl's entrance? Why does he begin with a detailed description of the mother in action? (3) How does White characterize his role as a writer? How do his role and attitude differ from those of an advance agent publicizing the circus? (4) How does he exemplify his assertion that out of the wild disorder of the circus comes an order that approximates "the world in microcosm"? What does this suggest about the nature of art? Does White draw any other analogy

between the girl's performance and the artist's experience? (5) How do you account for his choice of these words or phrases: "harumphing," "desultory treadmills of afternoon," "mild spectacle," "improving a shining ten minutes," "without benefit of strap," "the land of the sustained sibilant"? How does White sustain the sibilance? (6) How does he relate his experience at the circus to his picture of the South?

SUGGESTIONS FOR WRITING

Most of the discussion questions in the preceding section may also serve as topics for critical writing. The suggestions in the following lists are related to the selections from White but do not necessarily require critical comment on them. Though many of the topics are phrased as titles, there is no intention of denying the student the right to phrase his own.

I. SAYING THE WORDS

A.
1. Of Literary Bondage
2. Why I Want to Write
3. My Affair with Grammar
4. The Trouble with My Writing
5. A Fashionable Idiom
6. Analysis of a Passage of Contemporary Prose
7. The Poetry of Advertising
8. A Defense of Offbeat Language
9. The Difference Between Irony and Sarcasm
10. The History of a Word
11. Discussion of an Item in a Dictionary of Usage
12. Teaching Me to Read

B.
1. A Scene from Two Points of View
2. A Topical Parable
3. Answer to a Letter (Real or Imaginary) from the Dean
4. A Special Day of the Year
5. An Ironic Viewpoint
6. Machines in My World

II. THE CAREFUL FORM

A.
1. Description of a Dwelling or Neighborhood
2. The Adventures of a Night
3. Consultation with a Specialist
4. What Do I Want?

5. Editorial for a Student Newspaper
6. Soundtrack
7. The Morality of Science
8. A Design for Freedom
9. Is There a New Freedom?

B. 1. Report of a Student Meeting
2. Interview with a Celebrity
3. Definition of an Abstract Word
4. A Short Division
5. A Collection Classified
6. Implications of a Brief News Item
7. A Firsthand Experience with Government
8. Two Schools in My Life
9. Portrait of a Crusader
10. Are Brotherhoods Obsolete?
11. The Shape of a Student Constitution
12. How Decisions Are Made in Student Government

C. 1. Life Among the Quadrupeds
2. A Firsthand Encounter with Death

III. ONE MAN'S WORLD

1. A Journal for a Week
2. Organizing My Life
3. My Affair with Numbers
4. My Vocation and My Avocation
5. Confessions of a Young Salt
6. Profile of an Eccentric
7. Portrait of the Artist from His Book
8. A Teacher's Philosophy in Action
9. Homogenized Culture
10. A Parody of E. B. White
11. Sick Humor and Healthy
12. A Book I've Lived With
13. Visit to a National Shrine
14. Slight Sounds and Loud Noises

15. My Last Resort
16. A Meeting of North and South
17. Death of a City
18. A Magic Moment
19. The Split-Level Life
20. Another Place Like Home
21. The Wonderful World of Ersatz
22. The Air We Breathe
23. Poisons and Panaceas
24. Fishing in the Stream of Time
25. A Childhood Haunt Revisited

INDEX

About Myself, 95–98, 315
Across the Street and into the Grill, 215–218, 327
Adams, Franklin P., 206–207, 220
Age of Dust, The, 76–78, 313
Ain't, 7–8
Allusions, 309, 322
Analogy, 114, 305, 324
Analysis, cause-and-effect, 129–130; defined, 128–129; examples, 140–144; methods, 129–130; vs. other ways of development, 129
Angle (point of view), 24–26
Approach to Style, An, 13–17, 304–305
Appropriateness, 6–8, *see* Language; Style; Usage
Archy and Mehitabel, 205–211
Argument, 72
Attitude (tone), 24, 30–32, *see* Tone
Autobiography, examples, 172–190; methods, 171–172

Bedfellows, 147–157, 321
Beloved Barriers, 127–128, 320
Beside the Shalimar, 119–120, 319
Brevity, 201–202
Burning Question, The, 38–40, 309–310
Business Show, 58–59, 311

Calculating Machine, 20–22, 305–306
Camp Meeting, 120–127, 319–320
Canby, Henry Seidel, 7–8, 220
Cities, The, 251–252, 329
Classic Waits for Me, A, 213–215, 326–327
Classification and division, defined, 104–105; examples, 105–109; relation to comparison and contrast, 115; relation to illustration, 109
Clinical "we," 10–12, 24
Coinages, 18, 305

Colby, Frank Moore, 221–222
Cold Weather, 255–258, 330
Coleridge, Samuel Taylor, 90
Colloquialisms, 6
Comparison and contrast, defined, 114; examples, 116–128; methods, 114–116
Conrad, Joseph, 53, 185
Consonance, 279
Contact, 7
Contractions, 6
Contrast, *see* Comparison and contrast
Coon Hunt, 61–66, 311–312
Creative writing, 14
Criticism, language of, 18–19; meaning of, 153, 212–213

Day of Days, The, 37–38, 308–309
Deadwood, 202
Death of a Pig, 157–166, 321–322
Definitions, examples, 100–104; importance, 134–135, 138, 275–276; methods, 98–100; relation to comparison and contrast, 115
Democracy, 102–103, 316
Description, 53–59; concrete language in, 53–54; defined, 53; details in, 54–55; dominant impression, 54; examples, 56–59; order, 54; relation to exposition, 78; technical, 54
Design, a suitable, 144–147
    See also Form
Development, analysis of, 128–144; classification and division, 104–109; comparison and contrast, 114–128; definition, 98–104; illustration, 109–114; reporting the facts, 89–98; ways of, 88–144
Dialect humor, 224–225
Division, *see* Classification and division
Dominant impression, 55–56
Don Marquis, 205–211, 326
Door, The, 263–268, 331

Double entendre, 313–314
Doyle, Sir Arthur Conan, 209
Dudes and Flapsails, 100–101, 315–316
Dunne, Finley Peter, 225
Duty of Writers, The, 4–6, 303

Editorial "we," 10–11
Education, 116–119, 318–319
English Usage, 7–8, 303–304
Essay, 10, 24, 26, 258
Euphemisms, 132, 322
Exposition, defined, 78; examples, 79–88; tone, 78–79

Fact (the fact that), 203
Facts, reporting, 89–98
Familiar essay, *see* Personal essay
Farewell, My Lovely!, 40–47, 310
Fascism, 103–104, 316–317
Faulkner, William, 15–16
Figures, 183–184, 323–324
Figures of speech, *see* Analogy; Simile; Metaphor
Finalize, 18
First World War, 172–180, 322–323
Fitzgerald, F. Scott, 14, 145
Flesch, Rudolf, 21–22
Flocks We Watch by Night, The, 193–198, 325
Form, defined and discussed, 51–52, 144–147, 220–221; descriptive, 53–56; of exposition, 79; narrative, 59–60
Forms, of discourse, 53–88; of description, 53–58; of exposition, 78–88; of narrative, 59–72; of persuasion, 72–78
Freedom, 82–88, 314
Free verse, 207, 209, 212–215, 279, 281–282
Frost, Robert, 16, 37, 308–309
Future of Reading, The, 23–24, 306

Gibbs, Wolcott, 19

Grammar, 7–8, 17
    See also Usage
Guest, Edgar A., 106

Hemingway, Ernest, 15–16, 212, 215–218
Here is New York, 253–255, 330
Housman, A. E., 90
Humor and humorists, 5–6, 30–32, 79, 205, 208–209, 212, 218–226, 278–285, 310, 327

I, 10–12, 24
Illustration, defined, 109; examples, 110–114; relation to classification, 109; relation to comparison and contrast, 115
Imitation, 52
Incoming Basket, 182–183, 323
Informal essay, *see* Personal essay
Interior monologue, 331
Internal rhyme, 279
Irony, 30–32
It is her, she, 7–8

Jargon, 78–79

Language, abstract vs. concrete, 53–54, 90; advertising, 17–19, 303, 305; business, 18, 303, 305; criticism, 18–19; legal, 18, 36–37; levels or varieties, 6–8, 308; offbeat vs. standard, 17–19
    See also Style; Usage; Words
Lardner, Ring, 222–223, 225
Law and Justice, 101–102, 316
Levels of language, 6–8, 308
Light verse, 278–285
    See also Poetry and poets
Lime, 111–114, 318
Lindbergh, Anne, 274–275
Lippmann, Walter, 136
Listener's Guide to the Birds, A, 282–285, 332–333

Main intention, 52
Maugham, W. Somerset, 8
Metaphor, 99, 114, 306
Motor Cars, 79–82, 313–314
Mrs. Wienckus, 110–111, 317–318

Narrative, in *Death of a Pig,* 146–147; defined, 58; examples, 61–72; unity, 58–59
Nasby, Petroleum V., 223–225
Naturalness, 3, 8–10, 190
    See also Writing
Neologisms, *see* Coinages

Offbeat language, 17–19
Old Dameron, 191–193, 325
On a Florida Key, 245–251, 329
Once More to the Lake, 286–293, 333
Order, in description, 55; in narrative, 59–60
    See also Form

Paine, Thomas, 14–15
Parable, defined, 26; examples, 28–30, 259–263
Parody, 212–218, 220
Parts of speech, 7, 17, 303, 305
Passive voice, 25
Personalize, 21, 305
Personal essay, 10, 24, 26, 258–259
Personal pronouns, 10–12, 24–25
Persuasion, vs. argument, 72; defined, 72–73; examples, 74–78; relation to exposition, 78
Plain English, 16, 36
Poetry, 105–108, 317
Poetry and poets, 5–6, 90, 105–108, 211, 213–215, 220–221, 278–283, 308–309, 332
Point of view, 10, 24–26; in description, 55–56; in narrative, 60
Portraits, 191–211, 325
Possessive case, 203–204
Prefer the Standard to the Offbeat, 17–19, 305

Process, analysis of a, 129
Pronouns, personal, 10–12, 24–25
Puns, 313–314

Questionnaire, 184–187, 324

Reading, easy and hard, 20–22; experts, 20–22; importance of, 23–24; speed, 19–20
Red Cow Is Dead, The, 280–281, 332
Redundancy, 201–202
Removal, 180–182, 323
Reporting the facts, 89–98
Rhythm, 14
Ring of Time, The, 293–301, 333–334

Salt Water Farm, 56–58, 310–311
Sea and the Wind that Blows, The, 187–190, 324
Second Tree from the Corner, The, 66–72, 312
Security, 108–109, 317
Self-portraits, 171–190
Sentence structure, 14–16
Shakespeare, William, 186
Shape of the U.N., The, 130–139, 320
Shepherd's Life, A, 139–144, 320–321
Simile, 114
Simplicity, 3, 14, 16
    See also Writing; Naturalness
Slight Sound at Evening, A, 234–244, 328–329
Some Remarks on Humor, 218–226, 327–328
Sootfall and Fallout, 268–278, 331–332
Sound, 75–76, 312–313
Sound of words, 7, 14–16
Standard English, 17–19
Stein, Gertrude, 106–108
Stream of consciousness, 331
Study of the Clinical "We," A, 10–12, 304

Style, defined and illustrated, 12–17; in advertising and business, 17–18, 303; in criticism, 18–19; in exposition, 78–79; in "the little book," 200–205; offbeat vs. standard, 17–19

Suggestions for writing, 335–337

Supremacy of Uruguay, The, 259–263, 330–331

Symbols, 307

Technical description, 54

Tennis, The, 281–282, 332

Theme topics, 335–337

Thoreau, Henry David, 22, 53, 212
    See also Walden

Thurber, James, 31

Tone, consistency of, 25; defined, 24, 30–32; in exposition, 78–79; in persuasion, 73; serious vs. solemn, 30, 332

Town Meeting, 91–93, 314

Trance, 252–253, 329–330

Twain, Mark, 222–226

Twins, 93–94, 315

Two Letters, Both Open, 32–37, 308

Unity, in description, 54–56; in narrative, 59–60
    See also Design; Form

Update, 18

Usage, 17–19, 200–205, 326; correct, 6–8, 204
    See also Language; Style

Varieties of language, 6–8, 308

Vers libre, see Free verse

Verse, *see* Free verse; Poetry and poets

Walden, 226–233, 328
    See also Thoreau, Henry David

"We," clinical and editorial, 10–12, 24

Western Unity, 26–28, 306–307

Whitman, Walt, 16, 212–215

Wild Flag, The, 28–30, 307–308

Will Strunk, 198–205, 325–326

Withholding, 74–75, 312

Wolfe, Thomas, 15

Word-Handler's Aim, The, 9–10, 304

Wordiness, 201–202

Word order, 14–16

Words, abstract vs. concrete, 53–54, 90, 99; arrangement, 14–16; choice, 31; dangerous, 101–102; importance, 132; setting, 18; specific, 90
    See also Definition; Language; Usage

Writers and writing, aim, 9–10; approach to reader, 22; definition of a writer, 17, 185–187; duties of writers, 4–6, 22, 187; genesis of writing, 51

Yeats, William Butler, 52

82 83 84   20 19 18 17 16 15